Limits

to LIBERATION

IN SOUTHERN AFRICA

Limits

to LIBERATION

IN SOUTHERN AFRICA

The unfinished business of
democratic consolidation

Edited by Henning Melber

Compiled by the Democracy & Governance Research Programme,
Human Sciences Research Council

Published by HSRC Press
Private Bag X9182, Cape Town, 8000, South Africa
www.hsrcpublishers.ac.za

In association with the Journal of Contemporary African Studies,
Institute of Social and Economic Research, Rhodes University,
Grahamstown 6140, South Africa

First published 2003

ISBN 0-7969-2025-7

Cover by Flame Design
Cover photograph by Kelly Walsch

Production by comPress
www.compress.co.za

Distributed in Africa by Blue Weaver Marketing and Distribution,
P.O. Box 30370, Tokai, Cape Town, 7966, South Africa.
Tel: +27 21-701-4477, Fax: +27 21 701-7302, email: booksales@hsrc.ac.za

Distributed in the United States of America and Canada by Independent Publishers Group,
814 North Franklin Street, Chicago, IL 60610, USA. www.ipgbook.com.
To order, call toll-free: 1-800-888-4741
All other enquiries, Tel: +1 312-337-0747, Fax: +1 312-337-5985,
email: frontdesk@ipgbook.com

Distributed worldwide, excluding Africa, Canada and the United States of America by
The Nordic Africa Institute, Box 1703, SE 75 147 Uppsala, Sweden.
Tel: +46 18 562200, Fax +46 18 552290, email: orders@nai.uu.se

Contents

Tables

Figures

Acknowledgements

It took just over a year between the conference on '(Re-)Conceptualising Democracy and Liberation in Southern Africa' in July 2002 in Windhoek and this publication of revised versions of most of the papers originally presented there. This required the concerted efforts of many persons and institutions. *The Nordic Africa Institute* provided the bulk of the material and administrative support to organise the event within its research network on 'Liberation and Democracy in Southern Africa'. Arne Wunder and Charlotta Dohlvik were in charge of the practical arrangements of bringing the participants to Windhoek. The local organisation was achieved in collaboration with *The Legal Assistance Centre* (in particular, its director, Clement Daniels) and the *Namibia Institute for Democracy* (in particular, its directors, Theunis Keulder and Doris Weissnar). The role played by Lennart Wohlgemuth, not only as a conference participant and director of the Nordic Africa Institute, was motivating and encouraging throughout. The emotional and very practical support by Sue Melber made her once again a true companion also to the benefit of my employer and the other participants. Without the assistance of all those mentioned, the original conference would have been not only different but far less enjoyable.

I am grateful to Roger Southall for agreeing to the production of a special issue of *The Journal of Contemporary African Studies (JCAS)* based on contributions to the conference, as well as to *Taylor and Francis,* publishers of *JCAS,* for agreeing to the co-publication of the issue as a book by the *Human Sciences Research Council* (HSRC). Likewise, I am grateful to The Swedish International Development Authority (Sida) for their financial support to the project support through the Nordic Africa Institute.

Last but not least, the contributors to this volume displayed a high level of efficiency and professionalism in their contribution to this project.

Complemented by the extraordinary skills and commitment of Nova de Villiers who undertook the first edit of the chapters, this final product will hopefully offer a meaningful contribution to a necessary debate.

Finally, I dedicate this humble intellectual contribution to the cause of democracy, equality, freedom and human rights and to all those who take personal risks to bring us closer to such goals.

Henning Melber

Acronyms

ANC	African National Congress
BAC	Basutoland African Congress
BCP	Botswana Congress Party
BIDPA	Botswana Institute for Development Policy Analysis
BNF	Botswana National Front
BNP	Basotho National Party
CKGR	Central Kalahari Game Reserve
CoD	Congress of Democrats
COSATU	Congress of South African Trade Unions
CSI	Civil Society Initiative
DTA	Democratic Turnhalle Alliance
FNLA	*Frente Nacional de Libertação de Angola*
FRELIMO	*Frente de Libertação de Moçambique*
GDRC	Global Development Research Unit
GEAR	Growth Employment and Redistribution
ILO	International Labour Organisation
IMF	International Monetary Fund
LCD	Lesotho Congress of Democracy
LDF	Lesotho Defence Force
LLA	Lesotho Liberation Army
MDC	Movement for Democratic Change
MDM	Mass Democratic Movement
MFP	Marematlou Freedom Party
MISA	Media Institute of Southern Africa
MK	*Umkhonto We Sizwe*
MMD	Movement for Multi-Party Democracy
MPLA	*Movimento Popular da Libertação de Angola*
MWT	The Marxist Workers' Tendency

NAPWU	Namibia Public Workers Union
NCA	National Constitution Assembly
NDB	The National Development Bank
NEC	National Executive Committee
NEPAD	New Partnership for Africa's Development
NGOs	Non Governmental Organisations
NLMs	National liberation movements
NNP	New National Party
OAU	Organisation of African Unity
OM	Operation Mayibuye
PAC	Pan African Congress
RC	Revolutionary Council
RENAMO	*Resistência Nacional Moçambicana*
SAAF	South African Air Force
SACP	South African Communist Party
SADC	Southern African Development Community
SADF	South African Defence Force
SANDF	South African National Defence Force
Sapa	South African Press Association
SAPs	structural adjustment programmes
SHHA	Self-Help Housing Association
SWAPO	South West African Peoples Organisation
UDF	United Democratic Front
UNCHS	United Nations Centre for Human Settlements
UNDP	United Nations Development Programme
UNECA	United Nations Economic Commission for Africa
UNEP	United Nations Environmental Programme
UNITA	*União Nacional para a Independência Total de Angola*
UNTAG	United Nations Transitional Assistance Group
ZANU	Zimbabwe African National Union
ZANU-PF	Zimbabwe African National Union-Patriotic Front
ZAPU	Zimbabwe African People's Union
ZCTU	Zimbabwe Congress of Trade Unions
ZIPRA	Zimbabwe People's Revolutionary Army
ZUM	Zimbabwe Unity Movement

Introduction

Henning Melber

During 2001, the Nordic Africa Institute (previously the Scandinavian Institute of African Studies) initiated a research project around the theme "Liberation and Democracy in Southern Africa".[1] A network of scholars from mainly southern Africa was involved and a first consultative workshop was convened in December 2001 in collaboration with the Centre for Conflict Resolution in Cape Town.[2] This provided a platform for an initial conceptualisation of the issues which led, in turn, to a second gathering in Namibia in July 2002. With a focus on "(Re-)Conceptualising Democracy and Liberation in Southern Africa", it was held in collaboration with the Namibia Institute for Democracy and the Legal Assistance Centre as local civil society agencies.[3]

Most of the contributions to this volume are revised versions of papers originally given at the Namibian meeting.[4] They highlight political issues and processes in parts of southern Africa since the end of white-minority and/or colonial rule. Particular but not exclusive attention is paid to the post-independence records of governance of the Namibian and Zimbabwean liberation movements. Re-cast as political parties, they have since taking power in their respective domains sought to gain predominance in both the political arena, as well as within most, if not all, state and parastatal structures. In these two areas they have largely prevailed while also securing a power of definition in the political arena through the shaping or manipulation of public political discourse to suit their ends.

This brings us to the core focus of this volume, namely, the contradiction represented by the fact that the Namibian and Zimbabwean liberation movements which spearheaded mass popular struggles for liberation from colonial rule have, in power, developed into authoritarian and, to varying degrees, corrupt ruling regimes. By contrast, countries like Botswana and Lesotho which attained independence by negotiation and without mass mobilisation bear all the features of being multi-party democracies. Why this is so is a concern of the contributors to this volume. Why, some of its authors enquire, have the South West African Peoples Organisation (SWAPO) and Zimbabwe African National Union (ZANU) in power not displayed a consistent commitment to democratic principles and/or practices? In particular, they examine why these movements have deviated from their originally-declared democratic aims as well as largely abandoning their once-sacrosanct goal of socio-economic transformation aimed at reducing inherited imbalances in the distribution of wealth.

In examining these issues, the contributors probed beyond the myths and legends which have long surrounded southern Africa's liberation movements to take on board the fact that while these organisations were waging war on systems of institutionalised injustice, they did not themselves always display a sensitivity to human rights issues and democratic values. Nor did it prevent them from falling prey to authoritarian patterns of rule and undemocratic (as well as sometimes violent) practices towards real or imagined dissidents within their ranks.

Time and new data has also revealed that even the popular support for the struggle expressed by local groups was at times based more on coercion and the manipulation of internal contradictions among the colonised than on genuine resistance to the colonial state. Norma Kriger (1992) argues as much in reference to Zimbabwe while Lauren Dobell (1998) and Colin Leys and John Saul (1995) have exposed the level and degree of SWAPO's internal repression during its exile years. Some of these anti-democratic tendencies are detectable of late in South Africa. A recent study suggests a high degree of political intolerance among South Africans who, it seems, dislike political enemies a great deal and perceive them as threatening. As a result, the combination of dislike and threat "is a powerful source of political intolerance" (Gibson and Gouws 2003:71).

An argument presented in this volume is that the political change which has occurred in those southern African societies shaped by settler colonialism, can be characterised as a transition from controlled change to changed control. What this means is that a new political elite has ascended the commanding heights and, employing selective narratives and memories relating to their liberation wars, has constructed or invented a new set of traditions to establish an exclusive post-colonial legitimacy under the sole authority of one particular agency of social forces (see Kriger 1995 and Werbner 1998b for Zimbabwe; Melber 2003a for Namibia). Mystification of the liberators has played an essential role in this fabrication. As Werbner (1998a: 2) has noted: "The critique of power in contemporary Africa calls for a theoretically informed anthropology of memory and the making of political subjectivities. The need is to rethink our understanding of the force of memory, its official and unofficial forms, its moves between the personal and the social in post-colonial transformation".

What these elites have also done is develop militant notions of inclusion or exclusion as key factors in shaping their post-colonial national identities. Early post-independence notions of national reconciliation and slogans like "unity in diversity" have given way to a politically-correct identity form defined by those in power along narrow "we-they" or "with-us-against-us" lines. Simultaneously, the boundaries between party and government have been blurred and replaced by a growing equation of party and government. Opposition or dissent has come increasingly to be considered as hostile and the dissenter sometimes branded an "enemy of the people". In a recent University of Amsterdam doctoral thesis on the violent campaign waged by the Mugabe government on Matabeleland in the immediate years after independence, K.P. Yap (2001: 312–13) argued that:

> whilst power relations [in Zimbabwe] had changed, perceptions of power had not changed. The layers of understanding regarding power relations, framed by socialisation and memory, continued to operate. ... actors had changed, however, the way in which the new actors executed power in relation to opposition had not, as their mental framework remained in the colonial setting. Patterns from colonial rule of "citizens" ruling the "subjects" were repeated and reproduced.

Coinciding with this tendency towards autocratic rule and the subordination of the state to the party, a reward system of social and material favours in return for loyalty has emerged. Self-enrichment by way of a system of rent-or sinecure-capitalism has become the order of the day. The term "national interest" has been appropriated and now means solely what the post-colonial ruling elite decides it means. It is used "to justify all kinds of authoritarian practice" while the term "anti-national" or "unpatriotic" is applied to any group that resists the power of the ruling elite of the day (Harrison 2001: 391).

These selective mechanisms for the exercise and retention of post-independence power are not too dissimilar from the commandist notions that operated during the days of the liberation struggle in exile. As one South African political commentator noted: "Many of my former comrades have become loyal to a party rather than to principles of justice. (…) Unfortunately it is true that those who have been oppressed make the worst democrats. There are recurring patterns in the behaviour of liberation parties – when they come to power they uphold the most undemocratic practices". (Kadalie 2001; see also Kadalie 2002). Another put it this way: "It is interesting to see who still carries their own briefcase. These are people I've known for years when we were in the field. Some of them are still great but some of them have become very pompous. When you have a car and a driver and you're travelling first class, some people change" (Younge 2001).

Simultaneous to the above, outside of the inner sanctum of the political arena and within civil society, critical voices have emerged, including even those of some who played roles as active supporters of the liberation struggle, and others who followed it, with great sympathy. A new and sharper debate has emerged, one which deals increasingly with the post-colonial content of liberation, questions the validity of the concept of solidarity based on a shared past, and calls for the end of the cultivation of "heroic narratives" (Harrison 2001; Kössler and Melber 2002). The much-celebrated attainment of formal independence is no longer unreservedly equated with liberation, and neither with the creation of lasting democracy. Now, closer scrutiny is paid to both the inherited and self-developed structural legacies which have imposed limits to the realising of real social and economic alternatives in the post-colonial era.

One of these involves a growing recognition that armed liberation struggles operating along military lines in conditions of clandestinity were not suitable breeding grounds for establishing democratic systems of governance post-independence and that the forms of resistance employed in the struggle were themselves organised on hierarchical and authoritarian lines. In this sense, then, the new societies carried within them essential elements of the old system. Thus it should come as no surprise that aspects of the colonial system have reproduced themselves in the struggle for its abolition and subsequently, in the concepts of governance applied in post-colonial conditions.

There is a parallel here to de Tocqueville's celebrated retrospective on the shortcomings of the French Revolution. It reflected the frustration provoked by the restoration of old power structures under Louis Napoleon after his *coup d'etat* in 1851 and provides relevant insights to our southern African cases.[5] De Tocqueville argued that the French revolutionaries in the process of implementing the structures of the new system retained the mentalities, habits, even the ideas, of the old state even while seeking to destroy it. And they built on the rubble of the old state to establish the foundation of the new society. To understand the revolution and its achievement, he concluded, one has to forget about the current society and instead interrogate the buried one. His conclusion was that the early freedom of the revolution had been replaced by another form of repression. Revolutionaries in the process of securing, establishing and consolidating their power bases had sacrificed the declared ideals and substantive issues they were fighting for in the name of revolution.

This, however, is a process not confined to the spheres of conscious and deliberate effort. It is also a result of particular socialisation processes. In a recent journal article, Abrahamsen (2003) has suggested that the recognition of the relationship between power, discourse and political institutions and practices has much to contribute to the study of African politics. She argues that "postcolonial approaches illustrate the inadequacy of the conventional binary opposition between domination and resistance, and show how resistance cannot be idealized as pure opposition to the order it opposes, but operates instead inside a structure of power that it both challenges and helps to sustain" (209). She suggests that these internalised dispositions carry a price and contribute to a perpetuation of structures beyond the abolition of the very system which produced them. Hence, she suggests that the seizure of state power and control over means of production does not secure a solution, since a "change of economic and political structures of domination and inequality requires a parallel and profound change of their epistemological and psychological underpinnings and effects" (ibid.).

It is in this context that the essays in this volume reflect on the state of the democratisation process in post-colonial southern Africa. In his introductory overview, political scientist Kenneth Good argues that the predominant party systems in southern Africa through the 1990s produced a high degree of non-accountability of political elites who were bent mainly on the retention of their power. This has developed to the point where he argues that it is well nigh impossible to control their lust for never-ending power. "Singularly and collectively, the ruling elites of southern Africa have shown that their chief concerns are with self-interest and retention of power, and constitutionalism counts for little".

Echoing this theme, Amin Kamete maps out developments in urban governance and electoral democracy in Zimbabwe's capital city, Harare. He tracks the developments which have lead to ZANU's loss of legitimacy and support among the majority of the urban population in the capital. He then looks at efforts by the government to win back that constituency and how, having failed, it has systematically set about disenfranchising the urban electorate. This he describes as a deliberate perversion of the democratic process and one designed to frustrate the proper expression of the electorate's will.

Complementing that case, Suzanne Dansereau examines the role of the Zimbabwean labour movement in its resistance to the Mugabe government's policies. She traces how the movement frustrated in its objectives developed a party political arm in order to compete for power. She questions the degree to which the Zimbabwean government can claim legitimacy in a situation where the working class has switched sides and now forms the backbone of organised opposition.

In contrast to the Zimbabwean cases where the post-independence era has been characterised by a high degree of contestation between contending forces, accompanied by severe levels of repression, Ian Taylor looks at the Botswana Democratic Party's (BDP) single-party domination within a constitutional framework of politics in Botswana. He argues that it is the policies pursued since independence by the BDP which have fostered an enabling role for the state in promoting socio-economic development and which have earned it thereby a high degree of legitimacy. They have, he argues, disbursed benefits to wide portions of the citizenry. Nonetheless, Taylor notes, they have also generated profound inequalities and vast differences in life chances within the social formation and provoked some disillusionment with the much-vaunted "Botswana miracle".

Not as thematically remote as it might look at first sight, Francis Nyamnjoh emphasises the importance of a comparative approach towards re-conceptualising democracy and liberation in southern Africa. He offers an analysis which recognises traditional, un-elected chiefs as agents of change and the institution of chieftaincy as dynamic within a process of negotiation and conviviality between "tradition" and "modernity". He argues that in an ongoing process of power brokerage, traditions in southern Africa are being modernised and modernities traditionalised. The dichotomy between "citizen" and "subject" is hence a matter of negotiation and implies changing identities depending on the situation.

Roger Southall locates his case study of Lesotho within an analysis of two competing paradigms of legitimacy in southern Africa. One is the paradigm of liberation which, he argues, is predominant. It is authoritarian in nature, prioritises the past over the present, glorifies the ruling party and justifies its present excesses in terms of its heroic past. The other is that of democracy which stresses the right to rule by reference to the rulers having secured a mandate from the people "in cleanly fought ... popular elections". Southall details the long, messy and sometimes bloody struggle to achieve the domination of the democratic model over the liberation paradigm, the latter represented by the Basotho Congress Party (BCP) and its armed offshoot, the Lesotho Liberation Army (LLA). This latter, while having its origins in the unlawful denial of power to the BCP after it won the 1970 general election, allowed itself to become a surrogate force in the apartheid regime's counter-revolutionary war machine which sought so bloodily in the 1980s to frustrate the attainment of democracy in South Africa.

In his chapter on Namibia, Melber demystifies the post-colonial consolidation of the socio-political system in Namibia and argues that, as a process, it has only translated controlled change into changed control. Basing its legitimacy on its liberation past, SWAPO as an agency for post-colonial emancipation and development has, according to Melber, displayed an increasingly authoritarian tendency while spawning a new elite which offers less in the way of meaningful socio-economic transformation than the colonised majority was led to expect.

Martin Legassick's chapter looks at the impact of the armed struggle, and particularly at certain decisions taken by the ANC in relation to the tactics and strategy for the conduct of that struggle, on the democratisation process in South Africa. In Legassick's view, the transition in South Africa has been a revolution aborted. It has not produced true national and social liberation in the form of a democracy reflective of "working class power ... the precondition for socialism". What it has generated, instead, is a bourgeois democracy implementing neo-liberal policies akin to those advocated by major international financial institutions. This betrayal by the ANC of the working class was not, Legassick argues, a self-conscious strategy but one forced upon the ANC which, given its lack of an armed mass base, had no choice but to opt for a negotiated settlement within a capitalist framework. This lack of choice, in turn, stemmed from flawed strategic decisions adopted in the 1960s and early 1970s which resulted in the ANC not opting for a form of guerrilla warfare which would have led to "the taking of state power by the masses".

Raymond Suttner's chapter is in a somewhat similar vein in that he focuses on some largely hidden practices, traditions and cultures (including belief systems) of the ANC in exile and their impact on the current character of the party and its degree of political mobilisation. He shows how different internal and exile backgrounds and experiences informed the attitudes and expectations of the membership which in turn, shaped the character of the movement. These experiences produced political cultures which were not in sync with one another, generating conflicts and tensions which have been played out in the post-1994 era. The predominance of one tradition over the other has, Suttner argues, shaped the nature of the democratisation process in the country since 1994.

In the concluding chapter to the volume, Krista Johnson takes this argument forward and specifically traces the influence of vanguardism within the South African liberation movement in general, and the ANC in particular. She demonstrates that despite its radical ideological posturing and its rhetoric of popular democracy and people-driven transformation, the actions of the ANC leadership and the forms of representation and participation within in the party make it little different from elitist, liberal political parties elsewhere. She argues that the challenge remains to transform the basis of state/society relations by conceptualising new forms of political organisation.

As the sub-title to this volume suggests, there remains much in the way of unfinished business in regard to consolidating democracy in post-colonial southern Africa. This applies not only to the political process but also to our analytic understanding of the dynamics of the process. These essays represent a start with a grappling of the issues. The recognition that the model of liberation democracy as developed in Namibia and Zimbabwe is inherently elitist and potentially authoritarian is a significant step forward in the debate. The debate needs to go on and be further developed. Other southern African cases, most particularly Mozambique, need to be scrutinised and brought into the analysis while a critical eye needs to be kept on South Africa as it completes its first decade of democratic rule. Are the seeds of democratic decay set to germinate or is the democratic tradition of South Africa's civil society sufficiently resilient to overcome the authoritarian tendencies in the liberation paradigm of commandism favoured by some in the leadership of the ANC? There is still much work for the scholarly community concerned with these issues to undertake.

Notes

1   See for a first result in the initial stages of conceptualisation Melber and Saunders 2001. More details on the project can be obtained from the Institute's web site (www.nai.uu.se).

2   See for a summary the conference report in *News from the Nordic Africa Institute*, no. 2/2002. Most presentations to the workshop were published in various Discussion Papers (Davids et.al. 2002, Neocosmos et.al. 2002).

3   For a conference report see *News from the Nordic Africa Institute*, no. 3/2002.

4   An exception was the earlier publication of an unabridged paper (Legassick 2002), which in a considerably shorter version is included here again. The papers presented on Namibia have been edited as part of a separate book volume, published in English and German versions (Melber 2003b).

5   Roland Apsel made me aware of the inspiring comparative aspect through his reference to an article by the psychoanalyst Erdheim (1991). See on Tocqueville's political philosophy Siedentop (1994).

References

Abrahamsen, R. 2003. "African Studies and the Postcolonial Challenge." *African Affairs*, vol. 102. 189–210.

Davids, Y.D., Keulder, C., Lamb, G., Pereira, J. and Spilker, D. 2002. *Measuring Democracy and Human Rights in Southern Africa*. Compiled by Henning Melber. Uppsala: The Nordic Africa Institute (Discussion Paper no. 18).

Dobell, L. 1998. *SWAPO's Struggle for Namibia, 1960–1991: War By Other Means*. Basel: P. Schlettwein.

Erdheim, M. 1991. "Revolution, Totem und Tabu. Vom Verenden der Revolution im Wiederholungszwang." In *Herrschaft, Anpassung, Widerstand. Ethnopsychoanalyse 2*. Frankfurt/Main: Brandes & Apsel. 153–66.

Gibson, J. L. and Gouws, A. 2003. *Overcoming Intolerance in South Africa. Experiments in Democratic Persuasion*. Cambridge: Cambridge University Press.

Harrison, G. 2001. "Bringing Political Struggle Back in: African Politics, Power & Resistance." *Review of African Political Economy*, no. 89. 387–402.

Kadalie, R. 2001. "Interview." *Focus*, no. 24 (published by the Helen Suzman Foundation, Johannesburg) (http://www.hsf.org.za/focus24interview.html).

Kadalie, R. 2002. *Citizenship, Living Rights and the Public Intellectual – the role of the public intellectual in South Africa.* Paper presented to the Annual Congress of the South African Sociological Association, East London.

Kössler, R. and Melber, H. 2002. "The West German Solidarity Movement with the Liberation Struggles in Southern Africa. A (Self-)Critical Retrospective." In Ulf Engel/Robert Kappel (eds), *Germany's Africa Policy Revisited.* Münster/Hamburg: LIT. 103–26.

Kriger, N. 1992. *Zimbabwe's Guerilla War. Peasant Voices.* Cambridge: Cambridge University Press.

Kriger, N. 1995. "The Politics of Creating National Heroes: The Search for Political Legitimacy and National Identity." In N. Bhebe/T. Ranger (eds), *Soldiers in Zimbabwe's Liberation War.* London: James Currey/Portsmouth: Heinemann/Harare: University of Zimbabwe Publications. 139–62.

Legassick, M. 2002. *Armed Struggle and Democracy. The Case of South Africa.* Uppsala: The Nordic Africa Institute (Discussion Paper no. 20).

Leys, C. and Saul, J. 1995. *Namibia's Liberation Struggle. The Two-Edged Sword.* London: James Currey.

McGregor, J. 2002. "The Politics of Disruption: War Veterans and the Local State in Zimbabwe." *African Affairs*, vol. 101. 9–37.

Melber, H. (ed.) 2002. *Zimbabwe's Presidential Elections 2002. Evidence, Lessons and Implications.* Uppsala: The Nordic Africa Institute (Discussion Paper no. 14).

Melber, H. 2003a. ""Namibia, land of the brave': Selective memories on war and violence within nation building." In: J. Abbink/M. de Bruijn/K. van Walraven (eds), *Rethinking Resistance: Revolt and Violence in African History.* Leiden: Brill. 303–27.

Melber, H. (ed.) 2003b. *Namibia. Grenzen nachkolonialer Emanzipation.* Frankfurt/Main: Brandes & Apsel (English edition Uppsala: The Nordic Africa Institute; forthcoming).

Melber, H. and Saunders, C. 2001. *Transition in Southern Africa – Comparative Aspects.* Uppsala: The Nordic Africa Institute (Discussion Paper no. 10).

Neocosmos, M., Suttner, R., and Taylor, I. 2002. *Political Cultures in Democratic South Africa.* Compiled by Henning Melber. Uppsala: The Nordic Africa Institute (Discussion Paper no. 19).

Siedentop, L. 1994. *Tocqueville.* Oxford: Oxford University Press.

Werbner, R. 1998a. "Beyond Oblivion: Confronting Memory Crisis." In R. Werbner (ed.), *Memory and the Postcolony. African anthropology and the critique of power.* London & New York: Zed Books. 1–17.

Werbner, R. 1998b. "Smoke from the Barrel of a Gun: Postwars of the Dead, Memory and Reinscription in Zimbabwe." In R. Werbner (ed.), *Memory and the Postcolony. African anthropology and the critique of power*. London & New York: Zed Books. 71–102.

Yap, K. P. 2001. *Uprooting the Weeds. Power, Ethnicity and Violence in the Matabeleland Conflict 1980–1987*. Amsterdam (PhD thesis).

Younge, G. 2001. "Life after Mandela", *Guardian* (London), 16 May.

Democracy and the Control of Elites

Kenneth Good

Controlling elites seems impossible in Anglo-American liberal democracy, where ruling elites today are celebrities, and people are spectators inside, notably, the "big tent" politics of Tony Blair. Britain's first "post-ideological prime minister" abandoned the idea of equality in favour of the vagaries of "fairness", and believes that what counts in government is simply "whatever works" (Bagehot 2002). Bold new ideas may occasionally be adopted – such as an ethical foreign policy – then abandoned without shame or explanation at the first sign of opposition or opportunity, whether over, say, Chechnya or Kosovo, or for the sake of arms sales to Indonesia. President Bill Clinton, before him, based his "triangulation" on interlinking those whose support he already had, with those whose support he wished to obtain. Public health care was promoted with fanfare in 1993 and quickly dropped when opposition arose from private insurers and medical practitioners. Then, three years later, he signed Republican-inspired welfare "reforms", which saw the number of welfare recipients nationally falling by more than half – "moms on the move" – over the next five years (*The Economist* May 25, 2002).[1]

The interlinkage is commonly achieved through an abandonment of old working-class constituencies; Blair gained power through New Labour as Clinton did through the New Democrats. Politics of these terms is essentially "the manipulation of populism by elitism" (Hitchens 1999:23). Obscurantism is in-built in these democracies. Clinton left office on a record of immorality and corruption – sexual exploitation, perjury, abuse of office, facilitating genocide in Rwanda in 1994[2] – and with the highest approval ratings of any two-term president in modern history.

Elites subordinate the people through structural and institutional factors as well as through celebrity and glamour. Limited, divided, checked and balanced, and federalised, government in the United States entailed limited democracy also.[3] Two major parties share predominance and alternate in power in Washington. At the end of the twentieth century America possessed the largest inequalities of income in the developed capitalist world, and the society both admires winners and despises losers (see Good 2002a:ch.3). Wealth counted enormously in this democracy.

An estimated $3 billion was spent on presidential and congressional campaigns in 2000, of which George W. Bush, for instance, raised $100 million for his primaries, Jon Corzine spent $60 million to become a senator from New Jersey, and later Michael Bloomberg laid out $70 million to succeed Rudy Giuliani as mayor of New York (*The Economist* November 11, 2000 and January 5, 2002).

Three groups of "insiders" were highly advantaged: the very rich, who can finance their own costly campaigns; "legacies" or "inheritors", such as the sons and wives of presidents; and incumbents, who can exchange the power of their office for campaign contributions – in House races in 2000, incumbents spent nine times as much as their challengers did. Together, the "iron triangle" consisted of legislators, lobbyists and fund-raisers on and for whom American democracy operated (*The Economist* November 11, 2000). Non-participation by the majority is a structured aspect of this system. Only 38 per cent of Americans bothered to vote in 1998; strong campaigning by both Bush and Al Gore saw turnout rise to 50 per cent in 2000 (*The Economist* July 29, 2000).

Just in case, the process of congressional redistricting allowed "representatives", in explicit reversal of the liberal norm, to choose their voters. Using regular 10-yearly census data and improved computer software, state legislators produce electoral maps that are exact in their partisanship. The parties are agreed on the need to maximise the number of safe seats for each side, drawing competitive districts only if they cannot avoid it. The 2002 redistricting plans were said to be making an already change-resistant Congress even more immutable. Only six sitting-congressmen were defeated in 2000, a re-election rate of 98 per cent – it had averaged above 90 per cent since 1952 (*The Economist* April 27, 2002). In California, for instance, a map had been approved with only one competitive district out of 53 seats in Congress. This was tough for the "outsider" majority. "If the average Californian doesn't like his congressman," said Dan Schnur, a Republican adviser, "the only option is to call the moving vans." America's North-Korean-like re-election rates, its ever-costlier election campaigns, and its "astoundingly low voter turnout", all went together (*The Economist* April 27, 2002).

Remnants of decided "unfairness" permeated Tony Blair's big tent. In 2002 the nation celebrated the 50-year reign of its hereditary head of state, and long-overdue reforms of the House of Lords were contemplated. These faced difficulties. With 705 members, it was the world's largest second chamber, some of whom might be offered inducements of up to 100 000 pounds each to quit (Wintour 2002). British democracy was also highly elitist. On an impressionistic examination of its ruling class over the 20-year period till 1992, change in its composition appeared "not just ... slow [but] almost non-existent" (*The Economist* December 19, 1992).[4] Life within the new value-free democracy seemed unattractive to British voters too. Turnout in general elections in 2001 fell from the previous level of 71 per cent in 1997, to 59 per cent. This was "the lowest turnout ever" in the country, and on the judgement of Patrick Dunleavy and colleagues, Britain was at "a nadir in its history as a liberal democracy". Just 25 per cent of the electorate voted for New Labour, but the prime minister described the result as "a remarkable and historic victory for my party" (*Guardian Weekly* June 14 and 21, 2001).

The United States and Britain are leading examples of weak democracies combined with strong capitalist economies (Swift 2002:ch.3). Here popular sovereignty is restricted and limited by the individual right to accumulate property, and it holds sway over the collective rights of the community to, say, adequate public health care or decent transportation. This classification usefully stresses the market underpinnings, as does the terminology liberal/ electoral/representative democracy as interpreted here; a system hinging upon open elections, which functions primarily to elect and legitimise political elites, and which fails to address the inequalities inherent in the capitalist economy (Macpherson 1966:46–8).

Predominant Party Systems in Southern Africa

Controlling leadership is almost equally impossible within the presidentialist and predominant party democracies of southern Africa today.[5] Namibia paved the way for democratisation in the contemporary period. It began well in 1990, acquiring an advanced liberal democratic constitution which vested "all power" in the people. This was broadly and meaningfully understood as participation in activity "intended to influence the composition and policies of the government", and in "the conduct of public affairs" both directly and through chosen representatives.[6] Members of the National Assembly were described as being the "servants of the people", endowed with notable powers to fulfil that task. Cabinet ministers were required to attend Assembly meetings and to respond to "any queries and debates" on the "legitimacy, wisdom [and] effectiveness" of government policies. Parliament could "require any senior official ... to appear before any of [its] committees to account for and explain his or her acts and programmes", and the president too was obliged to "report" on government policies annually and "to respond to questions". The president was obliged to assent to any Bill correctly adopted by parliament, and while he could dissolve the chamber under certain circumstances, both the president and the assembly would then face a national election within 90 days. Executive power was vested in "the president and the cabinet", and the former was "obliged to act in consultation" with the latter. The president was directly elected by the people, on 50 per cent or more of the votes cast, and tenure was limited to "not more than two terms".

But the sovereignty of the people and parliament's enforcement powers soon counted for little against the predominance of SWAPO – which won 72.7 per cent of the votes, and 53 out of a total of 72 seats in the Assembly in 1994 – and the pre-eminence of President Sam Nujoma, who polled 76.33 per cent at the same time. The use of the party-list system of proportional representation, without constituencies or provision for by-elections, placed great powers of preferment in the hands of the executive; around 1995 some 40 Assembly members were ministers or their deputies, and sovereignty was less with the people than with the ruling elite. Half way through his second term, President Nujoma indicated that he contemplated remaining in office, the party's central committee and its subordinate organs rallied behind him, and presented the issue publicly as simply the president's physical capacity to continue in office and his proclaimed indispensability. Despite the opposition of civil society, the constitution was soon amended in parliament to meet his wish (Good 1997b:556, 562). The people and the law were as nothing compared to the president's preferences and his party's predominance.

Hopes were high in Zambia, too, in November 1991, when the 27-year rule of Kenneth Kaunda was brought to an end by the Movement for Multi-Party Democracy (MMD) led by Frederick Chiluba (Anders Andreassen, Geisler and Tostensen 1992). Thousands had flocked to their meetings under the slogan, "The Hour Has Come", as people sought a new dawn for the impoverished nation.[7] Turnout was about 50 per cent of registered voters, the MMD won

125 seats in the 150-member parliament, and Chiluba got some 80 per cent of the presidential vote.[8] They promised not only multipartyism, but also judicial independence and press freedom, but were otherwise silent on governmental structure (MMD 1991:2–3, 11). Chiluba himself was already known as a "conservative" trade unionist, and "something of an autocrat who does not normally consult his colleagues on sensitive policy issues" (Mthombothi 1991).

Autocracy was evident in his changing of the constitution in 1996 to ensure that the aged Kaunda could not stand again in elections, and in his frequent sacking of ministers – two were ousted in February 2001 for "impertinence"; to encourage conformity further, those sacked were often investigated for corruption, and their soft loans called in (*The Economist* March 17, 2001). During the previous year he had expelled leadership rivals from the ruling party, and banned internal party debate over his succession. In October he told state television: "we have been around for only nine years. The country is moving forward … but we need more time for an impact to be seen" (*Business Day* October 9, 2000).[9]

Another amendment to the constitution in 1996 stated: "no person who has twice been elected as president shall be eligible for re-election to that office". A founding idea of the MMD was popular opposition to presidents-for-life (*The Economist* May 5; Nawakwi 2001). But with the MMD's parliamentary majority standing at 143 out of 158 seats, changing the constitution seemed no bigger problem for Chiluba than it had been for Nujoma. As lawyers, churches, trade-unionists, and students demonstrated against a third term, large numbers of the party's senior officials declared their opposition to the move. But district administrators, and "party cadres" – both newly installed by Chiluba – called for a further term, and he replied that he would bow to the "wish of the people"; on BBC television he claimed that what was happening was democratic since it was the people who were asking him to stand again (*Business Day* April 12, 2001; *Sunday Times* May 6, 2001). According to ex-Labour-Minister Nawakwi, opposition to Chiluba from within the rank and file of the MMD was firm (2001). By early May 2001 the vice-president and some eight other ministers had been sacked, demonstrations spread throughout Lusaka, and armed police were deployed outside strategic points.

Broad-based popular protest forced Chiluba to renounce a third term, but it did not prevent him from placing his chosen successor, Levy Mwanawasa, as MMD presidential candidate in subsequent general elections. Turnout was around 80 per cent, but opposition parties damaged themselves by fielding 10 presidential candidates. Mwanawasa monopolised government resources in his campaign,[10] but scraped home by just 34 000 ballots with only 29 per cent of the vote; in parliament, the combined opposition obtained 81 seats and the MMD, 77. The voting and counting process was deeply flawed, and the observer mission of the European Union concluded that the results were "not safe" (Lee 2002).

The saga was perhaps not over for the autocratic Chiluba. Retention of power was only part of his equation. As president he enjoyed immunity from prosecution, and he left office surrounded by allegations of corruption.[11] His ex-wife, Vera, for instance, claimed in a public affidavit that he had salted away some $2.5 billion from state coffers while in power (Donaldson 2002a, 2002b). Profligacy characterised Chiluba's government. Like his predecessor, President Chiluba left State House a wealthier man, and Zambia a poorer nation (Games 2001; Donaldson 2002a, 2002b).[12]

Autocracy wellnigh characterised the region.[13] President Bakili Muluzi presided over a corrupt and mismanaged government in Malawi and, towards mid-2002, appeared to be embarked on a rerun of the Chiluba scenario.[14] Elected in 1994 as successor to President-for-Life Hastings Kamuzu Banda, narrowly re-elected in 1999, he was constitutionally required to step down in 2004. But the ruling United Democratic Front was endeavouring to raise parliamentary support to change the law, and senior members of Muluzi's administration were said to have openly backed an amendment. The move against the constitution also faced "strong criticism from a vast majority of Malawians", including "many members" of the ruling party; civic and religious groups were among those who opposed (Thipha 2002a, 2002b). Muluzi was said to have banned all demonstrations for and against a third term, and like Chiluba, he expressed a specious neutrality and populism: "I am a civilised and experienced politician ... whose only commitment is to serve Malawians" (cited by Hogarth 2002).[15]

In Angola, President Jose Eduardo dos Santos headed the ruling party and government, and was at the centre of an "oiligarchy" of vast corruption. About 800 000 barrels of oil were produced in Angola each day, and on each one of these, $3 was channelled into Dos Santos's personal account (research by Global Witness 1999, 2002). For the "tiny elite" around the president, the long-running war with the rebel UNITA movement, plus the booming oil industry, "allowed the amassing of great fortunes" (*The Economist* November 10, 2001). When elections were last held in the early 1990s, the Angolan people mocked the choice offered them with the slogan: "UNITA kills. The MPLA steals" (*Guardian Weekly* November 29, 2001). When the president actually announced, near the end of 2001, after 22 years in power, that he would voluntarily step down when elections were held at some indeterminate time in the future, many people suspected that he could yet be "persuaded" to change his mind. Doubts about his sincerity were fuelled, it was said, by his failure to groom anyone to succeed. Instead, he too over the years has dealt severely with any insider who posed any challenge to his incumbency (*The Economist* November 10, 2001).

Mozambican President Joaquim Chissano had been in power for 18 years by 2001, and, by that time, the country's constitution limited incumbency to two consecutive five-year terms. He reportedly told a closed-door central committee meeting of his ruling Frelimo party, in May of that year, that he would not run again at elections in 2004 (*Business Day* May 10, 2001). But this "No" too lacked conviction and credibility, and near the end of the year he was said to be considering his position, awaiting the call of his people, as it were, to continue in office (Editorial, *Business Day* October 5, 2001). Almost all his brother presidents in southern Africa were acting similarly. Sam Nujoma, who had initiated the practice of constitutional denial, was ready to continue even beyond his acquired third term in power. He told a BBC interviewer in early 2001 that he was physically fit, and when asked if he would seek a fourth term in 2005, when he would be 77, he said: "I am always at the disposal of the Namibian people" (*Business Day* April 11 and October 5, 2001).

Singularly and collectively, the ruling elites of southern Africa have shown that their chief concerns are with self-interest and retention of power,[16] and constitutionalism counts for little by comparison. Botswana was exceptional in its generally good governance and in the regularity and openness of its elections; but here, too, executive power was highly centralised in the duopoly of state and ruling-party presidencies, the opposition had never come close to winning in free elections over almost 40 years, and towards 2002 it barely existed as a credible force (for example, see Good 1999; Darnholf and Holm 1999). South Africa was also different with the strongest economy on the continent and an advanced liberal constitution, but "the aristocrats of the revolution" – Zakes Mda's phrase – had gained power in 1994, and the ruling party appeared determined to extend its predominance through every institution in the country and to stifle, not foster, opposition.[17] As much or even more than in Botswana perhaps, a voter faced an absence of real choice in national elections – the governing party seemed certain to win in the foreseeable future.[18]

Predominance and Presidentialism in Extremis: The Mugabe Regime

Dealing with despotism in Zimbabwe has drawn the regional leaders together in remarkable unanimity, and in the process thrown clear light on their values. President Dos Santos might well be the greater kleptocrat – Mugabe has no oil to exploit, and made do with a share of the Congo's mineral wealth – but no others display the same intensity of state lawlessness, economic destructiveness, and contempt for their people in sustained and awful combination. Zimbabwe in 1980 had the second most advanced economy in Africa, and he has brought it down in his striving to retain presidential power at any cost. He has repeatedly expressed his contempt for the rule of law – the basis of society and government – and has corrupted the police and the independence of the judiciary in so doing. When an organised democratic movement developed in the late 1990s, steadily increasing its popular support, he harassed its members and meetings, tortured and killed its supporters, and ensured through various stratagems that it was denied electoral victory in March 2002 (Good 2002b).

When American Secretary of State, Colin Powell, said that there was "overwhelming evidence that the [March election] was neither free nor fair", the South African Deputy President, Jacob Zuma, called them "legitimate" and congratulated Mugabe (*The Star* March 15, 2002). This warmly supportive position is upheld not only against manifest reality but also despite repeated warnings concerning the import of it all. For Tony Blair, Zimbabwe is a "major issue" for Africa; if African leaders were ambivalent towards good governance, "it will undermine the confidence of the West" (*The Star* March 6, 2002). The ANC went determinedly in the opposite direction: "The will of the people of Zimbabwe had prevailed", it declared on its website,[19] and it lambasted Britain and the United States for what it termed their "attempts to destabilise Zimbabwe" (*The Star* March 19, 2002; *Business Day* March 20, 2002).[20]

President Mbeki had already described fellow Commonwealth leaders who favoured firm action against Mugabe as inspired by notions of "white supremacy" (*Washington Post* March 13, 2002). When calls were made from inside the country for civil protest, cabinet spokesperson Joel Netshitenzhe urged Zimbabweans not to take part. Trade and Industry Minister Alec Erwin said that Pretoria was preparing an aid package for Zimbabwe (*Business Day* and *Mail&Guardian* March 22, 2002), at a time when other countries were applying sanctions, and Mbeki and President Obasanjo endeavoured to promote the idea of talks between the Zimbabwean ruling party and the Movement for Democratic Change (MDC), in order apparently to present Mugabe in a favourable light (Fabricus 2002; Mothibeli 2002; Munusamy 2002a).

Australian Prime Minister John Howard reportedly told Mbeki and Obasanjo, when they met together in London in March 2002, that the voting figures in Zimbabwe had been massively rigged, but when President Mbeki's spokesperson, Bheki Khumalo, was asked to comment, he said: "We don't want to be part of what we consider malicious gossip." Data then suggested that some 426 000 votes had been added to the count over 72 constituencies, while about 186 000 had disappeared over 48 constituencies (Matisonn 2002). R.W. Johnson's critique of the election (2002) appeared a little earlier, and noted that about 1.8 million of the names on the official voters' roll were those of people who "do not really exist", that the opposition MDC was physically prevented from monitoring 52 per cent of all polling stations, that "the name of the game was stuffed ballot boxes", and that "between 900 000 to 1.1 million votes were manufactured".

Repression continued unabated in Zimbabwe after the presidential elections of 2002, including the persecution of journalists. But at a Commonwealth conference on Parliament and the Media, in Cape Town, delegates from South Africa, Mozambique, Namibia, and other African countries declared that any response should be left to governments to make, not individuals (*Business Day* April 18, 2002).[21]

The presidents tried repeatedly to restrict debate on Zimbabwe to themselves, and to either say nothing or to support Mugabe. Mbeki's economic adviser, Wiseman Nkuhlu, said that African countries wanted to be left alone to deal with African issues such as Zimbabwe "in their own way".[22] What this way might be was soon suggested before the annual meeting of the United Nations Human Rights Commission in Geneva. The 14-member African bloc in the

53-member commission, tabled a "no-action" motion on a European Union proposal to send a human rights expert to Zimbabwe. The African group earlier stipulated that only they had the right to table issues of concern to the continent. The commission then voted 26 to 24 against the probe. Nigeria, the leader of the bloc, was said to have portrayed the European Union's move as "politically motivated". The Mugabe government saw this step as welcome support (*Mail&Guardian* April 19 and 26; *Business Day* April 22, 2002). President Mugabe had cause for even bigger celebration when Zimbabwe, in insult to all the realities, was elected to membership of the Human Rights Commission – Justice Minister Chinamasa claimed that this showed "confidence in Zimbabwe and its role in international affairs" (Mapenzauswa 2002).

The seizure of commercial farms, and their allocation to people in or close to the ruling elite, went ahead. At the end of April 2002 at least 150 farmers had reportedly been forced off their properties in a new wave of illegal evictions; Vice-President Simon Muzenda himself led a group of officials to seize Chindito farm from its owner (*Business Day* April 28, 2002). Among the latest recipients of these unlawful take-overs were the vice-president, the Ministers of Defence and of Higher Education, a retired brigadier and MP; a general and politburo member, and other similar high-ranking members of the in-group. Information Minister Jonathan Moyo explained that, since all Zimbabweans were entitled to land, there was no reason why top officials should be excluded; he was awaiting his turn too (*The Sunday Independent* April 28, 2002; *Zimbabwe Independent* May 31, 2002). As of late June 2002, the list of officials and associates of Mugabe who had benefited from the latest land-grabs totalled 181 (Matison and Marquez 2002; Babineaux 2002).

It was also reported that the country's GDP was expected to fall by $1.12 billion in 2002 largely due to agricultural decline attributable to farm seizures (*The Sunday Independent* April 28, 2002). The Amani Trust noted that political violence in Zimbabwe had worsened since the March election (*Business Day* April 30, 2002). In mid-2002 Mugabe escalated his destruction far further, when 2 900 remaining commercial farmers were ordered to cease all productive activities, regardless of the maize and other crops in the ground – including some 24 000 hectares of vital wheat – and the cattle that they owned, and at least 232 000 farmworkers rendered jobless as starvation rose in the land.[23]

The African leadership's support for Mugabe continued, and it was perceived as such internationally. That they had chosen support for their fellow president in Zimbabwe over the Zimbabwean people's attempts to realise democracy and good government was affirmed with unanimity in Windhoek at the end of May. A meeting of the ruling parties from Angola, Botswana, Malawi, Mozambique, Namibia, South Africa, Tanzania and Zimbabwe congratulated President Mugabe on his "convincing" win "against all odds" in the March elections. They condemned the "grossly fabricated and far-fetched propaganda deliberately perpetrated against the government", and what they called "attempts to install puppet regimes that guarantee the exploitation of our resources" (Resolution of the meeting, in *Zimbabwe Independent* May 31, 2002).

Since the rise of the broad-based democratic movement in Zimbabwe in the late 1990s, the regional leaders have scorned the problems that Zimbabweans faced, and extended support to the despot. All facts concerning land seizures for self-enrichment, lawlessness, destruction, and election-rigging have been almost studiously ignored. International appeals to rethink this ultimately self-destructive posture have been spurned.[24] The real values that they hold at home in, say, Namibia, Malawi or Zambia, may be disguised or ignored, but towards the "litmus test" of Zimbabwe they have been glaringly revealed – non-accountability, bad government when profitable, one-party predominance, and perpetuity in presidential office if achievable.[25] Zimbabwe is a test case, not because Blair or Powell think so but because of how the Zimbabwean people have striven for democracy, and how they have been abandoned by almost all African ruling elites. In Botswana and South Africa the presidents indicate an occasional indifference to democracy. But towards the making of democracy in Zimbabwe the whole region has shown actual hostility. Perhaps it's the very strength of these popular forces that most disturbs an Mbeki or Obasanjo, their bases in an organised trade union movement and in urbanised civil society. The extremity and irrationality of their views ultimately implies a contempt for the rights of all people in the region.

Participatory Democracy

The people can control elites, in actuality or realistic aspiration, where the value of equality is upheld and organisations exist to further this. Elites of wealth, status, and education will exist in a society, but for real democracy to prevail they must be prevented from using their endowments for unfair political advantage. Consider two examples: Athenian democracy, 508 to 322 BC; and the United Democratic Front in South Africa, from 1983 to 1991, just after the return of the "revolutionary aristocrats".

The institutions of democratic Athens were important, but the principles guiding them and the society were perhaps of greater long-term relevance. Democracy came into being through a largely "leaderless uprising", preceded by reforms which, as Ober suggests, made Athenians "potentially responsible for one another's welfare" (Ober 1999:28–9). Ordinary citizens acquired political, legal and ideological power, in a class-based, imperialistic and – the conditions of the time – slave-owning society. Within a defined citizenship,[26] it upheld a "stern ethical code predicated on duty to self and community". Elites of wealth and education were socially active, litigious, and critical in speech and writing, but they were prevented from achieving political dominance. People's courts existed, composed of a jury of some 200 to 500 randomly chosen citizens, who were also the judges. They met almost daily, and decisions were by majority vote in secret ballot. They prescribed large fines, banishment and death. The citizen-juror tended to be deeply suspicious of the wealthy as a class. Both ideology and practice, Ober says, "encouraged voluntary redistribution of wealth and limited the political effects of wealth-inequality", chiefly through taxation and fines.[27]

Political life, he notes, was hard, but it was also voluntary. A rich or educated individual could choose to pay his taxes and keep out of politics. He was free to criticise democracy, as did Plato – the first elite theorist – in speech and writing, but not to take his criticism into the public domain or encourage the overthrow of the system, as Socrates was adjudged to have done. The educated held big advantages in public speaking, but Athenians believed in the wisdom of mass audiences, and educational attainment was not deemed necessary for collective decision-making.[28] Any citizen was free to speak at the Assembly, which drew 6 000 to 8 000 participants, remunerated on a daily basis so that none would be excluded for financial reasons. All business was decided here, by simple majority. Every citizen over 30 was expected to hold an office, and most official positions were chosen by lot, on the principle of political equality. Elections were viewed in Athens as an aristocratic method of selection, which conferred unfair advantage on the well-born, prominent and wealthy – the celebrities of advanced capitalist democracies today.

The Council of 500 was the highest decision-making body, and it prepared the agenda for the meetings of the Assembly. Like the courts, its members were chosen by random selection, on a rotational basis. The rule that no man could be a councillor more than twice in his lifetime meant, according to Mogens Hansen, that "every second citizen over 30, that is, something like every third citizen, served at least once as a member of the Council, and three-quarters of all councillors in any one year had to serve for a night and a day [as president of Athens]" (quoted in Fishkin 1995:54). Thus, every fourth Athenian citizen could expect to be state president for 24 hours during his lifetime.[29]

The participatory element in decision-making in Athens was, according to Fishkin, remarkable. Between one-fifth and one-tenth of the citizenry participated in any one meeting of the Assembly, which met between 30 and 40 times each year. The courts, the Council and various legislative commissions are described by him as "deliberative microcosms of the entire citizenry"" (Fishkin 1995:55).

For Ellen Meiksins Wood, what was distinctive about this democracy was that "the majority of its citizens were people who worked for a living". There existed a "union of labour and citizenship", focused specifically upon the "peasant-citizen". The Athenian state brought landlords and peasants together in one civic and military community. Democracy coexisted with slavery, in this undeveloped pre-capitalist society, but it also limited "the ways in which slavery could be utilised, especially in agriculture". The citizen majority could use their political power to resist the dominance of the rich. Status and wealth were present, but were not allowed to count politically (1995:183–8). Democracy represented all culturally defined citizens, regardless of their class or status. The power of the majority was enhanced inside the state as simultaneously the influence of elites was checked and diminished. It was a dynamic and revolutionary democracy over almost two centuries. It was the antithesis of the insider–outsider dichotomy that characterises American liberalism.

As a property-owning middle class is vital for liberalism and liberal democracy, as many thinkers have emphasised, so too, an organised working class imbued with the principle of equality is vital for active participatory democracy. Rueschemeyer and colleagues' definition of democracy is increasing political equality, and they found that urban workers were "the most frequent proponent of the full extension of democratic rights" (Rueschemeyer, Huber Stephens and Stephens 1992:5–6), well beyond the necessary but decidedly insufficient stage of periodic voting. Such extension holds out the prospect, demonstrated in South Africa in the 1980s, of engaging people in politics, of expanding civil society – consistent with the furthering of economic development – and, perhaps too, of controlling elites.

Urbanisation, educational advance, and the formation of a working class showed outstanding growth in South Africa through the 1970s and 1980s. The number of secondary schools in greater Soweto, for instance, grew from eight in 1972, to 20 in 1976, and to 55 by 1984, and total non-agricultural employment reached five million in 1985, when trade union membership touched 1.4 million workers, for a unionisation density of 27.6 per cent. The most rapidly growing unions became affiliated with the Congress of South African Trade Unions (COSATU) formed in 1985, and pursued what has been termed a "radical vision of a future society" to be achieved by "incrementalist" means (Webster and Adler 2002; see Good 2002a:175–90). It was a grassroots movement and a new type of politics "rarely seen among the powerless", which "stresse[d] the ability of ordinary men and women", rather than great leaders, "to act to change their world" (Friedman 1987).

Formed in 1983, the United Democratic Front (UDF) also encouraged sustainable forward movement in which the broadest number of people governed themselves in the here and now. Together with trade union action in the workplace, they aimed, as they said in 1986, to build a politics grounded in participation. Their popular democracy involved people acquiring control over their own lives in their neighbourhoods, schools and factories.

The UDF also recognised that elitism constituted a substantial barrier to the successful development of participatory organisations. Because organisation was the weapon of their struggle with a powerful state, as with the trade unions too, and because it was essential for democracy throughout civil society and eventually in government, elitism was inevitably a problem within the democratic bodies themselves. But rather than resign themselves to oligarchy and presidentialism, the UDF endeavoured to confront and check the danger through its "basic principles of our organisational democracy". As described by Morobe in 1987, these were: Elected Leadership, periodically re-elected and recallable; Collective Leadership; Mandates and Accountability; Reporting and Reporting Back; and Criticism and Self-Criticism. They constituted, he said, "fundamental weapon[s] of our struggle" (see Good 2002a:177–8).[30]

The UDF, and COSATU to a lesser extent, faced enemies on two fronts. The most obvious in the 1980s was heavy state repression. A first state of emergency in 1985–86 saw the detention of about 8 000 activists, and in the second in 1986–87, over 25 000 were detained. An identified core of active leaders, approximately 200 nationally, were held for prolonged periods. Others were kidnapped, assassinated or disappeared. Nearly 70 per cent of detainees, by late 1987, were believed to be members of UDF affiliates. Then in February 1988, the UDF itself, and 16 of its affiliate organisations across the country, were banned, and prohibited from "carrying on or performing any activities or acts whatsoever". Different restrictions were simultaneously imposed on COSATU, effectively prohibiting activities not confined to employment and workplace issues (Good 2002a:179; Webster and Friedman 1990:18–9, 25–7, 39).

State repression ensured that power shifted in practice within the UDF to key acting officials, among them Morobe for publicity and Azhar Cachalia as treasurer. But the principles of reporting back to the members, and of criticism and self-criticism of leaders, remained of active importance (see Good 2002a:179 for examples). The Front continued to operate weakly and unevenly during 1988, links with COSATU were strengthened, and then formally constituted in a new body, the Mass Democratic Movement (MDM). After the Front declared itself unbanned at the start of 1989, the UDF–MDM operated in tandem.[31] This was a significant constituency for participatory democracy. The UDF represented at its peak some estimated 700 affiliated groups and around two million people, and COSATU could claim a paid-up membership of the same order in the 1990s; the two together constituted just short of the combined populations of Mauritius, Namibia and Botswana.

Compelling expression of the principle of criticism of leaders was made by this coalition in February 1989, when Morobe, together with the co-president of the UDF and the president of COSATU, issued a public statement in the name of the MDM, describing and condemning the "reign of terror" of Winnie Madikizela-Mandela in Soweto. The statement said that "we are not prepared to remain silent where those who are violating human rights claim to be doing so in the name of the struggle". She had "abused the trust and confidence of the community", and the MDM therefore "distanced itself from Mrs Mandela and her actions". Morobe was already on record as saying: "We do not believe that any of our members are beyond criticism; neither are organisations and strategies beyond reproach" (see Good 2002a:99–100).

The UDF also faced latent opposition from the ANC. The ideas and practice of openness and accountability were unattractive to the great leaders in jail and exile. The UDF's formation was greeted with surprise and consternation by Thabo Mbeki, and its autonomy was judged threatening to the pre-eminence of the ANC within the liberation movement. The party accepted that leaders decided alone, secretly if necessary. The open and critical style of the UDF was unattractive to Nelson Mandela, as Meredith indicated when he made contact with its members in the last year of his imprisonment, and he responded to the MDM's criticism of the "Mother of the Nation" by actively seeking her promotion (Good 2002a:96–100, 119).[32] The process of secret talks after 1985, between Mbeki and Mandela, each separate from the other, and various governmental officials and supporters, both elevated the ANC leadership and relegated the UDF to the sidelines.[33] State power was the goal of the ANC's armed struggle, and parliamentary democracy was represented as its adequate accompaniment. Seekings speaks of a mutual dislike between the ANC and the UDF, but underplays their great disparities in outlook, practice and power. The Front was disbanded just a year after Mandela's release. But their ideas – and COSATU – remain,[34] and are of increased relevance in a time when predominance bulks ever larger, but elites are no longer protected by that aura of revolutionary sacrifice.

Democratising Liberal Democracy

Practical devices involving electoral systems, referenda, and deliberative systems are in use or under consideration in a variety of countries, that can enhance the influence of voters and broaden the scope of decision-making.[35] But rather than extending and deepening civil society, the trend in South Africa today, under Mbeki's presidentialism and ANC predominance, is in the opposite direction. Civil society is much smaller and less active than through the 1980s. Far more people probably discussed politics then, says Friedman with certain accuracy, than now. Research carried out by the Institute for Democracy in South Africa shows that 70 per cent of citizens today do not participate in civics (Friedman 2002:21–2). Much evidence points to the fact, furthermore, that civil society is no longer an independent critical voice relative to government, but merely its appendage, perhaps a partner with government in delivery (Friedman 2002:25). In the longer established liberal democracy in Botswana, with no heritage of past struggle, the quietism is worse.

Swift notes that opposition to the extension of democracy in contemporary circumstances is a lot like the liberal and elitist ideas previously put forward against the introduction of any democracy at all – "the people are not educated enough, they are too apathetic, too easily misled, the issues are too complex" (Friedman 2002b:96). Arblaster reached a similar conclusion earlier.[36] The likes of a Clinton and Blair enjoy their domination, and their charm and celebrity are there to disguise the fact that they would prefer to extend rather than to reduce it: the opposition of African ruling elites to the people is blatant. Resistance to them all is thus necessarily unending.

Notes

1   In seven states the fall was 70 per cent. Current law requires that 50 per cent of a state's welfare recipients work at least 30 hours a week – the more they work, goes official thinking, the more respected they will be.

2   The United States "coldly presided over the worst atrocity of the past 20 years, going out of its way to suppress all efforts to call the crime by its name while it was in train". It was "the defining scandal of the Clinton Presidency" (Melvern 2000 and review by Braeckman 2001).

3   For Daniel Lazare, actually "a counter-democratic regime of infinite duration". "America the Undemocratic" (1998:31 and 37).

4   By 2002 the proportion of top-job-holders educated at the old elite schools had fallen, but "social mobility ha[d] slowed", and the "gap between rich and poor people's education [had] widened" (*The Economist* December 7, 2002:15).

5   The phenomenon of one-party predominance under democratic conditions existed in the North – notably in Sweden, Italy and Japan – before it appeared in Botswana and then in Namibia and South Africa (Pempel 1990). The Northern form has not been characterised by the same degree of calcified presidentialism as in Africa.

6   The people's right to "directly" influence government was important, and there were other participatory elements. All people had "the freedom to form and join associations or unions", workers had a legal right to strike, and press and academic freedom were guaranteed. Quotations are from the constitution, as detailed in Good 1997a:ch.4.

7   Zambia had, for instance, acquired foreign reserves of 2 billion British pounds at independence, but Kaunda left a foreign debt of almost US$ 8 billion at the end of 1991 (Bridgland 1991).

8   In a population of 7.8 million, 2.9 million were registered to vote (*Business Day* November 6, 1991).

9   GDP a head had fallen from $390 in 1991 to $330 in 1999 (*The Economist* March 17, 2001).

10 Mwanawasa thought it "proper" that he enjoyed official planes, cars, security guards, and fawning coverage from state media; "What would you expect?" he declared just before polling day (*The Economist* January 5, 2001).

11 Transparency International ranked Zambia among the 10 most corrupt countries of the 90 it monitored (*The Economist* January 5, 2001).

12 GDP, for example, was $3 288 million in 1990, and $3 150 million in 1999; life expectancy was 49 years in 1990, and 38 in 1999; the infant mortality rate was 107 (per 1 000 live births) in the first year, and 114 in the latter; and foreign direct investment had fallen from $203 million to $163 million (The World Bank 2001:229).

13 The outstanding exception was Mauritius, where governments had actually changed hands through the ballot box.

14 Some donors had withdrawn aid to the country in 2001 citing "lack of good governance, corruption and political intolerance". Muluzi had chosen to sell 167 000 tons of the country's emergency grain reserves, and the proceeds apparently disappeared. Three cabinet ministers had been sacked in November of that year. One, earlier very close to the president, referred at his trial to the involvement of "bigger fish" in corruption (Thipha 2002a, 2002b).

15 He then ordered police to arrest those who publicly objected to his moves (*The Economist* June 8, 2002).

16 A measure of the scale of the problem was offered by Nigerian President Obasanjo in Addis Ababa in June, when he said that some $140 billion had been stolen by corrupt African leaders and banked abroad. He wanted the African Union to seek the return of this money (*Business Day* June 14, 2002). About $4 billion in state funds had been looted in Nigeria by his predecessor, President Sani Abacha (ibid June 27, 2002).

17 It was sometimes suggested, not least by President Nelson Mandela in his address to the 50th national conference of the African National Congress in Mafikeng in December 1997, that rule by the ANC was sufficient grounds for democracy, and those who opposed its government were inherently anti-democratic and racist (considered further in Good 2002a:ch.5).

18 The ANC gained 63 per cent of the national vote in 1994, and increased that to just short of a two-thirds majority in 1999. Steven Friedman notes that "the outcome of elections is at present pre-ordained" (Graham and Coetzee 2002:22).

19 A judgement reiterated in a motion passed in parliament soon after.

20 Flagrant approval of Mugabe was expressed by member of the ANC's National Executive Committee, Dumisani Makhaye, who urged some 800 party delegates to support Mugabe's "liberation struggle"; and declared that "the West wants to impose presidents of their choice" in order "to weaken governments and parties of the former national liberation movements in southern Africa". He also referred to the MDC leader, and former trade unionist, in explicitly racist terms as Morgan "Sixpence" Tsvangirai (*The Sunday Independent* March 31, 2002).

21 A week or so later, the Committee to Protect Journalists, a United States-based group, rated Zimbabwe the seventh-worst place in the world to be a journalist (*The Economist* May 11, 2002).

22   Sole presidential dissenting voice on Zimbabwe was that of Senegal's Abdoulaye Wade, who actually said: "Mugabe did not respect the rules. The opposition could not wage its campaign. There were many deaths. Electoral laws were changed. We can't call that an election." Calling a spade a spade, he added: "I refuse to belong to this trade union of presidents" (speaking in Dakar April 2, and quoted in the *New York Times* April 10, 2002).

23   Farmers who endeavoured to attend to their crops or livestock faced among other things two years in jail (Peta 2002a, 2002b; Babineaux 2002; Muleya 2002).

24   The leaders, typified by Thabo Mbeki, had painted themselves into a corner by March 2002 – claiming to uphold specific values while negating them repeatedly in practice – and they have only worsened their predicament subsequently. Their repeated response has been to assert that Zimbabwe was only one case, for which they could not be held accountable – "held hostage", as they chose to call it. But the supposed exceptions have increased and worsened. When a dispute arose in July with Colonel Gaddafi, the greatly rich Libyan dictator, who described the New Partnership for Africa's Development (NEPAD) as a product of "former colonisers and racists", Mbeki said: "The matter is really quite irrelevant. It will be wrong that any determination should be on [the basis of] any particular country" (Munusamy 2002b). Yet the president recognises that South Africa's policy towards Zimbabwe is vital if his long-touted African Renaissance cum NEPAD was to succeed, as he said when introducing his budget vote in parliament in June (Hartley 2002).

25   Viewed presidentially, "Mugabe's poll position" looked pretty good: to deny him victory in March would be "to question every African election to-date and [thus] take away the legitimacy of nearly every African leader". Letter from V.K. Maukonen in *Guardian Weekly* June 16, 2002. Recall the election of President Obasanjo which returned Nigeria to democracy in 1999: some 50 million people were believed eligible to vote; turnout in Nigeria has usually been low, and a 40 per cent vote was thought high. But in 1999 nearly 30 million ballots were said to have been counted, for a participation rate of 60 per cent, and the gap between the winner and loser was seven million votes. The only arithmetical conclusion was that about "half the votes counted ... must have been fakes" (Elizabeth Blunt, noted in Good 2002a:7).

26   Which excluded women, as did all other advanced societies until well after the end of the nineteenth century.

27   Athenian democracy and Ober's work is considered in detail in Good 2002a:167–70.

28   Growing up in democratic Athens was a form of on-the-job training, and an "idiot" was someone ignorant of public affairs.

29   The president, among other things, presided over all Assembly meetings.

30   The notions of organisation as a weapon of the weak, and that real democracy is inconceivable without it, are derivative of Robert Michels, as was the supposed inevitability of oligarchy.

31   Popo Molefe, general secretary of the Front, wrote later of the effects of state repression: "layer after layer of activists rose to the challenge ... even at times when almost every

leader was either on trial or in detention. The success of the UDF was due in part to the nurturing of successive tiers of leadership". (Seekings 2000:Foreword, 3, 228).

32 Martin Meredith: *Nelson Mandela: A Biography* (discussed in Good 2002a:96–100, 119).

33 By 1988 the initiative in opposition politics had "clearly shifted to the ANC" for the first time, according to Seekings, and talks became "the exclusive preserve of that party" (considered in Good 2002a:102–3).

34 Morobe and Cachalia presented detailed criticism of Madikizela-Mandela before the Truth and Reconciliation Commission in November 1997, the latter saying: "A part of me now wants to forget the nightmare [of her actions in Soweto], but another part says we cannot go forward until there's some accountability". He recommended disqualification from public office for gross human rights violators (Good 2002a:119–23).

35 For example, in Switzerland, a wealthy and conservative country, referenda have been used for over 150 years, at national and cantonal levels, and on citizen and governmental initiative.

36 The powerful "do not want" direct democracy, and "actively resist any attempt to bring it into being" (Arblaster 1987:89).

References

Anders Andreassen, B., Geisler, G. and Tostensen, A. 1992. *Setting a Standard for Africa? Lessons from the 1991 Zambian Elections.* Bergen: Christen Michelsen Institute.

Arblaster, A. 1987. *Democracy.* Milton Keynes: Open University Press.

Babineaux. 2002. *Mail&Guardian* (Johannesburg), June 28.

Bagehot. 2002. *The Economist* (London), May 4 and 18.

Braeckman, C. 2001. "Review of a People Betrayed (Melvern 2000)", *New Left Review*, 9, May/June.

Bridgland, F. 1991. *Business Day* (Johannesburg), October 24.

Darnolf, S. and Holm, J. 1999. "Democracy Without a Credible Opposition", *The Journal of African Policy Studies*, 5, 1 and 2.

Donaldson, A. 2002a. *Sunday Times* (Johannesburg), March 31.

_____ 2002b. *The Star* (Johannesburg), May 10.

Fabricius, P. 2002. *The Star* (Johannesburg), May 13.

Fishkin, J. 1995. *The Voice of the People.* New Haven and London: Yale University Press.

Friedman, S. 1987. *Building Tomorrow Today: African Workers in Trade Unions, 1970–1984.* Johannesburg: Ravan Press.

_____ 2002. "Consensus on and Participation in Popular Self-Government". In Graham, P. and Coetzee, A. (eds.) *In the Balance? Debating the State of Democracy in South Africa.* Cape Town: IDASA.

Games, D. 2001. *Business Day* (Johannesburg), May 11.

Good, K. 1997a. *Realising Democracy in Botswana, Namibia and South Africa.* Pretoria: The Africa Institute.

_____ 1997b. "Accountable to Themselves: Predominance in South Africa", *The Journal of Modern African Studies*, 35,4:556, 562.

_____ 1999. "Enduring Elite Democracy in Botswana", *Democratization*, 6,1, Spring.

_____ 2002a. *The Liberal Model and Africa: Elites Against Democracy.* London: Palgrave.

_____ 2002b. "Dealing with Despotism: The People and the Presidents". In Melber, H. (ed.) *Zimbabwe's Presidential Elections 2002: Evidence, Lessons and Implications.* Uppsala: Nordic Africa Institute.

Global Witness. 1999. Research in *The Star* (Johannesburg), December 6.

_____ 2002. Research in *The Star* (Johannesburg), February 25.

Graham, P. and Coetzee, A. (eds.) 2002. *In the Balance? Debating the State of Democracy in South Africa.* Cape Town: IDASA.

Hartley, W. 2002. *Business Day* (Johannesburg), June 19.

Hitchens, C. 1999. *No One Left to Lie To.* London and New York: Verso.

Hogarth. 2002. *Sunday Times* (Johannesburg), June 2.

Johnson, R. 2002. *Business Day* (Johannesburg), April 4.

Lazare, D. 1998. "America and the Undemocratic", *New Left Review*, 232:31–37.

Lee, R. 2002. "Tough Choice". *BBC Focus on Africa.* April–June 13, 2. London.

Macpherson, C. 1966. *The Real World of Democracy.* London: Oxford University Press.

Mapenzauswa, S. 2002. *Business Day* (Johannesburg), May 2.

Matisonn, J. and Marquez, J. 2002. *The Sunday Independent* (Johannesburg), April 7.

Maukonen, V. 2002. *Guardian Weekly* (London), March 28.

Meiksins Wood, E. 1995. *Democracy Against Capitalism: Renewing Historical Materialism.* Cambridge: Cambridge University Press.

Melvern, L. 2000. *A People Betrayed: The Role of the West in Rwanda's Genocide.* Cape Town and London: NAEP and Zed.

Movement for Multiparty Democracy (MMD). 1991. "Manifesto". Lusaka: Campaign Committee: 2–3, 11.

Mothibeli, T. 2002. *Business Day* (Johannesburg), May 13.

Mthombothi, B. 1991. *The Star* (Johannesburg), November 4.

Muleya, D. 2002. *Business Day* (Johannesburg), July 2.

Munusamy, R. 2002a. *Sunday Times* (Johannesburg), May 26.

_____ 2002b. *Sunday Times* (Johannesburg), June 16.

Nawakwi, E. *Business Day* (Johannesburg), May 10.

Ober, J. 1999. *The Athenian Revolution.* Princeton, NJ: Princeton University Press.

Pempel, T. (ed). 1990. *Uncommon Democracies: The One-Party Dominant Regimes.* Ithaca and London: Cornell University Press.

Peta, B. 2002a. *The Sunday Independent* (Johannesburg), June 23.

_____ 2002b. *The Star* (Johannesburg), June 24.

Rueschemeyer, D., Huber Stephens, E. and Stephens, J. 1992. *Capitalist Development and Democracy.* Cambridge: Polity Press.

Seekings, J. 2000. *The UDF: A History of the United Democratic Front in South Africa, 1983–1991.* Cape Town: David Philip; Oxford: James Currey; Athens, Ohio: Ohio University Press.

Swift, R. 2002. *The No-Nonsense Guide to Democracy.* London: New Internationalist and Verso.

Thipha, R. 2002a. *Business Day* (Johannesburg), May 30.

_____ 2002b. *The Economist* (London), June 1.

Webster, D. and Friedman, M. 1990. "Repression and the State of Emergency: June 1987–March 1989". In Moss, G. and Obery, I. (eds.) *South African Contemporary Analysis.* London: Hans Zell.

Webster, E. and Adler, G. 2002. *Trade Unions and Democratisation in South Africa, 1985–1996.* London: Macmillan.

Wintour, P. 2002. *Guardian Weekly* (London), May 23.

World Bank, The. 2001. *The Little Data Book 2001.* Washington, DC: The World Bank.

Liberation and Opposition in Zimbabwe

Suzanne Dansereau

President Mugabe characterises the present crisis in Zimbabwe as Western intransigence in the face of his resolve to correct the ills of colonialism once and for all, by returning land to the peasantry, originally taken without compensation by British colonial power. According to him, it is a continuation of the national liberation struggle waged by the Zimbabwe African National Union–Patriotic Front (ZANU-PF) and peasants against colonialism, and then kept up throughout the 23 years of independence by attempts to reform the country's colonial legacy. Pitted against them are foreign and colonial interests, represented by the Movement for Democratic Change (MDC), seeking to overthrow an elected government and restore colonialism, with the support of workers and urban dwellers who contributed little to the liberation struggle and are without interest in, or links to, the peasantry.

This simple characterisation into a series of bifurcated forces: urban or rural, national or international, worker or peasant, might be a useful simplification for a group trying to generate legitimacy in the face of growing popular dissatisfaction, yet it hides much about the complex national and international forces contributing to the present crisis. It ignores the deep involvement of ZANU-PF with those same external donors, the growing externalisation of the economy since the adoption of structural adjustment in 1990, and the way the ruling elite has been able to make use of its monopoly over external and state resources to become increasingly entrenched. Most importantly, it fails to acknowledge the emergence of an internal national opposition with a mass base in the labour movement. It denies labour's role in the anti-colonial struggle and fails to acknowledge labour's gradual distancing from the ruling party as it has sought to overcome growing hardship among workers and others faced with falling wages, unemployment and inflation, eventually turning to other social groups to create a broad national alliance aimed first at reforming the constitution, then at engaging in a direct electoral challenge in the face of ruling party intransigence. Crucial to a proper understanding of Zimbabwe's current crisis is the need to understand this internal struggle as a struggle over democratisation – between an entrenched elite seeking to retain power and a national opposition seeking to dislodge it. Workers, peasants and donor agencies may be pawns or even players in this struggle.

President Mugabe and ZANU-PF call on the memories of the liberation struggle in their search for legitimacy. Yet we have seen throughout southern Africa how effective liberation movements have been in consolidating their dominant position to remain in power and establish a new neo-patrimonial system, resulting in liberation without democracy (Melber 2002). But problems with democracy in Africa are not unique to either southern Africa or post-liberation societies. Some are due to the nature of the ruling elite, sometimes commonly referred to as a kleptocracy by the likes of *Time* magazine, or state merchant capital (Moore 2001), or politics of the belly (Bayart 1993). All refer to a state elite described as a petty bourgeoisie reliant on political power and corruption for its basis of accumulation as it permits access to public resources (Szeftel 2000). This reliance on the state for access to economic power makes the Western democratic notion of a rotating elite an unlikely prospect, especially in the African context, given the absence of alternative sources of independent economic power or opportunities. This would be even more relevant when the transition from bush to State House was short and direct and undertaken by a group totally excluded from economic and political power under settler colonialism, as was the case in Zimbabwe, and throughout much of southern Africa.

The entrenchment of a ruling elite has in fact been aided by the truncated democratisation associated with the imposition of multipartyism within the "good governance" agenda, associated with the implementation of structural adjustment programmes (SAPs) throughout sub-Saharan Africa. The narrow approach to democratisation put forward by donor agencies and countries as articulated in the good governance model requires multipartyism, competing institutions, and a state role reduced to the protection of private property and the support of market forces. The void created by state withdrawal is to be filled by the private sector – the market will regulate economic activity and government services will be provided by non-governmental, non-profit organisations or for-profit agencies involved in a variety of services ranging from water and electricity distribution, to care-giving and education. Privatisation of state services provides new economic opportunities to the ruling elite. Yet the similar privatisation of the state's political functions to a civil society, called upon to participate in policy-making in order to enhance government accountability, is a controlled form of participation limited to activities such as "stakeholder processes", and serves to thwart the demands for more fundamental forms of participation and democracy (Dansereau 2002). The promise of greater political space is largely reserved for groups representing elite interests while excluding mass-based organisations, which are geared to mobilising the many into more meaningful participation (Sachikonye 1995). These more popular mass-based groups, such as trade unions, quickly reach the limit of the narrower form of participation included in the good governance agenda at the same time as the state is required to abandon its developmental role, leaving it with reduced capacity to address social problems associated with structural adjustment, and respond to the demands of a mass-based opposition. The result in many cases is increased instability as popular groups resort to demonstration and rising opposition as increasing numbers are excluded from the benefits of the new economic dispensation (Schmitz and Hutchful 1992). By contrast, an elite has been able to benefit from the new dispensation and to use structural adjustment to entrench itself further as the group through which the aid flows (Campbell 1995). This does not result in improved norms of public behaviour but in new forms of corruption (Szeftel 2000). It also results in an increased reliance on repression as a protection against widening opposition which, given its mass base, could not be incorporated into elite circles. In the case of Kenya, for example, donors played a central role in impeding an opposition victory and full transition to democracy by knowingly endorsing unfair elections as they advanced the cause of multipartyism thereby undermining domestic efforts to secure greater reforms and allow an opposition victory (Brown 2001).

The following chapter will document the struggle in Zimbabwe, not between dichotomous internal and external forces but between an emerging elite on the one side, making use both of the rhetoric of the liberation struggle and its temporary but recurring alliances with foreign capital to consolidate its power soon after reaching State House, and the collapse of its initial attempts to introduce a redistributive development agenda. And on the other side, a labour movement that gradually moved away from its alliance with the ruling party and eventually turned to outright opposition, in alliance with other social groups, as it failed to improve workers' deteriorating shopfloor conditions and when its growing resistance was met by exclusion and intimidation by the ruling party.

Early Development Period: The 1980s

The colonial period had been marked by significant strikes and African-led trade union activity which played a leading role in the mobilisation of workers, and provided an alternative to the more elitist African organisations. Colonial fear of a linkage between trade unions and nationalist parties led to serious repression against African trade unionism with frequent detention and deportation of leadership (Sachikonye 1986:251). On the eve of independence in 1980, unions were in a relatively weak position as the job colour-bar excluded African workers from most skilled jobs; the 1934 Industrial Conciliation Act excluded them from collective bargaining (Dhlakama and Sachikonye 1994:149); and most unions, even the nonracial ones, became dominated by white skilled workers after 1950 (Wood 1987:53). In spite of significant strikes, the combination of state repression and bureaucratic leadership kept the unions weak (Mitchell 1987:106).

The ZANU-PF government assumed power in the newly independent country with promises to redress colonial injustices and bring about a socialist transformation, including greater worker and peasant participation. High worker expectations led to a series of 178 strikes and work stoppages between March and October 1980, lasting into 1981, affecting the whole country and all major economic sectors (Sachikonye 1986:252). Demands focused largely on wage increases, and changes to the worst excesses of racist and abusive managers. Many strikes were spontaneous, leaving union leadership behind as workers demanded to meet directly with the new government. Government initially responded with promises to reform the collective bargaining structures, yet it soon took a tougher stand, sending police against strikers and threatening stronger measures as it declared that workers' needs were to be subsumed under the "national interest" and that workers' demands should be "reasonable" and not disrupt production, as this would discourage investment. At the same time, government established a minimum wage, resulting in wage increases among the worst paid (Mitchell 1987:109).

Many workers and trade union leaders took an active part in the liberation struggle, yet labour issues were relegated to secondary importance, along with urban and even women's issues – all subordinated to the broad nationalist struggle, articulated around rural issues (Raftopoulos 1994). This subordination became embedded in the first planning document *Growth with Equity* in 1981, in which workers were described as "a small and privileged urban wage-income elite and efforts must be made to avoid perpetuating this situation" (Government of Zimbabwe 1981). Both workers and peasants were seen as participants in post-colonial reforms, yet under the protection of the state, which would take a greater role in the economy to "alleviate economic exploitation ... and the grossly inequitable pattern of income distribution and of predominant foreign ownership of assets" (ibid). In the 1982 Transitional National Development Plan, the state was established as the engine of growth and transformation, directing national and foreign companies into a national development strategy through the creation of key institutions and direct state involvement in several economic, and especially strategic, sectors. ZANU-PF articulated this position clearly in 1983, when it reiterated its commitment to class struggle, yet claimed that workers who were lazy were the same as exploiters and that "co-operation between the workers and employers in economic activities of the country is essential" (*Zimbabwe News* July 1983; Mitchell 1987:105).

The promised improvements in workers' conditions were brought about by reforming industrial relations to include African workers as employees, excluded since the passage of the Industrial Conciliation Act in 1934. Industrial relations structures were modified by introducing a tripartite structure, thereby limiting employers' powers, strengthening workers' positions in collective bargaining, and strengthening the state's role in labour matters. A powerful retrenchment committee was established to review all employer-proposed retrenchments, and labour boards were transformed into tripartite National Employment Councils, charged with collective bargaining for the entire industrial sectors. Pass laws for African workers were abolished. Trade testing and access to apprenticeship and education programmes were provided for African workers as a way of overcoming the job colour-bar based on the wide skills-differential between European and African workers. Companies were also required to reduce the use of expatriate labour in favour of promoting and training internally. Companies would also be compelled to improve living and working conditions for workers and their families and to institute measures to allow for the emergence of a skilled, stable workforce (Government of Zimbabwe 1982).

The state also involved itself in affairs of the labour movement. Its enthusiasm for workers' committees, established during the early post-independence strikes and capable of communicating with workers and persuading them to end their strikes, while trade unions could not, led the government to establish these committees nationwide to promote peace and dialogue between management and workers. However, trade union structures continued to be the organs solely responsible for wage negotiations (Mitchell 1987:111–112).

In *Growth with Equity* (Government of Zimbabwe 1981), government indicated its support for unions and adopted measures to strengthen them. It supported the emergence of one union per sector and one national union federation to overcome the fragmentation of the pre-independence movement. At independence, there were five separate federations, most linked to different political factions. The government pushed for their amalgamation and in 1981 they came together in a fragile alliance as the Zimbabwe Congress of Trade Unions (ZCTU), dominated by the affiliate formerly linked to ZANU. Albert Mugabe, the prime minister's brother, was named as their first general secretary. At the ZCTU's founding congress in 1981, there was a recognition of the need to accept the authority of the ZANU-PF government if they were to be allowed to pursue union activities (Wood 1987:73). Non-ZANU-PF unionists accused the then Minister of Labour, K. Kangai, of having manipulated the process by nullifying the credentials committee during the congress, and causing the non-ZANU unions to disappear in the process of union amalgamation and the emergence of one union per sector (Mitchell 1987:114–5).

Between 1981 and 1985, the ZCTU was plagued by corruption, embezzlement, maladministration and authoritarianism resulting from problems arising from total dependence on external funding as well as internal dissension and organisational weakness. The government dismissed the congress leadership, appointed senior industrial relations officers to sort out the financial affairs and to organise its second congress (Sachikonye 1986:265). By 1985, a new federation leadership, composed of representatives from among the country's now-strengthened sectoral affiliates, began distancing itself from the governing party, but it was not until a change in culture in the union movement more generally at the end of the 1980s that it became more clearly independent (interview with Morgan Tsvangirai, July 20, 1994). Prior to that, there was a belief among unionists that workers were unwilling to criticise government, seeing it instead as a possible solution to their problems. At best, government involvement in union affairs and the setting of minimum wages created confusion among workers, who wondered, "What then is the role of unions?" (Government of Zimbabwe, Ministry of Labour 1984:62). Workers were also sensitive to government accusations of laziness when they were compared to "the hardworking peasants" and to allegations that their job stoppages were damaging the "national interest". Workers turned instead to "work-ins" in an attempt to draw attention to their grievances as they did in 1985 when the country's largest furniture manufacturing company threatened retrenchments. Workers called on the workers' committee to lead the action and ran the company without managers while petitioning government to take control and transform it into a co-operative, in order to prevent retrenchments (*The Guardian* October 9, 1985).

Tensions between workers and government increased with the passage of the new labour law in 1984. Both unions and employers deplored government's increased role in labour relations under the new law. Government argued that workers still needed to be protected. The Bill gave it the right to intervene in the administration of trade unions, to fix wages, and to alter annual collective bargaining agreements if they were deemed not to be in the national interest. It also removed the right to strike from a broad range of sectors considered "essential services". In order to protect the economy in general, all unions would now have to apply to government to obtain the right to strike.

This coincided with the growth and development of the union movement throughout the 1980s as it increased both in membership and strength so that by the end of the decade it represented at least 33 per cent of the active labour force of 1.2 million (out of a population of 10 million at the time). This was in spite of the absence of the closed shop, requiring individual member union registration, and government regulations preventing the 180 000 public sector workers, including nurses and teachers, from becoming part of the ZCTU (Dhlakama and Sachikonye 1994:160). The ZCTU itself had developed as an organisation, bringing together 35 affiliates who retained their own structures and control over dues collection. Workers' committees were seen as less of a threat as most worked with the union though they were still subject to government manipulation (interview with Morgan Tsvangirai, April 9, 1994). By the end of the 1980s, the unions felt strong enough to stand up to company pressure and began urging government to withdraw from the collective bargaining process, and especially from the establishment of minimum wages, so that they could act as true worker representatives. At the same time, worker dissatisfaction grew as wages failed to keep up with high rates of inflation. By 1987 average real earnings fell to Z$2 091, below the pre-independence figure of Z$2 756 in 1979. Unemployment grew as a result of the large number of retrenchments in 1982–84, in spite of government attempts to limit them through the work of the Retrenchment Committee. Employment creation produced only 10 000 new jobs annually in the first decade of independence and did not keep up with either the population increase or the large numbers of school-leavers, who were estimated at 300 000 per annum in the early 1990s. Unemployment was estimated at 25 per cent of the workforce in 1991 (Kadenge, Ndoro and Zwizwai 1992:9).

This was the result of economic problems that set in soon after independence. Early optimism about the possibility of change and development was fuelled by growth in the first two years of independence averaging 12 per cent a year in 1980 and 1981. Yet the world recession, falling mineral prices and drought produced an economic contraction of 4.2 per cent in 1983, precipitating a foreign currency crisis (Kadenge, Ndoro and Zwizwai 1992:7). Government then approached the International Monetary Fund (IMF) in 1983, resulting in a shift in development directions. IMF loans carried with them stiff conditions, including the reduction in government spending on infrastructure and food subsidies, falling in real terms by 18 per cent during the first year of these measures (*Africa Research Bulletin* 1983). The government was also required to put the lid on yearly minimum wage increases, to increase taxes and divert spending to support export promotion (*Quarterly Economic Review* 1983). Loans from the IMF continued throughout the rest of the decade, interrupted only in 1984 when they were suspended by the IMF in response to government restrictions on profit repatriation and ongoing exchange controls, undertaken to avert another foreign currency crisis. Loans resumed in 1986 and government plans were marked by a demonstrable willingness to incorporate austerity measures and support for the export sector. The dependence on foreign loans worsened the national debt-service ratio, which rose from 2 per cent in 1980 to 30 per cent in 1983 (*Africa Research Bulletin* 1983), remaining high throughout the 1980s and 1990s, averaging 28 per cent between 1990 and 1997 (World Bank 1999).

This *rapprochement* with the IMF and shift in economic development coincided with a hardening of government's response to opposition. The first two years of independence had been marked by a policy of national reconciliation between blacks and whites, and between the two principal political parties to emerge out of the war of independence and the 1979 elections – ZANU and ZAPU (Zimbabwe African People's Union). Yet the discovery of an arms cache in 1982 on land owned by ZAPU prompted ZANU to end this loose alliance by dismissing all ZAPU ministers from the cabinet. Members of the newly created national army that had been part of the former Zimbabwe People's Revolutionary Army (ZIPRA), the armed wing of ZAPU, deserted and started "dissident" activity in Matabeleland against the government, which responded by sending the army against them. These operations are now known to have resulted in executions, kidnappings, detention and torture between 1983 and 1986 (Lawyers' Committee for Human Rights 1986). Political violence spilled over into the run-up to the 1985 elections. Dissidents were reported to have killed three ZANU party officials in separate incidents in 1984. In response, ZANU party supporters, especially party youth, went on rampages in several communities, attacking those thought to be ZAPU members. Deaths were reported, and houses and cars burnt, while the police reportedly looked on. The elections themselves were conducted in an atmosphere of relative peace, but further attacks were made on ZAPU supporters, with destruction of property and the death of six people (Ncube 1991:163). This period came to an end only in 1987 with the Unity Accord, resulting in ZAPU joining ZANU-PF, bringing several ZAPU leaders into the cabinet and making ZAPU president and long-time liberation fighter, Joshua Nkomo, one of the country's two vice-presidents.

The ongoing influence of Western donors and a growing internal opposition, put pressure on ZANU-PF to abandon plans for a *de jure* one-party state in 1990, creating political space for opposition parties to contest the 1990 elections. Observers reported these elections to be neither free nor fair. Only two seats were won by the opposition Zimbabwe Unity Movement (ZUM). Problems were reported with ZANU-PF's use of state resources to fund its campaign and the use of political violence, mainly by the party's youth wing, as they engaged in running battles aimed at intimidating opposition organisers. Shots were fired at the opposition party's national organising secretary and its election director a few days before the vote, forcing other opposition candidates into hiding (Makumbe 1991:183).

Growth of Resistance: The 1990s

In spite of the condemnation of the 1990 elections, the IMF and World Bank went ahead with an SAP in 1991 which consolidated many of the trends begun during the 1980s. The programme required macro-economic adjustment and trade liberalisation aimed at stimulating investment activity and removing existing constraints on growth as stated by the Minister of Finance in 1990 (Government of Zimbabwe 1990), while purposefully moving away from the redistributive policies of the early independence period. The state was required to shift from a developmental state and large-scale public sector investment to activities aimed at encouraging investment in lagging productive capacity by doing away with many economic regulations to allow market forces to operate in directing the pace and course of economic activities (Government of Zimbabwe 1990).

The SAP contained the usual package of government cutbacks, including currency devaluation, reduction in the size of the civil service, and subsidies to parastatals in social services and in food subsidies which reversed many of the social gains made in the early period (Dansereau 2000). Economic priorities were now directed at trade liberalisation, export promotion, economic deregulation and the privatisation of many state assets. Investment promotion and incentives replaced policies aimed at government control of investment, originally instituted as part of government development planning. Monetary policy was now to be directed towards fighting inflation, and financial sector reforms would be geared towards facilitating new entrants into the financial sector.

Actions in the mining sector are a good example of this shift. In the early independence period, mining had been seen as a strategic sector, given its significance for foreign currency earnings, employment and energy. Government increased its intervention during the 1980s, becoming involved in production and marketing while linking extraction to manufacturing. Under structural adjustment, its sectoral policy shifted to creating an enabling environment to attract greater foreign investment so that producers would now benefit from tax credits, while government abandoned the idea of greater involvement in production. Instead the Ministry of Mines would seek to commercialise many of its services, in view of eventual privatisation (Government of Zimbabwe, Ministry of Mines 1999).

Structural adjustment brought few remedies to the Zimbabwe economy. It never reached the targeted growth rate of 5 per cent per annum, averaging only 1.2 per cent from 1991 to 1995, though the period was also marked by a severe drought. The trade deficit increased with a doubling of imports and decline of exports. Manufacturing fell as a contribution to GDP in that same period, while some other sectors such as tourism, transport and communication, and finance grew. Foreign debt rose from 8.4 per cent to 21.8 per cent of GDP between 1991 and 1996. In addition, there was a significant fall in social wages due to cutbacks in social services with the institution of cost-recovery programmes in health, education and other areas. Primary school drop-out rates increased, particularly among girls. Per capita spending on health dropped by 20 per cent in real terms between 1990 and 1995, at a time when the HIV/AIDS pandemic was becoming keenly felt. A brain drain set in, along with a sharp rise in crime (Bond 2000:179).

Workers and others were hurt by these economic problems. Persistent inflation and the elimination of subsidies and social programmes saw the cost of food increase by 516 per cent, and medical care, transport and education by 300 per cent. By 1995, 62 per cent of households could no longer afford all the basic necessities of food, clothing, shelter and transport at one time (Government of Zimbabwe 1995). This decline was linked to a further fall in real wages of 36 per cent between 1990 and 1996 (South African Press Association (Sapa) January 14, 1997), falling from an index of 122 in 1982 to 67 in 1994 (Kanyenze 2000). The ZCTU reported that on average their members had a real wage decline of 38 per cent in 1996, compared to 1980, and 40 per cent lower than in 1990. Those that suffered the biggest wage falls, compared to 1980, were civil servants losing 65 per cent, domestic workers 62, construction workers 56, teachers 50, farmworkers 48, miners 20 and manufacturing 19 (ZCTU 1996). Unemployment was reported to have risen between 35 and 45 per cent, resulting from a decline in manufacturing. Unemployment was further exacerbated by the announcement of job losses caused by the new SAP, with an estimated loss of 30 000 civil service jobs and another 2 000 among parastatal workers (Government of Zimbabwe 1990).

Labour initially welcomed government's claim that it would now take a "hands-off" approach to collective bargaining as part of economic liberalisation and reforms brought to the Labour Act in 1992. Yet the ZCTU noted that it continued to intervene in setting minimum wages while reforms to the Bill expanded the sectors now deemed essential and now ineligible to strike (Tsvangirai 1992). The reforms also abandoned the principle of one union per industry at the same time as government announced its intention to establish union-free export-processing zones.

Unions and government grew further apart after the adoption of structural adjustment. The ZCTU was under increased threats of deregistration with one union suspended after being accused of inciting members to strike. It was accused of partisan political motivations because of its opposition to the SAP. In 1994 the Reserve Bank blamed rising unemployment on workers' wage demands, concluding that these would lead to the failure of the programme (*Daily Gazette* September 5, 1994). Employers made a similar accusation, charging that it could not meet its SAP targets because of workers' excessive wage demands (*Sunday Gazette* August 14, 1994). Unions concluded that government objectives since the introduction of the SAP were to break the strength and unity of the labour movement, now using its more-developed labour relations apparatus to support management in collective bargaining (Tsvangirai 1992). This conviction was reinforced by declining real wages and employment levels and growing hardships experienced by large segments of the population as the effects of the programme deepened. A brief thaw occurred in the run-up to the 1995 elections when the union movement published a policy document on structural adjustment and attempted to engage the state and the international financial institutions in a more constructive debate on it. The government, fearing labour's strength, agreed to meet with labour leaders and attended May Day celebrations in 1995 for the first time since 1991 (Raftopoulos 2000:268).

Spurred on by the contrast between their falling real wages and the large wage increases that government awarded its own officials, workers and unions took increasingly large-scale industrial actions to recoup wage losses in both the private and public sectors. As these grew in size and intensity, defying existing labour laws, the government responded with an increasingly heavy hand, advising that workers should tighten their belts for the good of the nation. In 1994 a series of large strikes took place, starting in banking, followed by the construction and insurance sectors, with a significant strike by post and telecommunication workers. The government, as employer, dismissed all the workers and jailed the union leaders, but the strike nonetheless gained the support of both parliamentarians and the public and forced government to back down. Unions learnt an important lesson from that strike – that in spite of the stiff anti-strike measures in the labour law, the union had forced government to accede to worker demands, including the rehiring of dismissed workers.

Another strike wave occurred in 1996, mostly in the public sector, and quickly escalated into a national crisis that reflected the growing politicisation of labour relations as over 160 000 workers walked off the job in key government services. University students joined in and the teachers threatened to walk out as soon as their term break began. Government took a hard stand, threatening to fire workers, detaining union leaders, and refusing to negotiate. Yet government was again pushed to the bargaining table, where they finally conceded a 20 per cent wage increase, ending the strike after two weeks (Sapa, August 20–29, 1996). This strike dealt a further blow to government as the extent of disruption to crucial services made them appear to have lost control (John Makumbe, quoted in *Southern African Chronicle* September 6, 1996).

Strikes resumed in October in the public health sector. Nurses and junior doctors went out – responding to resentment built up over the years during previous strikes when they had been forced back to work (Dhlakama and Sachikonye 1994:162). This time they paralysed the hospital system for 49 days. Government once again refused to negotiate, dismissing 2 000 nurses and 200 junior doctors, advertising abroad for replacements and leaving the army in charge of patient care! The government interpreted the strike as a political challenge rather than an industrial dispute, claiming that it had been fomented by the opposition political parties and was causing unacceptable threats to public safety. In the end, the nurses and doctors had to beat a "tactical retreat" in the face of increasing public pressure. However, negotiations over the reinstatement of dismissed workers prolonged the strike (*Moto* December/ January 1996/97).

These strikes created an atmosphere of defiance in the last months of 1996. The ZCTU called a national strike and public demonstration in support of health workers. Government threatened military intervention and introduced a ban on demonstrations. The national strike never materialised – largely because government called out the military to quell any demonstrations. A few hundred people showed up for a rally and several union leaders were briefly imprisoned. Interestingly, though, these actions were taken in alliance with churches, students and human rights groups, bringing together those that would form the crux of the alliance to become consolidated into a national opposition movement to form the Movement for Democratic Change (Sapa, November 1–15, 1996).

The economy continued to deteriorate in 1997 with a 74 per cent fall in the value of the currency and rapidly rising inflation (Bond 2000:182). Over 100 job actions accompanied by several demonstrations, national stay-aways and consumer boycotts (*Financial Gazette* February 11, 1999) took place as the unions widened the scope of their activity to address the general economic decline of members, aiming at government instead of individual employers as the problem was now seen as one of macro-economics. The ZCTU demanded participation in the Tripartite Negotiating Forum, a committee bringing together government and employers in discussions around a social contract and macro-economic issues (Morgan Tsvangirai, quoted in *Financial Gazette* April 9, 1998). Labour was eventually invited to participate but this was short-lived. The ZCTU withdrew in February 1999 when the government allowed further price increases in basic goods, despite union opposition. The ZCTU claimed that the government was dithering on crucial matters to arrest the escalating rate of inflation, the severe national debt, the day-to-day increases in the prices of basic commodities, the devaluation of the local currency, corruption and scandals, the land question and other issues. It announced it would stay away from the Tripartite Negotiating Forum until the government lifted the ban on mass actions that had been imposed in 1998 after a three-day stay-away in which the government called in riot police (ZCTU 1999).

Emergence of National Opposition

This inability to solve workers' economic problems coupled with increasing repression against strikes and demonstrations, as well as the failure to effect change via tripartite negotiations at the macro-economic level, pushed the labour movement to see the need for change at the political level. Yet problems with elections, including the low turnout of the 1990 elections (only 54 per cent), marked what Makumbe (1991:180) calls the "beginning of authoritarian rule in post-independent Zimbabwe". The 1995 elections, boycotted by five main opposition parties that alleged the playing field was too uneven, left a weak opposition made up of only a few individual candidates to face intimidation, and resulted in a low turnout of 57 per cent – yet a turnout of which Makumbe and Compagnon (2000:290, 236) are suspicious, given the government's concern with the need to reverse the decline in turnout. In spite of government's declared commitment to multiparty democracy the unions and citizens' groups, not surprisingly, became increasingly convinced of the inability to bring about change via the electoral route. This prompted the emergence of an extra-parliamentary opposition as those in opposition felt that the current context was one of corruption and abuse of power resulting in increasing poverty, hunger and riots, and that these required constitutional change aimed particularly at limiting the power of the president (Makumbe and Compagnon 2000:318). The alliance brought together 96 organisations such as labour, churches, co-operatives, citizens' groups, human rights organisations, and student groups into a broad coalition organised into the National Constitutional Assembly (NCA) in 1998. The ZCTU's Morgan Tsvangirai became president of the new organisation, whose objective was to push for a full representative constitutional review. The government, in an attempt to regain the momentum and deflect the support for more radical constitutional change proposed by the NCA, set up its own review, appointing 400 people to a Constitutional Assembly who, after holding a national consultation, would draw up a draft constitution to be put to a national referendum in February 2000.

Once the ZCTU withdrew from tripartite national discussions in 1999, and in an attempt to go beyond the constitutional debates of the NCA, it convened a broader convention of trade unions and opposition groups. The outcome was the formation of the National Working Peoples' Convention in May 1999 with the mandate to map out strategies to protect workers from the biting economic conditions and put into place a strong, democratic popularly-driven and organised movement of the people. In this early period, it concentrated on mobilising and educating for social change and engaging in a campaign for democratisation, emphasising social democratic, human-centred development, political pluralism, participatory democracy, accountable and transparent governance. In September 1999, at a ZCTU congress, the union gave its support for it to become a fully-fledged party. With participation by 40 popular groups and at an event attended by 20 000 people, the MDC was officially launched, declaring it would contest the 2000 parliamentary elections (*The Worker* September 1999).

The MDC entered the election period a few months later, with activists and members coming from a diverse set of interest groups. Current leadership reflects the MDC's close association with the labour movement. The current president and vice-president of the movement – Morgan Tsvangirai and Gibson Sibanda – holders of the two top positions within the ZCTU, had been key to distancing the union from the ruling party. In addition, eight other trade unionists are members of the MDC executive. Several trade unionists were among the MDC candidates of the 2000 parliamentary elections, and several won, including Gibson Sibanda, now House Leader for the MDC (as Morgan Tsvangirai did not win his seat). In addition to the trade unionists, the diverse group of MDC members who went to parliament included Roy Bennett (a white commercial farmer) and Munyaradzi Gwisai (a member of the Trotskyist International Socialists). Others were educators, entrepreneurs, professionals, ex-civil servants, clergy and former NGO workers.

This group reflects the broad coalition that makes up the MDC. In addition to trade unionists, the alliance over constitutional issues within the NCA brought in several constitutional specialists, university lecturers, and former members of the students' association, many of whom play a prominent role in the movement, as well as human rights groups in response to demands for greater political freedom. Alliances over general economic hardships and the battles to have the government impose price controls brought in activists from consumer groups, teachers, NGOs, students, the co-operative movement, some of the churches, and others. Regional branches of national organisations have also joined, even if the national organisation did not, including branches of the Commercial Farmers' Union, the Zimbabwe Farmers' Union and the Indigenous Commercial Farmers' Union (interview with R. Makuwadza, August 2, 1999). This diversity expanded further after February 2000 with the start of land invasions and attacks against white commercial farmers, many of whom then openly supported the MDC. Other forms of financial support came from indigenous business people, though not from the main associations grouping indigenous business people.

While trade unionists, or former trade unionists, clearly head the organisation, the MDC manifesto reveals that labour is but one set of interests within this broad national alliance. The movement is not a workerist party, but a common front of various political and economic interests, coming together in a social democratic platform that emphasises popular participation to reclaim "peoples' power" and economic justice. The MDC manifesto claims this will be achieved via a mixed economy that recognises a stronger state capable of limiting the excesses of the marketplace, providing conditions for economic and social development and poverty alleviation while calling on international trade and national capital to develop a local manufacturing sector to create employment (MDC 2000).

The positions in the MDC manifesto reflect this loose alliance, combining social justice priorities with commitments to national development, articulated loosely from a socio-democratic position. Yet its principle organising slogan *Chinja Maitiro* (Change) provides a powerful rallying cry, around which it attempts to maintain the support of the divergent groups which currently support it. The trade unions have begun to wonder if it is hiding behind the excuse of violence to postpone the emergence of clearer policy proposals (*The Worker* February 2001). Yet events since February 2000 have postponed any such discussion as the MDC faces the increased intransigence of the ruling party.

Just before the parliamentary elections in 2000, Mugabe's government was faced with criticism at home and abroad, especially from 1997 onward, because of the growing economic crisis prompted by several unbudgeted items. The first was the decision to award compensation packages (representing 2.6 per cent of GDP) to the increasingly vociferous war veterans. This was followed by the decision to expropriate 1 471 commercial farms, and to continue its costly involvement in the Democratic Republic of the Congo (World Bank 2000). These actions made it difficult to meet donor conditions to reduce budget deficits and led to the IMF suspending aid in 1999 (*The Star* February 9, 2001).

Government's failure in the constitutional referendum in February 2000 was ZANU-PF's first loss at the polls since 1980, one which it felt might be a warning of things to come. For the first time the party recognised the depth of popular dissatisfaction. It marked the end of government's willingness to be bound by good governance criteria and the political conditionalities of the SAP, as it was unable to balance the demands of the international donor community with those of internal forces. It chose then to abandon its alliance with international donors in favour of a clear nationalist programme involving alliances with war veterans and a return to liberation war slogans.

Invasions of commercial farms by war veterans began shortly thereafter, with land squatting in the name of the much-promised land reform programme, which would now be fast-tracked. Mugabe refused to dislodge the land invaders. He claimed they were really protesting against Zimbabwe's colonial heritage (*Daily Mail&Guardian* March 20, 2000) and that the government would move in later to subdivide the land (*Financial Gazette* March 16, 2000). This nationalist language was carried through to the election campaign as Mugabe vowed the country would never again be colonised. Britain was presented as the enemy, as the country originally responsible for land theft, and commercial farmers and the MDC were its agents of neo-colonialism.

The IMF continued to insist that major economic reforms, such as a significant dollar devaluation and drastic cuts to the government budget deficit, be undertaken in exchange for economic aid. The government refused to accede to this until after the parliamentary elections scheduled for later that year (*Financial Gazette* February 24, 2000). The IMF added that government's refusal to end the fast-track land reform programme and to co-operate with the United Nations Development Programme to find a peaceful solution to the land problem would also prevent the resumption of donor funding. Squatter actions had been judged to be illegal by the Zimbabwe Supreme Court, and government's refusal to abide by its judgment threw the country into a constitutional crisis (*Financial Gazette* February 8, 2001). A campaign of intimidation was then aimed at the judiciary, forcing the chief justice into early retirement and two other judges to resign (*Daily Mail&Guardian* February 16, 2001).

The parliamentary elections of 2000 were marked by significant violence and intimidation, yet the MDC won an unprecedented 57 seats out of a total of 120 contested (30 seats being appointed by the Council of Chiefs and by the president). The MDC president, Morgan Tsvangerai, formerly general secretary of the ZCTU, challenged Robert Mugabe in the 2002 presidential elections. The run-up to the elections held in March 2002 continued the pattern of poorly concealed legality. The government hurriedly passed two Bills which significantly curtailed civil liberties. The first one banned all correspondents from foreign and domestic news organisations. The remaining Zimbabwean journalists would now have to be licensed, at the discretion of the Information Minister. The second Bill – the Public Order and Security Bill – dramatically increased government's sweeping powers of detention and seizure. Welshman Ncube of the MDC stated that these two Bills, "when taken together ... complete the transition from a form of democratic society to a total dictatorship and fascist state" (quoted in *The Times* January 7, 2002).

During the elections, most foreign correspondents either reported clandestinely, or used Zimbabwean journalists. The Security Bill was used extensively against the MDC to break up training sessions for polling agents and even small gatherings in private homes. It had a significant impact on the party's capacity to organise. In addition, pre-poll violence was used to intimidate. During the elections, 1 400 MDC polling agents and election observers from civil society organisations were detained (*Financial Gazette* March 14, 2002). The MDC estimates that in 52 per cent of rural stations its polling agents were prevented from reaching the stations in time for the start of polling and that 40 per cent of rural stations remained without effective MDC polling officers throughout the voting process. Newly promulgated regulations allowed voting to go on even in the absence of a political party's polling agents. The elections were widely condemned by international observers (Southern African Development Community 2002). While Mugabe gained a formal victory, there was little legitimacy. In spite of this victory, however, intimidation and violence aimed at MDC supporters and organisers continued after the elections. Several were arrested, charged with treason and murder, and at least eight journalists were charged with infringing the new information law. The MDC is now making claims of systematic torture being used against its parliamentarians and supporters.

The Zimbabwe government's willingness during the electoral period to ignore all outside pressure and any semblance of legality, entrenching itself in an anti-colonial stance, has left the country in an impasse with both the international community (as it drew in other African heads of state) and with internal forces, with little obvious sign of resolution. Post-election negotiations between ZANU-PF and the MDC, brokered by Nigeria and South Africa, have not ended the political impasse, leaving the country in a weakened condition to deal with looming food shortages, an unresolved land situation, high unemployment, inflation, and a parallel currency market.

Conclusion

This article has sketched a very different scenario from the one presented by ZANU-PF. It has outlined the emergence of a national opposition, not solely as an agent of international donors but representing a broad alliance of organisations, many of which have a mass constituency. This alliance was initially led by labour, seeking first to bring constitutional change but faced with an increasingly entrenched elite, turning to direct electoral challenge. It thus becomes clear that Mugabe's characterisation of the MDC as an agent of international donors contributes to an interpretation of the current political climate as an extension of the struggle waged during the war of liberation. In contrast, this analysis has demonstrated that the struggle is now between a growing national opposition and an entrenched elite that was able to make use of its ties with international agencies to consolidate its power. It relinquished those international ties only when it became clear in February 2000 that it could no longer maintain a veneer of democracy, demanded of a "good governance" agenda, when faced with the impending loss of upcoming parliamentary and presidential elections. To augment its chances of emerging victorious, ZANU-PF appealed to the ideals of the liberation struggle – the promise of land. By moving towards a fast-tracked land reform programme it aimed to regain the favour of the biggest section of the electorate, the land-starved peasants, who continue to represent 70 per cent of the population.

This meant marginalising workers and urban dwellers, characterised by ZANU-PF as self-interested labour aristocrats, both during the war and after independence. This version of history excludes labour not only from the independence struggle but from the entirety of the country's colonial history. Understanding the independence struggle as multifaceted, with roots in both the countryside and the urban areas, with a variety of social and political messages, helps us to see the more elitist nature of ZANU-PF leadership, both before and after independence, with a purely nationalist message, led largely by intellectuals. Once it came to power in 1980, ZANU-PF's programme of "growth with equity" – in spite of its socialist language – served to expand the role of the state rather than establish worker or peasant control. In the end, this facilitated elite entrenchment and was consolidated by the eventual adoption of structural adjustment.

Many of these same dangers face the MDC. Labour has played a pivotal role in founding the movement, after a long period of struggle and radicalisation. Yet it must be remembered that the movement is a broad alliance of groups with various socio-economic interests, united in their opposition to ZANU-PF and maintaining their resolve in the face of growing repression. Faced with the need to weather the current storm and to maintain the struggle for change, and even survival, they have put off until a later date the arduous process of transformation from movement to political party, with fully articulated positions. Such a process will mean a struggle between competing economic and political interests within the movement, to which will be added the inevitable pressure from donor agencies. It remains to be seen whether the mass membership of groups in the movement, including labour and citizens groups, will participate in these discussions; or if the leadership will become divorced from it and seek refuge in elite politics. To do so will mean embarking on a well-trodden and narrow path, the results of which have left little leeway to even the most astute of political figures in sub-Saharan Africa.

References

Bayart, J-F. 1993. *The State in Africa: Politics of the Belly*. London: Longman.

Bond, P. 2000. "Zimbabwe's Economic Crisis: Outwards vs Inwards Development Strategy for Post-Nationalist Zimbabwe", *Labour, Capital and Society*, 33,2:162–91.

Brown, S. 2001. "Authoritarian Leaders and Multiparty Elections in Africa: How Foreign Donors Help to Keep Kenya's Daniel arap Moi in Power", *Third World Quarterly*, 22,5:725–40.

Campbell, B. 1995. "Guinea's Economic Performance under Structural Adjustment: Importance of Mining and Agriculture", *Journal of Modern African Studies*, 33,3:425–50.

Dansereau, S. 2002. "Democratisation in Zimbabwe: Limits of the Good Governance Agenda". In MacLean, S., Parker, H. and Shaw, T. (eds.) *Advancing Human Security and Development in Africa: Reflections on NEPAD*. Halifax: Centre for Foreign Policy Studies, Dalhousie University: 183–202.

_____ S. 2000. "State, Capital and Labour: Veins, Fissures and Faults in Zimbabwe's Mining Sector", *Labour, Capital and Society*, 33,2:216–54.

Dhlakama, L. and Sachikonye, L. 1994. *A Collective Bargaining in Zimbabwe: Procedures and Problems in Political Transformation, Structural Adjustment and Industrial Relations in Africa*. Geneva: International Labour Organisation: 147–68.

Government of Zimbabwe. 1981. *Growth with Equity: An Economic Policy Statement*. Harare: Government Printer.

_____ 1982. *Transitional National Development Plan, 1982/83–1984/85*. Harare: Government Printer.

_____ (Ministry of Labour, Department of Research and Development). 1984. *Labour and Economy: Report of the National Trade Union Survey*. Harare: Government Printer.

_____ 1990. *Economic Policy Statement: Macro-economic Adjustment and Trade Liberalisation Including the Budget Statement 1990*. Harare: Government Printer.

_____ 1995. *Poverty Assessment Study Preliminary Report*. Harare: Government Printer.

_____ (Ministry of Mines, Environment and Tourism). 1999. *Client's Charter*. Harare: Government Printer.

Kadenge, P., Ndoro, H. and Zwizwai, B. 1992. *Zimbabwe's Structural Adjustment Programme: The First Year Experience*. Harare: Sapes.

Kanyenze, G. 2000. "The Implication of Globalisation on the Zimbabwe Economy". Harare: Zimbabwe Human Development Report.

Lawyers' Committee for Human Rights (LCHR). 1986. *Zimbabwe: Wages of War*. New York: LCHR.

Makumbe, J. 1991. "The 1990 Zimbabwe Elections: Implications for Democracy". In Mandaza, I. and Sachikonye, L. (eds.) *The One-party State and Democracy: The Zimbabwe Debate*. Harare: Sapes: 179–88.

Makumbe, J. and Compagnon, D. 2000. *Behind the Smokescreen: The Politics of Zimbabwe's 1995 General Elections*. Harare: University of Zimbabwe.

Melber, H. 2002. "From Liberation Movements to Governments: On Political Culture in Southern Africa", *African Sociological Review*, 6,1:161–72.

Mitchell, B. 1987. "The State and Workers' Movement in Zimbabwe", *South Africa Labour Bulletin*, 12,6/7:104–22.

Moore, D. 2001. "Is the Land the Economy and the Economy the Land? Primitive Accumulation in Zimbabwe", *Journal of Contemporary African Studies*, 19,2:253–66.

Movement for Democratic Change (MDC). 2000. *Manifesto*. Harare: MDC.

Ncube, W. 1991. "Constitutionalism, Democracy and Political Practice in Zimbabwe". In Mandaza, I. and Sachikonye, L. (eds.) *The One-Party State and Democracy: The Zimbabwe Debate*. Harare: Sapes: 155–78.

Raftopoulos, B. 2000. "The Labour Movement and the Emergence of Opposition Politics in Zimbabwe", *Labour, Capital and Society* 33,2:256–86.

_____ 1994. "Nationalism and Labour in Salisbury, 1945–1965". Unpublished paper presented at St Antony's College, Oxford University.

Sachikonye, L. 1995. *Democracy, Civil Society and the State*. Harare: Sapes.

_____ 1986. "State, Capital and Trade Unions". In Mandaza, I. (ed.) *Zimbabwe: The Political Economy of Transition 1980–1986*. Dakar, Senegal: Codesria: 243–74.

Schmitz, G. and Hutchful, E. 1992. *Democratization and Popular Participation in Africa*. Ottawa: North-South Institute and Partnership Africa–Canada.

Southern African Development Community (SADC). 2002. "Analysis of Zimbabwe's Presidential Election, March 9, 10, 11, 2002 in Terms of SADC Parliamentary Forum, Electoral Recommendations". Harare: SADC.

Szeftel, M. 2000. "Between Governance and Under-Development: Accumulation and Africa's Catastrophic Corruption", *Review of African Political Economy*, 27,84:287–307.

Tsvangirai, M. 1992. "The Labour Relations Amendment Bill 1992". Published in the proceedings of the Conference on *ESAP, Industrial Relations and Employment Creation* organised by the Employers' Confederation of Zimbabwe and the F.N.Stiftung Foundation, August 17–19, 1992.

Wood, B. 1987. "Roots of Trade Union Weakness in Post-Independence Zimbabwe", *South African Labour Bulletin*, 12,6/7:47–92.

World Bank. 1999. *Global Development Finance: Country Tables.* Washington DC: World Bank: 600–2.

_____ 2000. *Zimbabwe-Enhanced Social Protection Program, Project ZWPE68947 June 29.* Online www.worldbank.org. March 16, 2002.

Zimbabwe Congress of Trade Unions (ZCTU). 1999. *The ZCTU in 1999 and Beyond: An Update.* Harare: ZCTU.

_____ 1996. *Beyond ESAP.* Harare: ZCTU.

Newspapers/Publications

Africa Research Bulletin, Blackwell Publishers, Oxford.

Daily Gazette, Harare.

Daily Mail&Guardian, (online).

Financial Gazette, Harare.

Mail&Guardian, Johannesburg.

Moto, Harare.

AIA's Southern African Chronicle, (Africa Information Afrique, independent newswire service) Harare.

South African Press Association (Sapa). Johannesburg.

Sunday Gazette, Harare.

The Guardian, London.

The Star, Johannesburg.

The Times, London.

The Worker, (ZCTU monthly publication), Harare.

Quarterly Economic Review, London.

Zimbabwe Independent, Harare.

Zimbabwe News, (ZANU-PF publication), Harare.

Interviews

R. Makuwadza, General Secretary, Chemical Workers' Union. Interviewed by S. Dansereau, August 2, 1999.

Morgan Tsvangirai, President of the Movement for Democratic Change. Interviewed by S. Dansereau, July 20, 1994.

In Defence of National Sovereignty?
Urban Governance and Democracy in Zimbabwe

Amin Kamete

Elections are usually regarded as an important measure of democracy as they constitute a "general indicator of the relationship between state power and different groups in society" (Laakso 1999:9). Democracy – however it is defined (Joseph 1999) – is in turn an indicator of urban governance. Using this framework of liberal democracy, pre-independence Zimbabwe can be judged as having been very undemocratic (Swilling 1997) and therefore badly governed (Global Development Research Centre (GDRC) 2000). The black majority did not have the vote in either national or local government elections. They were excluded through the adoption and application of several restrictive qualification criteria that included race, land tenure, income and property ownership. During the 1960s and 1970s, liberation movements waged a long struggle of independence, one of whose major aims was the extension of the vote to the black majority. Following independence and the triumph of the Zimbabwe African National Union–Patriotic Front (ZANU-PF), one of the two liberation movements, the urbanites who had been given the national vote through the promulgation of universal adult suffrage were not immediately granted the local vote. Understandably, the former liberation movement sought first to address pressing national issues before turning attention to local issues such as municipal council elections.

This chapter reviews in detail how and why the local vote was eventually granted and democracy was ushered in to urban Zimbabwe after the restrictive qualification criteria were dropped or relaxed. It then examines how the relationship between the ruling former liberation movement – perhaps buoyed by regional and tribal politics as well as the euphoria of independence – and the urban masses was initially cosy before widespread disenchantment produced apathy and then total and open hostility from the angry urbanites as they sought to dispose of the former liberation movement. The discourse peers into the souring relations and the continuously widening fault lines. It discusses how these developments have generated "unfriendly" responses among the ranks of the ruling party. The chapter suggests that it is these unfriendly reactions that might be regarded as the recanting of the major aims of the liberation struggle by ZANU-PF, in particular those relating to human rights and electoral democracy.

Factored into the analysis are issues relating to urban governance. Here, it is explained that the deterioration of the national macro-economic situation under the management of the former liberation movement, coupled with a persistently atrocious record of urban governance under a local administration that was almost entirely made up of representatives from the ruling party, resulted in the "informed" urban masses dumping the ruling party *en masse* and opting for change, a move that – perhaps curiously – was in accord with sections of the urban population that could be labelled as reactionary by the former liberation movement. The chapter then examines the reaction of the ruling party as it sought to win back the urban masses, and how, after failing dismally as reflected by the pattern of national and local government elections, the government presided over by the former liberation movement embarked on a strategy of systematically disenfranchising the urban electorate through legal, physical and administrative instruments.

It is at this point that the discussion critically examines the question as to whether the former liberation movement is adopting reactionary tactics that could be viewed as a blatant reversal of the gains of the liberation struggle or whether the movement is simply guarding those gains and consolidating its post-independence achievements.

The discussion seeks to develop a balanced view of matters while leading to a conclusion that is backed by events and processes on the ground. The conclusion revisits the emerging view that the concept of democracy is being abused or twisted to suit selfish and corrupt agendas by politicians from the liberation struggle era. It also looks critically at a variant of this view that insists that the former liberation movement is inexplicably going where everybody else is coming from, and how it is reverting to the history of the liberation war to justify its every (untenable?) move that is causing untold suffering and frustrations among the embattled urban populace.

Urban Governance and Electoral Democracy

Electoral democracy cannot be separated from issues of governance, which in this case is more than the "act of ruling" (Onibokuni and Faniran 1995:3). To lay the framework for the ensuing discourse on elections and democracy, it is important that governance as a concept be examined in greater detail.

Many discussions dealing with governance rightly focus on the relationship between "the governors" and "the governed" (see Olowu and Akinola 1995). Governance relates to the whole spectrum of civil and political institutions, relationships and processes. This brings to the fore the central role governance plays in democracies. However, the concept of governance is neither simple nor free of controversy (United Nations Centre for Human Settlements (UNCHS) 2000:1). The definition of governance by the United Nations Development Programme (UNDP) (1997:2–3) is one of the most comprehensive attempts so far. The agency defines governance as:

> The exercise of political, economic and administrative authority in the management of a country's affairs at all levels. It comprises the mechanisms, processes and institutions, through which citizens and groups articulate their interests, exercise their legal rights, meet their obligations and mediate their differences. In a commentary on this definition another UN agency [UNCHS 2000:8] emphasises the distinction between *governance* and *government* and points out that in the concept of governance power is viewed as existing within government as well as outside it. Besides government other institutions that are seen to have power include civil society and the private sector. Informal institutions are also factored into the decision-making and power-brokering formulae. The argument is that relationships and processes between the stakeholders are (or should be) the basis of decision-making. In the light of this, one source maintains that governance: "is about roles, rules and relationships" (GDRC 2000). One of the key roles stakeholders play is the organisation and control of, as well as participation in, the events and processes involving the selection of those who will govern. This is accomplished through the electoral process.

Governance has been appropriated into the urban arena, where it is regarded as reflecting "the sum of the many ways individuals and institutions, public and private plan and manage the common affairs of the city" (UNCHS 2000:9). Involved as it is with diversity, urban governance inevitably incorporates the resolution of conflicts and accommodation of diverse interests in order to promote "co-operative action". The mediation of differences is increasingly becoming a common trait in the discussions of urban governance. It is as important as the articulation of interests and the exercise of legal rights and obligations (GDRC 2000).

The debate on urban governance has assumed normative overtones through the search for "good" urban governance. Among the numerous prescriptions for good urban governance are attributes such as transparency, popular accountability, efficiency, participation, trust, reciprocity, legitimacy and representativeness in the conduct of public affairs, as well as respect for human rights and rule of law (Olowu and Akinola 1995:20; Harpham and Boateng 1997; Wekwete 1997; GDRC 2000). The UNCHS has gone beyond this to search for what it considers should be the norms of good urban governance. From the agency's viewpoint: "good urban governance is characterised by sustainability, subsidiarity, equity, efficiency, transparency and accountability, civic engagement and citizenship, and security, and ... these norms are interdependent and mutually reinforcing" (2000:11).

Diversity in urban areas necessitates the incorporation of the mediation, management and resolution of conflict as an integral component of urban governance. It also makes it imperative that all different groups, interests and viewpoints are taken on board in the planning and management of the common affairs of the city. It is not surprising therefore that the Global Campaign for Good Urban Governance amplifies the concepts of the "inclusive city" and "inclusive decision-making" to deal with the "messy reality of competing interests and priorities" in order to "balance, reconcile and trade off the competing interests" (UNCHS 2000:9). The Sustainable Cities Programme describes the outcome of this strategy as "broad-based local governance" (UNCHS and United Nations Environmental Programme (UNEP) 2000:2).

Among the key attributes of good urban governance are indicators that have to do with the involvement of the general population in the running of cities and towns. Attributes such as civic engagement, governability, accountability, participation and legitimacy (GDRC 2000; UNCHS 2000) imply, among other things, the existence of democratic processes. These are sustained by a system of electoral democracy (see Young 1999:40). This enables residents to have a strong say in deciding who rules them and how they are governed. This they do through voting. It is here that the issue of citizenship comes in. As will be demonstrated, citizenship can be used or abused by those in power to enhance or erode the principle of democratic governance, especially in the electoral processes.

Electoral Democracy and Urban Governance in Zimbabwe

The electoral system in Zimbabwe is depicted in Figure 1. As the diagram shows, there are two levels of election in Zimbabwe: national and local. Each of these levels has two types of election. The principal decisions for both levels are made by the nation state, especially in the national legislature. For this reason, national elections are perceived as having more at stake than local ones. They are thus more popular and more bitterly fought. Not surprisingly, they get a greater proportion of attention and are subject to more rigorous and detailed analyses than local government elections (see Darnolf 1997; Laakso 1999). National elections have wider socio-spatial and temporal implications. They afford the opportunity for more significant decision-making on more fundamental issues. They also have greater impact on shaping national identity; they are decisive in the crafting of national legislation; and they are critical in defining access to national resources, power and influence across space, society and time. In view of this, it is understandable that since the dawn of Zimbabwe's politically exciting times in the year 2000, parliamentary and presidential elections have aroused more interest than mayoral and council elections.

However, this should neither downplay nor diminish the importance of local elections. It is at the local level that issues of governance and democracy are more acutely felt. Local government is heavily involved in the day-to-day life of the population, as it grapples with critical issues of service delivery and management. It is also at the local level – though within the parameters set by the centre – that the wellbeing of the population is moulded. Perhaps more significantly, local government elections, which often take place more frequently than national ones, are more important as quick indicators and gauges of public opinion and political allegiances than parliamentary and presidential elections.

Figure 3.1 Levels and types of elections in urban Zimbabwe

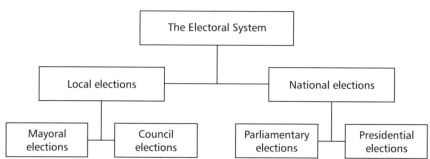

Under Colonial Rule: No Vote for the Majority Blacks

During the various colonial regimes, urban electoral democracy was a preserve of whites. Race was the single most important qualifying criterion. In the very first elections in 1899 the vote was open only to literate male British subjects who were over 21 and were economically independent in terms of property or income (Laakso 1999:30). Little wonder then, that out of a population of more than 500 000 people, fewer than 5000 qualified to vote.

Buttressing the race card was a host of legislative and administrative instruments, chief among which was the constitution. For example, the Land Tenure Act designated urban areas as "white only" areas, blacks being allowed only to provide labour there with the understanding that they would retire "home" once their usefulness ran out. Being aliens in urban areas, blacks could not own property there. Consequently, they could not vote in urban local government elections. This was effectively ensured by the infamous Land Apportionment Act that legalised the expropriation of land from the blacks and its re-allocation in such a way that urban areas ended up in white areas. To emphasise the point that blacks did not "belong" to the towns and cities, the townships set aside for housing blacks in urban areas were run not by the respective urban local authorities but directly by the Department of Native Affairs situated in central government.

Independent, but still no Local Vote

It thus came as no surprise that part of the agenda of the national liberation struggle was "one man one vote", which in essence meant expanding the vote to millions of disenfranchised blacks (Sellström 1999). Although the most pressing electoral priority of the liberation movements was the national vote, in particular general elections, it would not be inaccurate to state that local government was also on the agenda. A significant proportion of the nationalists and their leadership had been residents of urban areas and victims of the politics of racial exclusion and marginalisation at the local level (see Meredith 2002).

Zimbabwe's first post-colonial constitution, the Lancaster House Constitution, introduced universal adult suffrage. It was this provision that allowed the majority blacks to vote in the 1980 general elections. The historic elections brought ZANU-PF to power – the larger of the two liberation movements. More than two decades later, it was this former liberation movement that still held the reins of power. In the course of time, the party's cosy relationship with the more enlightened urban electorate was to turn gradually into a lukewarm one before it quickly deteriorated into mutual hatred and distaste at the close of the twentieth century. The evolution of this relationship and its impact on the electoral system are the subject of the rest of this discussion.

As noted above, immediately prior to independence, the right to vote in general elections was extended to the indigenous black population. Residency, age and citizenship rather than race and property ownership became the new qualifying criteria. In addition to indigenous Zimbabweans, this democratisation saw many people of foreign origin, but with residency, coming to cast their vote. Notable among these were immigrant workers from neighbouring countries – mainly Malawi, Zambia and Mozambique. In addition to dominating the farming and mining sector, these foreigners constituted a significant proportion of the working class in the urban areas, including Harare.

The introduction of universal adult suffrage was not automatically extended to urban local government elections. The right to vote in urban local government elections in Harare, as in other cities, was for a time still based not only on residency but also on property ownership, which in the clauses of the operative legislation was an indication of the existence of a material stake. It is this stake that gave one the right to participate in the management of the common affairs of the city, which in essence meant the right to select representatives in local government elections. That a large number of blacks could not vote in local elections was a foregone conclusion. Most were tenants and lodgers. According to the law, they did not have a material stake in the urban system. This situation continued well into the late 1980s.

Finally, the Vote

ZANU-PF has always been a populist party. To underline this fact the party's long-standing slogan boldly proclaims "The People's Party". The leaders, most of whom are nationalists who directed the liberation struggle, love to show off the power of the party through its support base and dominance in decision-making structures. It was only a matter of time before the party decided to turn its attention to ensure its dominance in institutions of local governance in urban areas. There were good reasons for this. The party had most of its support from the low-income workers who, by virtue of not owning property, did not have the right to elect representatives to urban councils. The fact that most of the colonial period was characterised by racial discrimination under which blacks could not own property in "white-only" areas, meant that low-income groups would for some time continue to be in the minority with respect to property ownership in the urban areas.

To address this anomaly, the government tried to empower – economically and politically – urban low-income groups. First it promulgated the policy of homeownership under which all sitting tenants in council housing were to be afforded the chance to own the houses on a rent-to-buy basis (Zimbabwe Government 1995; National Housing Task Force 2000). The policy did help increase the number of home-owners among the low-income groups. However, in terms of electoral democracy there was an inherent limit to this policy. There could be only as many new voters as there were houses to be owned. The fact that by the end of the 1990s Harare's official housing waiting list had over 100 000 applicants emphasised the shortage of houses to own. Not surprisingly then, Harare continues to be dominated by lodgers who, according to a recent study, constitute more than two in three of all urban households (Mubvami and Hall 2000).

Consequently, the "right" to vote was limited to a few ratepayers whose allegiance to the party was not as fervent and obvious as that of the non-home-owning low-income majority. In any case, most of the ratepayers were whites in the middle- and low-density areas. And they did dominate local politics. Those blacks who had managed to climb up the socio-economic ladder were too few to make a difference. In any event, most of them were lukewarm in their support. Some displayed outright apathy to electoral issues. They saw no reason to go through the rigorous and tedious voter registration and voting process. It should be remembered that the Zimbabwean economy was still robust, and the predominantly urban manufacturing sector was still on an upward swing.

Table 3.1 Voter composition in Harare in 1990 and 2000

Area	1990		2000	
	Number	**Per cent**	**Number**	**Per cent**
High density	383 832	76	536 645	82
Medium & low density	121 054	24	118 375	18
Total	504 886	100	655 020	100

Source Kamete 2000a

What made the local vote undemocratic was the fact that the affluent groups who could vote in council elections were decidedly in the minority. Figures for the general elections, which, as noted above, had been democratised, reveal just how exclusionary the local electoral system was. In 1990, compared to the high-density-area voter population of about 400 000, the total number of eligible voters in affluent medium- and low-density areas was less than 122 000 (Table 3.1). In fact, the non-voting low-income groups made up more than 75 per cent of the registered voters in Harare. Ten years later this proportion had increased to over 80 per cent. A comparison of the composition of the Harare city council with the national legislature shows just how illogical the local electoral system was. The local council did not reflect the national situation.

In the national parliament there were overwhelmingly more urban members of parliament representing the disenfranchised groups than those that represented the privileged, affluent electorate. Members of parliament representing high-density (low-income) areas constituted 77 and 81 per cent of Harare's urban parliamentarians in 1990 and 2000 respectively (Table 3.2). Thus, while parliament was in step with the demographic and socio-economic composition of the city, council was not. The situation where representatives chosen by a minority ran the affairs of the city was clearly reminiscent of the colonial era.

Table 3.2 Constituency representation for Harare in parliament in 1990 and 2000

Year	Total in Harare urban	Distribution of constituencies			
		In high-density low-income areas		In other parts of Harare urban area*	
		Number	Per cent	Number	Per cent
1990	13	10	76.9	3	23.1
2000	16	13	81.3	3	18.8

*Includes medium-density (middle-income) and low-density (high-income) areas as well as commercial and industrial districts and institutions.
Source Kamete 2002a

Table 3.2 shows the electoral situation in Harare. The point here is that the high-density (low-income) areas are home to the majority of urban voters in Harare. As reflected in the table, out of the 13 constituencies (or geographical electoral districts) demarcated in 1990, 10 were in the high-density low-income areas. This translates to 77 per cent of the total voter distribution in geographical terms. In contrast, non-poor areas, which were privileged with the local vote, made up only 23 per cent of the constituencies. What this means is that 10 years after independence, the majority still did not have the vote.

Things had to change, but not entirely for altruistic reasons of good governance and democracy. In addition to democratising the urban electoral system, the "People's Party" needed to express its political dominance in numerical terms in the urban local authorities. The ZANU-PF government eventually gave the local vote to the urban masses at the close of the 1980s. This it did by relaxing property ownership as a qualifying criterion for voting. Legislation was passed that stipulated age and residency as the only requirements for participating in the urban local government electoral process. As envisaged, by the mid-1990s the party was dominating all urban local authorities. Only a sprinkling of independent councillors in cities such as Harare, Bulawayo and Mutare prevented ZANU-PF from having 100 per cent control over municipal councils.

Why Were Urban Local Elections "Democratised"?

While the idea that ZANU-PF gave the local vote to the "masses" because it wanted to "complete" the democratisation process cannot be dismissed out of hand, later developments in urban politics were to cast doubt on this observation. In using the wisdom of hindsight, it can be concluded that ZANU-PF gave the vote to the people because it wanted to stamp its authority on local authorities. Subsequent developments would reveal that the ruling party was determined to get its way in urban local government not only in terms of decision-making, but also to enjoy such benefits as free urban services, and access to land and employment.

By the beginning of the year 2002, for example, the ruling party and its leadership were in arrears in their rates and services accounts in virtually all urban centres. In Harare alone, ZANU-PF officials owed the city council about Z$300 million (about US$7.3) in unsettled bills (Zvauya 2002). This was about 40 per cent of all uncollected revenue in the city (Kamete 2002a:38). In addition, it later emerged that a large number of ruling party supporters got their jobs in Harare city council in circumstances that strongly reek of "cronyism" (Zvauya 2002). Just before the ruling-party-aligned commission running the city was replaced by an elected opposition-dominated council, it employed over 2000 labourers and a senior executive. When the new council resolved to fire the workers, the local government minister, himself a top-ranking member of the ruling party, issued directives reversing the decisions (Kamete 2002a).

Thus the party had more than a political motive in gaining control of urban councils. It also wanted to ensure that it could extract as much material capital as it desired without anybody standing in the way. Affluent, independent and business-minded voters had been bringing in independent and business-minded councils. Developments following the democratisation of local government elections suggest that politicians viewed the control of local resources by "the wrong people" as hindering their access to the coveted resources and opportunities. That had to change. There was no better way to do this than to overwhelm the system with the popular vote.

The party proceeded to democratise the urban electoral system because it was confident that the majority would vote for it. The good relations between the party and the majority of the urban residents assured the party that it would defeat most of its opponents in urban local elections. The results of the enfranchisement of the rest of the urban population vindicated the party's calculations. Before long, the party had under its control the majority of councillors, this in addition to its monopoly over urban parliamentary constituencies, virtually all of which were, by 1995, represented by ZANU-PF members of parliament. The urban populace was firmly behind the party that had selflessly liberated them from colonial rule.

Souring Relations

The cosy relationship between the party and the urbanites did not last long. Even in the heyday of good comradeship, there were signs that the populace was slipping in its support. First there was apathy. As the years wore on, the percentage of registered voters turning up to vote in urban constituencies progressively declined. From a massive 106 per cent turnout for cities and 113 per cent for other urban centres in 1985,[1] the turnout had by 1995 declined to 51 per cent for cities and 53 per cent for other urban centres (Laakso 1999:117,176). The rapid deterioration of the economy orchestrated by the 1997 slump of the Zimbabwe dollar was a major factor in the souring relations between the nationalist party and the urbanites. The economic plague saw the proportion of the urban poor rise from 41 per cent in 1995 to 63 per cent in mid-2001 (Kamete 2002b:14; see also Ministry of the Public Service, Labour and Social Welfare 1997; Consumer Council of Zimbabwe 2001). Amidst an unrelentingly skyrocketing cost of living, urban poverty began to be politicised (Nyakazeya 2001).

In February 2000 the urban electorate finally dumped ZANU-PF in a fiercely contested referendum over a new constitution. About two in three of the urbanites who voted rejected the constitution, this despite a massive campaign by ZANU-PF, which to all intents and purposes viewed the constitution as party business (Kamete 2002a:33; Meredith 2002:163). The newly formed labour-based MDC and the National Constitutional Assembly – a civic body advocating a new constitution – had successfully delivered the first dosage of defeat to the former liberation movement, which, prior to this historic event, had known nothing but victory in all elections.

For the ruling party worse was to come. The country's fifth parliamentary elections were held in June 2000. They were, arguably, by far the most fiercely contested general elections in Zimbabwe's history. When the results were announced the party had been booted out of almost every major urban centre. It lost everything in all the cities and only managed to scrounge something in the smaller urban centres. These "smaller" victories were obtained through gerrymandering, which resulted in urban constituencies being diluted by large swathes of rural territories. Notably, the turnout in these two historic voting processes was very high. The urbanites had turned up in large numbers and angrily passed a vote of no confidence in the party. No wonder then that the party detected a huge conspiracy to unseat it.

What amounted to a betrayal in the eyes of the party was to continue in urban local elections. Within two years the party lost mayoral elections in Masvingo, Bulawayo and Chegutu. It also lost all by-elections in Bulawayo, the second largest city. The minister responsible for the local government portfolio refused to officiate at the installation ceremonies for all but one of the renegade mayors.

Assault on Democracy in Harare?

The 2000 election outcome was a nightmare for the party. However, there was no time to wallow in self-pity, as there was to be a presidential poll in 2002. It was then that the party got to work. Three controversial developments took place which are variously interpreted. On one hand the party's opponents see them as a shameless descent into despotism. On the other, these same developments are viewed by the party as reflecting the former liberation movement's staunch and patriotic defence of the gains of independence and, indeed, national sovereignty. Table 3.3 summarises the three illustrative cases in Harare.

Table 3.3 The assault on democracy

Case	Events	Effect
The Harare Commission saga	Blocking of council and mayoral elections despite the obvious illegality and court orders	Denying people the right to choose their own representatives
Disenfranchisement	Stripping of citizenship from "foreigners' Reduction of polling stations by 40 per cent Disregard of court order	Denying people the right to vote
Ministerial directives	Vetoing of council decisions on finance and recruitment Barring mayors from attending Cabinet Action Committee meetings	Denying democratically elected representatives the right to decide and observe processes that affect their constituency

Denying People the Right to Choose:
The Harare City Commission Saga

In February 1999, the then Minister of Local Government and National Housing dissolved the entire Harare city council. The sitting councillors were victims of a public outcry that followed erratic water supplies to some high-density areas. The affected residents were incensed. Eventually they succeeded in having the executive mayor resign and forcing the minister to suspend the entire council (Kahiya 1999). Though the Combined Greater Harare Residents' Association finally engineered the downfall of the council, this historic event began in the high-density residential areas, where the low-income residents' disgruntlement was carried on to the streets and into town houses. In suspending the councillors the government was acting in sympathy with public sentiments. The minister appointed a commission to run the city and restore it to its former glory. The Harare City Commission was to hand over the "restored" city to an elected council. Considering the fact that the mayor and some of the councillors were high-ranking party officials, it can be concluded that the government was unusually sensitive to the needs of the people.

The law stipulates that an appointed commission has a limited lifetime, and its tenure cannot be extended indefinitely. This stipulation was to become a source of controversy and animosity in the city. Developments on the electoral front made it very unwise for the minister to call for early elections in the capital. The urban rebellion had happened during the tenure of the commission (Kamete 2002). The minister was supposed to call for elections within a year. The rejection of the constitution and the urban losses of ZANU-PF in the June parliamentary election, coupled with massive opposition victories in mayoral elections in Masvingo, Bulawayo and Chegutu, sent clear signals that the party stood no chance in mayoral and council elections in the capital. It came as no surprise that the minister resisted any calls to terminate the tenure of the commission and pave way for an elected council. That would be disastrous and embarrassing, especially in view of the fact that the 2002 presidential elections were imminent. Despite calls from residents, the opposition and civil society, the government refused to allow the residents of Harare to choose who would preside over their interests in council. The tenure of the commission was repeatedly and illegally extended.

Faced with what they perceived as an assault on democracy, various stakeholders, among them individuals, civil society and the opposition MDC, sought legal recourse. The High Court declared the commission illegal and ordered the holding of elections within specified dates. Government appealed the decision. Eventually the case went all the way to the Supreme Court, which again ordered that elections be held before the presidential poll. Government ignored the order and stood by its decision to hold council and mayoral elections simultaneously with the presidential election. Needless to say, this would be long after the expiry of the deadline set by the courts.

Denying People the Right to Choose: The 2002 Election Saga

The run-up to the 2002 presidential poll witnessed the most intensive efforts at disenfranchising the urban electorate. The government put in place legal, physical and administrative obstacles that were strategically meant to frustrate the urban electorate. First came the legal impediments. A change in citizenship laws disenfranchised large sections of the electorate. These were residents who were not Zimbabweans by descent and/or had dual citizenship. The law required such people to renounce foreign citizenship within a specified period. This was obviously targeted at white voters and some black immigrants whom the president had disparagingly described as "totemless".

The initial demands on citizenship constituted a straightforward and logical requirement. However, someone was bent on throwing a spanner in the works. The registrar-general's interpretation was that anyone *entitled* to any foreign citizenship had to renounce that entitlement. The timing of this pronouncement was such that it would be administratively impossible to complete the process before the end of the voter registration period. Foreign embassies made it clear that they could not complete the paperwork within the stipulated time. Consequently, tens of thousands of urbanites were disenfranchised.[2]

Then came the residential criteria, where all desiring to register to vote had to own property or have proof of residence. Commentators saw this as targeting the so-called "born frees" (young people born after 1980) most of whom were in the opposition camp and were non-property owners. These had to have collaborating evidence that they were indeed residents of urban areas.

The physical impediments came in the form of the reduction of polling stations. In Harare alone there was a 40 per cent decrease in the number of polling stations (*Daily News* March 29, 2002). To buttress what may be perceived to be a monumental electoral inconvenience, the Harare elections became administratively complex. The president had decreed that the election would be a tripartite poll where residents had to cast votes for the mayor, councillor and president.

Due to the complexity of the voting process, by the time the voting period officially came to an end, there were still long queues of voters in all polling stations in Harare. This was not surprising considering the fact that it reportedly took as long as 10 minutes to process one voter. In response to an urgent appeal from the opposition the High Court ordered that the voting days in Harare be extended by a further day. In a flagrant defiance of the order, the next day government opened polling stations late and closed them early.

The end result of the legal, physical and administrative impediments was a systematic disenfranchisement of more than a quarter of a million registered voters in Harare alone. Though it is difficult to estimate the combined numerical effect of the legal, physical and administrative strategies to deny the vote to the urban voter, it can be argued that in terms of electoral democracy the net effect was significant enough to constitute an assault on democracy.

Denying Council the Right to Govern: The Flood of Ministerial Directives

The former liberation movement won the presidential poll but suffered heavy defeats in the mayoral and council elections. The opposition snatched the coveted mayoral seat and all but one of the contested council wards. But the ruling party was not done yet. It was still determined to flex its muscles. Before the first democratically elected council in three years could settle down, the Minister of Local Government, Public Works and National Housing issued three directives in quick succession (Kamete 2002a). The first directive reversed a council resolution to cancel all recruitments and promotions effected by the commissions in the previous six months. The second one instructed council to refer to the minister all council resolutions dealing with human resources and financial matters. The third one banned all mayors from attending Cabinet Action Committee meetings. Mayors could attend only by invitation.

Commentators see the directives as an attempt to clip the wings of the new city administration, which – as events on the ground show – is out to undo what the previous administrations under the tutelage of the ruling party have done. The council may view its radical actions as heralding the introduction of efficiency into urban governance and management systems that had hitherto known nothing but misplaced patronage, corruption, incompetence and inefficiency. However, that is certainly not the way government sees the rapidly unfolding events. Victimisation and plain politicking is what the ruling party reads into the behaviour and actions of the new city administration.

Explaining the Party's "Undemocratic" Behaviour

The former liberation movement's behaviour since the year 2000 has led to critics the world over criticising it for behaving undemocratically, impoverishing the once-stable economy, and resorting to authoritarian tactics of governance. The imposition of "smart" sanctions (arms embargoes, financial sanctions and travel restrictions targeting the ruling party leadership and their interests) by, among others, the United States, New Zealand, Australia, the European Union and Switzerland, is a result of these accusations (Tostensen and Bull 2002). So is the suspension of the country from the Commonwealth. The accusations are based mainly on the conduct of the government immediately before, during and after the 2002 presidential poll.

The government and ruling party have not been taking this lying down. The whole country is now awash with what opponents of government consider to be blatantly shameless propaganda, but what the former liberation movement views as setting the record straight by telling it as it should be. The party claims that it is the champion not only of Zimbabwe's liberation struggle but also of defence against an attack on national sovereignty and the country's continued existence as an independent state. The following sections will examine these two perspectives.

Consolidating Gains and Defending National Sovereignty

ZANU-PF's explanation of its behaviour is based on what it perceives to be the nature of the opposition, its supporters and its sponsors. Ever since white farmers appeared on CNN happily making cash donations to the MDC, the opposition has been labelled a puppet of imperialists, while the farmers have been labelled enemies of the state. As early as 1999, President Mugabe spoke of some persons of British extraction who have been placed in our midst to undertake sabotage aimed at affecting the loyalty not just of the people but also that of the vital arms of government like the army, so that these can turn against the legitimate government of the country. (Cited in Meredith 2002:154)

Opposition party supporters, most of whom are young urbanites born after 1980, did not, according to the ruling party, experience – let alone participate in – the liberation struggle. Because of this they have been labelled as misdirected sell-outs bent on compromising the country's hard-won independence.

The puppet and sell-out tags have been used *ad nauseam* to discredit the opposition and its support base. Factored into the foreign sponsorship of the party have been British organisations such as the Westminster Foundation. "White Rhodesians" – as they are derogatorily labelled – from all over the world, but particularly those from Britain and South Africa, are seen as the real power behind the MDC. That the opposition party has substantial support from the white community and the international community is an undeniable fact. ZANU-PF loves to remind everyone who cares to listen about its not-so-adulatory interpretation of this kind of foreign support.[3]

The former liberation movement's trepidation, though paranoid, is not totally unfounded. The MDC's rags-to-riches story is sensational. As the ruling party regularly points out, this phenomenal rise is partly a result of foreign sponsorship or "foreign masters", as the party's propaganda machinery puts it. To underline this thesis, President Mugabe once described the MDC as being "as old and as strong as the forces and interests that bore and nurtured it; that converge on and control it; that drive and direct it; indeed that support, sponsor and spur it" (quoted in Meredith 2002:192).

The party that waged a liberation struggle that was entirely bankrolled by the same "force" now roundly condemns anyone who gets help from the same sources. In fact, so incensed was the party about the rechannelling of foreign support to the opposition that it banned the foreign funding of all political parties. This it did by rushing through parliament the Political Parties Finance Act in 2000. The fact that the ruling party openly continues to receive funding from foreigners despite the legal ban suggests that the piece of legislation was crafted with the opposition in mind.

In addition to the financial support from "enemy" quarters, what perhaps convinces ZANU-PF that its opponent is an imperialist puppet is the perceived support from the independent and international press. The ruling party's stalwarts insist that local independent newspapers – *The Daily News, The Financial Gazette, The Zimbabwe Standard* and *The Zimbabwe Independent* – which neither toe the party line nor applaud what the government is doing, are owned and operated by the enemies of the state. Descriptions such as "oppositional press", "Rhodesian-funded", "Rhodesian-owned", "white-owned", "white-funded", "British-funded", and "British-owned" newspapers or news media houses are common in the state media and in the speeches of party leaders. ZANU-PF's open hatred of independent media houses is based on this perspective. The birth of the Access to Information and Protection of Privacy Act in 2002 is in part an expression of this conviction.

Table 3.4 In defence of national sovereignty

Reason	Official refrain	Perceived threat
The nature of the opposition	"They did not fight the war"	No credentials and right to run the country
The nature of the opposition support	"Puppets of the British" "White sponsored"	Agents of neo-imperialism and neo-colonialism
The nature of the critics of the regime	"Oppositional press" "Rhodesian-owned newspapers" "Rhodesians" "British-sponsored newspapers" "The apartheid press" "White-owned newspapers"	Propagators of neo-colonialist and imperialist propagnda

It is not surprising, therefore, that the urbanites' rejection of the ruling party is viewed as a rebellion that is dangerous not only for the ruling party but also for national independence and sovereignty. Further, the support of a perceived puppet by the urban electorate is also regarded as a betrayal of the country and a lack of patriotism. The incessant calls for political re-education and national conscientisation of the urban masses are based on this view.

It is in light of the above that the government's actions and the behaviour of the former liberation movement become understandable. The assault on the democratic rights of the urban electorate is nothing more than a drastic action to protect the country's sovereignty, jealously guard its independence and self-determination as well as consolidate the gains of independence. Left alone the urbanites will sell the country to the highest bidders, who in this case, are the British from whose kith and kin the government of Zimbabwe is taking, or rather "repossessing", commercial farms. Thus, to its proponents, the party's desperate bid to neutralise the treacherous urban areas by stifling and paralysing them in electoral terms is a means to a noble end.

No Patriotic Agenda

Opponents of the party and critics of its seemingly desperate behaviour have little sympathy for this defensive view. To them, the ruling party is going back to the days of oppressive despotism experienced under the brutal colonial regimes. In this contrasting view, there is nothing patriotic about the former liberators' bid to stifle the urban population. The undemocratic behaviour is a result of fear and paranoia.

Above all, the leadership is afraid of losing a lucrative source of income. On numerous occasions the party's stalwarts have been labelled as thieves, described as corrupt and unscrupulous. Even the land redistribution programme is branded as a ploy by the party leaders to grab land for themselves rather than for the masses (*The Zimbabwe Standard* June 9, 2002). The fact that most well-known beneficiaries of properties seized from white farmers are party stalwarts lends credibility to this claim. The plundering and milking of state enterprises, the defective administration and awarding of tenders, the looting of the War Victims Compensation Fund, as well as the history of non-payment for services rendered by public sector institutions, including local government, are seen as evidence of the party's mercenary and kleptocratic tendencies.

To critics, the sad developments in the country are thus symptomatic of a desperate bid to hang on to power even at the expense of the wellbeing of the country. Here the urbanites are the prime target because they can see through the plot and have refused to be fooled, unlike the uninformed illiterate or semiliterate rural electorate. What is happening to the urbanites can thus not be separated from the systematic persecution of other enlightened opponents of the nationalist party such as reporters, leaders of civil society and opposition politicians.

Table 3.5 No patriotic agenda

Reason	Explanation
Fear of losing income	Desire to continue control of public coffers
Fear of retribution	On plunder and human rights abuses
Implausible evidence of threats to national sovereignty	Poorly scripted plots to incriminate opposition in anti-government activities
Paranoid tendencies	Unwarranted persecution of independent thinkers, reporters, the opposition

That Tony Blair, the British prime minister, who is among the fiercest critics of the regime, has come up for attack and accusation for practically all the maladies plaguing the country thus comes as no surprise to those who believe they can see through ZANU-PF's badly scripted act. Letters in the independent press and discussions at public forums ridicule some of the accusations against the British. Among these is one that insists that the economic mess in which the country finds itself is a result of British-sponsored economic sabotage. The abundance of what critics regard as unintelligently contrived plots (see box) to convince the world that the enemies of the state are at work around the clock, lends further weight to the dismissal of the perceived threats to national sovereignty and the gains of independence.

It is on the basis of these fictitious plots that the conclusion is reached that there is no threat to national sovereignty. Instead, the nationalist party is afraid of its people, especially the urbanites. Some imaginative observers even claim that the fear is born from prospects of retribution once the party is booted from power. The numerous and unrelenting calls and threats of justice (see *The Zimbabwe Standard* June 9, 2002) have, in the opinion of the party's critics, spurred the former liberators of the country to cling onto the reins of power by any means. If democracy and good governance fall victim to this spirited bid to resist an ouster, then too bad.

In the final analysis, this view argues that it is the fear and greed of paranoid nationalists that has orchestrated the country's tumble into what the proponents of this explanation regard as despotism (see Good 2002). It is fear

Neo-Imperialist Plots?

Among the most celebrated of these poorly constructed plots was a sensational revelation in the year 2000 in the principal daily newspaper of a document detailing a plot to destablise the country. The country did not believe it. The Minister of Information, during whose tenure the revelation was published, was never re-appointed to cabinet. Another state daily published an alleged plot to bomb buildings in the major cities. It appears the public was never convinced. No one was arrested. Some of the plots, including some that involve treason have gone to the courts (Kahiya 2002). As yet there has been no conviction. Large dosages of such plots regularly appear under what critics regard as the guise of investigative reporting.

of retribution and the desire to preside over the country's resources so as to ensure that the plundering of its wealth by a few continues, that underlie the behaviour of the former liberation movement. Anything that threatens the political and economic status of the party leadership is the enemy, not of the country but of the former liberation movement, especially the top brass. In this view, selfishness and personal ambition, rather than patriotism and the defence of national sovereignty, are the driving forces behind the persecution of urban residents and the atrocious record on urban governance and democracy.

Conclusion

It is a fact that the urban populations have rejected the former liberation movement. It is also a fact that the former liberation movement has been staging a spirited bid to remain in power. In the process, the party that brought independence and democracy to the country has become in every way as undemocratic as its colonial predecessors were. Falling victim to all this have been the institutions of democracy and democratic processes including the urban electoral system. These adversities have been to the detriment of the urban populace, especially the urban electorate and civil society, whose rights have been trampled on or snatched away.

What remains controversial, however, is whether ZANU-PF is engaged in a process that is seeing the reversal of all the good it brought at independence. Among the good things are the right to choose who governs, the right to participate in the running of the affairs of the urban areas and the country, as well as the right to associate and the right to speak (see Young 1999).

The party argues that it is protecting the country from a revival of neo-colonialism and the new imperialism. On the other hand, critics will continue to maintain that the party has no patriotic agenda. It is the fear of the people and the paranoia emanating from the desire to save the leadership's hide that is the driving force of the onslaught on the urban population.

The evidence at hand seems to agree with this contention. The ridiculous nature of the supporting evidence about the threats to national sovereignty is a strong indication that there may be absolutely no threat at all to nationhood and national sovereignty. The regular bizarre accusations that it is the enemies of the country, working through a puppet opposition, who are responsible for landing the country in its current socio-economic and political plight are less than convincing. This is especially so when the "enlightened" urbanites can point to the ruling party's own responsibility for plunging the country into its current state of economic disaster and political conflict and instability.[4]

Notes

1 The 113 per cent is explained by the fact that there was a larger voter turnout than anticipated according to the officially registered voters.

2 Among those who lost the vote was Sir Garfield Todd, a former prime minister of Southern Rhodesia who had supported the liberation struggle.

3 Following the 2000 parliamentary election, the president who is also the first secretary of ZANU-PF warned the party's central committee of the "forces ranged against us" which to him was a "resurgence of white power". He described the MDC as "a counter-revolutionary Trojan Horse contrived and nurtured by the very inimical forces that enslaved and oppressed our people yesterday" (quoted in Meredith 2002:191).

4 Among the sources of the current problems are (i) the fall of the Zimbabwean currency, which was precipitated by hefty payments to veterans of the country's war of liberation in November 1997; (ii) the country's entry into and involvement in the DRC war; and (iii) the invasion of commercial farms in February 2000. Some include in the list the victory of the ruling party's candidate in the March 2002 presidential elections.

References

The Consumer Council of Zimbabwe (CCZ). 2001. *Poverty Study Report.* Harare: CCZ.

Daily News. 2002. "Urban Dwellers Have Every Reason to Feel Cheated". Harare: March 29.

Darnolf, S. 1997. *Democratic Electioneering in Southern Africa: The Contrasting Cases of Botswana and Zimbabwe.* Göteborg: Göteborg University.

Good, K. 2002. "Dealing with Despotism: The People and the Presidents". In Melber (ed.) 2002.

Global Development Research Centre (GDRC). 2000. "Defining Urban Governance". Available at http://www.gdrc.org/u-gov/work-def.html.

Harpham, T. and Boateng, K. 1997. "Urban Governance in Relation to the Operation of Urban Services in Developing Countries", *Habitat International,* 21,1:65–77.

Joseph, R. (ed.) 1999. *State, Conflict and Democracy in Africa.* Boulder, Co: Lynne Rienner.

Kahiya, V. 1999. "Nkomo Suspends Tawengwa, Entire Harare Council", *Zimbabwe Independent,* Harare, February 26.

Kahiya, V. 2002. "Mandela's Lawyer to Defend Tsvangirai", *Zimbabwe Independent,* Harare, November 9.

Kamete, A. 2002a. "The Rebels Within: Urban Zimbabwe in the Post-Election Period". In Melber, H. (ed.): 32–47.

_____ 2002b. *Governance for Sustainability? Balancing Social and Environmental Concerns in Harare.* CMI Report 2002:12. Bergen: Christen Michelsen Institute.

Laakso, L. 1999. *Voting Without Choosing: State Making and Elections in Zimbabwe.* Helsinki: Department of Political Science, University of Helsinki.

Melber, H. (ed.) 2002. *Zimbabwe's Presidential Elections 2002: Evidences, Lessons and Implications.* Nordiska Africainstitutet Discussion Paper 14. Uppsala: Nordic Africa Institute.

Meredith, M. 2002. *Mugabe: Power and Plunder in Zimbabwe.* Oxford: Public Affairs.

Ministry of Public Service, Labour and Social Welfare (MPSLSW). 1997. *1995 Poverty Assessment Study Survey: Main Report.* Harare: Social Development Fund.

Mubvami, T. and Hall, N. 2000. "City Consultations on Urban Poverty in Harare". Harare: Municipal Development Programme.

National Housing Task Force (NHTF). 2000. *National Housing Policy for Zimbabwe.* (Final Draft). Harare: Ministry of Local Government and National Housing.

Nyakazeya, P. 2001. "Up to 60 per cent resort to walking to work", *The Zimbabwe Standard,* Harare, August 19.

Olowu, D. and Akinola, S. 1995. "Urban Governance and Urban Poverty in Nigeria". In Onibokuni and Faniran (eds.) 1995.

Onibokuni, A. and Faniran, A. 1995. "Introduction". In Onibokuni and Faniran (eds.): *Governance and Urban Poverty in Anglophone West Africa*. Ibadan: CASSAD: 1–19.

Sellström, T. 1999. *Sweden and National Liberation in Southern Africa: Volume 1: Formation of Popular Opinion 1950–1970*. Uppsala: Nordic Africa Institute.

Swilling, M. 1997. "Building Democratic Urban Governance in Southern Africa". In Swilling, M. (ed.) *Governing Africa's Cities*. Johannesburg: Witwatersrand University Press: 212–73.

Tostensen, A. and Bull, B. 2002. "Are Smart Sanctions Feasible?" *World Politics*, 54,3:373–403.

United Nations Centre for Human Settlement (UNCHS) (Habitat). 2000. "The Global Campaign for Good Urban Governance". Concept paper. Nairobi: UNCHS (Habitat).

_____ and United Nations Environmental Programme (UNEP). 2000. *Sustainable Cities and Local Governance*. Nairobi: UNCHS and UNEP (joint publication).

United Nations Development Programme (UNDP). 1997. *Governance for Sustainable Human Development*. New York: UNDP.

Wekwete, K. 1997. "Comments on the Outreach Research on Urban Governance in Zimbabwe". Mimeo. Harare: Department of Rural and Urban Planning, University of Zimbabwe.

Young, C. 1999. "The Third Wave of Democratisation in Africa: Ambiguities and Contradictions" In Joseph, R. (ed.) *State, Conflict and Democracy in Africa*. Boulder, Co: Lynne Rienner: 15–38.

Zimbabwe Government. 1995. *Zimbabwean Report to the Fifteenth Session of the United Nations Commission on Human Settlements (Habitat)*. Harare: Government Printers.

Zvauya, C. 2002. "ZANU-PF Officials Owe Council Z$300 million", *The Zimbabwe Independent*, Harare, March 31.

As Good as It Gets?
Botswana's "Democratic Development"

Ian Taylor

Botswana's growth record has been impressive. Analysis of this, and the developmental record that springs from such growth, has largely been favourable. Indeed, there is an identifiable school of thought which Penelope Thumberg-Hartland has termed the "African Miracle" school which is mainly positive and largely economistic in its approach (Thumberg-Hartland 1978; Picard 1985, 1987; Harvey and Lewis 1990; Danevad 1993; Stedman 1993; Dale 1995). Though of course this "school" is varied, it does in the main approach Botswana's post-independence from a positive and often uncritical stance, asking whether Botswana is indeed *A Model for Success?* (Picard 1987). Critical evaluations of Botswana's record – whilst acknowledging the positive aspects post-1966 – are thus needed (Good 1993, 1999, 2002; Mhone 1996).

From being one of the poorest countries in the world at independence, Botswana has enjoyed rapid economic growth and is now classified by the World Bank as an Upper-Middle-Income country, (one of five in sub-Saharan Africa), with a per capita GDP of more than $6000 (World Bank 1999). Yet, when it became independent, Botswana had a per capita income equivalent then to roughly US$80 (Republic of Botswana 2001). At the developmental level, Botswana has achieved a great deal. Educational and health services, absent at independence, have all been developed. There has been a relative autonomy which has allowed the political and bureaucratic elite to formulate policies that have benefited national development (even whilst benefiting traditional elites, for example, policies vis-à-vis cattle production). Acemoglu *et al* (2001:44) have put it thus:

> The members of the BDP [Botswana Democratic Party] and the political elite that emerged after 1966 had important interests in the cattle industry, the main productive sector of the economy.

This meant that it was in the interests of the elite to build infrastructure and generally develop institutions ... which promoted not only national development, but also their own economic interests. This development path was considerably aided by the fact that the constitution and policies adopted by the BDP meant that there were no vested interests in the status quo that could block good policies. The perspective adopted here is that even the most free capitalist democracy remains, in the final analysis, a veiled "dictatorship of the bourgeoisie". This is because the capitalist class, apart from owning and controlling the means of production, control through various mechanisms the main organs of the superstructure. The outward appearance of a democratic state in its liberal capitalist form – through the extensions of the franchise for instance – does not actually affect the dictatorial nature of the state to any *meaningful* degree, as it is the institutional form within which democratic competition plays out that is important. And in a capitalist society, the institutional form is one erected for, and defended by, the bourgeoisie. This is not to argue that capitalism precludes the feasibility of democracy, even if it is situated within a liberal capitalist milieu. Indeed, there are obviously potentialities open to advance a transformation of the state. This strategic position grants space (dependent upon the specific situation and the balance of class forces) that, though ultimately constrained by "determination in the last instance", means that democratic practice may well be pursued as an arena of struggle.

Having said that, the very limitations on Botswana's celebrated liberal democracy are profound. Although it is true that the state has provided social services in the form of schools and clinics to the populace, and has exhibited features of the "developmental state", major contradictions within the country's political economy and the qualitative nature of its democracy mean that the country exhibits authoritarian liberalism. Like the East Asian developmental states of Malaysia, Singapore, South Korea etc., Botswana has combined high growth rates and visible "development" with a structured autocracy that belies its benign image internationally. Picking out a number of these themes is the focus of this article.

Limitations on the Credibility of Democracy in Botswana

The autonomy of the state machinery has been largely facilitated in Botswana by the fact that civil society has been poorly developed and disorganised and democratic input weak (Holm and Molutsi 1989). Hence, there has been minimal opposition to the dominant elites' programmes. In addition, the fragmented opposition has meant that the Botswana Democratic Party (BDP) has enjoyed domination – if not wholly unchallenged – since independence (Mokopakgosi and Molomo 2000; Osei-Hwedie 2001). Opposition parties are generally weak due to interminable intra-party faction-fighting, internal splits, an unfavourable electoral system (i.e. "first past the post'), feeble organisational structures, and poor capacity to promote alternative policies. The failure of opposition parties to unite and the propensity of opposition leaders to put their egos before everything has meant that Botswana is, and has been since 1966, a de facto predominant-party system where the incumbent BDP has won each and every election by a landslide victory. Thus, in survey data which the United Nations Economic Commission for Africa (UNECA) has commissioned on Botswana (and on which the author has been working), the opposition was seen as ineffective. Indeed, over 50 per cent of respondents thought that the opposition in parliament was weak in its influence on government policy, programmes and/or legislation, with over 16 per cent claiming that the opposition had "no influence".

This has meant, as one BDP MP remarked, that it is BDP backbenchers who criticise the cabinet as "there is no opposition in parliament". Accordingly, the BDP back-bench had decided to criticise its cabinet to keep it active, whilst "the BNF legislators no longer had issues on which to attack the BDP because the ruling party had done so much for the people" (*Daily News* May 12, 2002). In essence, in Botswana it is the government's own back-bench who act as the opposition to advise the cabinet! Only 3 per cent of respondents in the UNECA survey thought that the opposition had a strong influence on the government, a reflection of the poor showing and behaviour of the opposition over the years.

As Chabal has noted: "the success of the state's hegemonic drive in post-colonial Africa [has] depended not so much on the exercise of what appeared to be its power as a state but rather its ability to minimise the threat of counter-hegemonic politics" (1994:226). What has occurred in Botswana has been two-pronged vis-à-vis this point. The potential of the traditional leaders as a counter-hegemonic site was destroyed early on in the post-colonial dispensation and, perhaps just as importantly, the opposition's ineptitude and factionalism has resulted in the emasculation of credible alternatives to the BDP (Selolwane 2001). It is only at the local level where the opposition has made any meaningful inroads into the BDP's power base (or even captured power).

Table 4.1 Number of seats won in Botswana's general elections

Party	1965	1969	1974	1979	1984	1989	1994	1999
BDP	28	24	27	29	28	31	31	33
BNF	–	3	2	2	5	3	13	6
BPP	3	3	2	1	1	0	0	–
BIP / IFP	0	1	1	0	0	0	0	–
BCP	–	–	–	–	–	–	–	1
BAM	–	–	–	–	–	–	0	0
Total	31	31	32	32	34	34	40	40

Table 4.2 Percentage of popular vote won by party in Botswana's general elections

Party	1965	1969	1974	1979	1984	1989	1994	1999
BDP	80	68	77	75	68	65	55	54
BNF	–	14	12	13	20	27	37	25
BPP	14	12	6	8	7	4	4	–
BIP / IFP	5	6	4	4	3	2	4	–
BCP	–	–	–	–	–	–	–	11
BAM	–	–	–	–	–	–	–	5
Other	1	0	1	0	2	2	0	0
Rejected	–	–	–	–	–	–	–	5

Thus the BDP towers over the political scene. The opposition suffers not only from poor leadership, but also from a lack of funds. In contrast, the BDP is wealthy and also enjoys logistics propitiated by the state. Political party funding is not provided by the state, and being the incumbent party, the BDP is able to attract generous donations from various sources. Because of its predominance and the seemingly hopeless chance opposition parties have of unseating them, alternative parties to the BDP attract virtually no donations. As a result, during elections the BDP is comparatively advantaged with a financial strength and visibility unmatched by any of the other parties. It is the BDP which deploys advertisements and election billboards, and drives around in new vehicles – all contributing to a high and active visibility which the opposition manifestly does not have. In addition, as a consequence of its long dominance, the BDP also enjoys considerable powers of co-option of alternatives. The party is able to use its predominance in government to appoint additional members ("Specially Elected Members"). These are four in number and could conceivably be used to tip the balance of power in favour of the incumbent party if ever there is a threat to its power.

Cushioned by the huge flow of income from diamonds, the BDP-controlled state enjoys a "comfort zone" which very few other African administrations can claim. This allows the BDP to effectively "buy" support, often through simply not implementing its own laws and regulations – which would be unpopular and would undermine its support. A good example is the way in which the ruling party has allowed millions of pulas in arrears to accrue through the Self-Help Housing Association (SHHA) programme. Through loans and monthly service charges, the SHHA has supplied decent, tenant-owned accommodation for many thousands of urban citizens, mostly low-income earners. According to some figures, the SHHA accounts for over 50 per cent of the housing stock in the urban areas – a considerable constituency (Mosha 1998:287). As a result, when the issue of arrears was brought up before the 1989 general elections, the BDP-dominated administration decided *not* to use the law to get back the state's money. Diamonds mean free money to the voters in some instances – particularly before an election. In a country where the ruling party has been so dominant for so long, the distinction between party and government interests is clearly blurred.

Indeed, the various parastatals and statutory bodies in Botswana are largely controlled by a small group of politically trusted senior technocrats closely connected to the BDP leadership. In Botswana's developmental state set-up, their influence is strengthened by their capacity to influence business opportunities, award contracts and, importantly, operate in a largely non-transparent fashion through the control of access to vital data and information. The control of vital information on state-owned and controlled companies is bolstered by the relatively weak state of the media (see below) and the deep reluctance of ministers to answer questions in parliament about matters relating to these bodies and companies – particularly if and when elements of the elite are involved in shady practices. Without comprehensive and accessible data and a clear regulatory mechanism to check the corporate activities of state-owned and controlled companies, any comprehensive assessment of their performance is problematic.

The Media and the Threat of Government Surveillance and Control

Obviously, the fairness of the democratic system in a country is affirmed not only by what happens at the polling station on the day of elections but by the broader milieu within which the political process plays itself out. In particular, access to information, freedom to campaign, and equal and fair access to the media are crucial features in this regard. In Botswana, with the exception of small localised private radio stations – such as Gabz FM – the electronic media is government-controlled. The national radio station Radio Botswana is a government mouthpiece, and so is the only daily newspaper the *Daily News.* Although opposition activities are covered, the overall perception of the contents of such media products is that the BDP government is given greater weight. Certainly, the government is perceived by the people to have an inordinate amount of influence over the press compared with the opposition parties (Leepile 1996).

There are, however, a number of private weekly periodicals which maintain considerable independence from the ruling party. It is these journals that have in the past exposed government corruption (such as the Botswana Housing Corporation scandal, the Mogoditshane land sales issue and the National Development Bank loans scandals involving very senior ministers).[1] Unfortunately, the immaturity of the Botswana press and its propensity for scandal and trivia centred around personalities undermines much of the potential that the media might have. The independent press frequently publishes gossip and innuendo as fact, rarely bothering to check stories, and sharp political analysis is rare. Having said that, "from independence up until the twilight of the twentieth century, the Botswana government has done little to promote or strengthen media freedom, diversity and expansion. It instead continues to thrive on restrictive media legislation, bureaucratic red tape and unclear policies" (Media Institute of Southern Africa n.d.). In this context, the media in Botswana are maybe the best that can be expected.

A number of restrictive laws continue to impinge on the free operation of the media in the country. Examples are: the National Security Act of 1986, which gives the state potentially repressive power to penalise legitimate reporting; the Anthropological Act of 1967, which restricts research and limits access to information; and Section 59 of the Penal Code, which provides for penalties for causing "public alarm". In addition, the Economic Crimes and Corruption Act of 1994 restricts both access and coverage of information regarding ongoing police investigations into corruption allegations.

Interference in media independence has been repeated. One of the latest incidents was the April 2002 cancellation of a "Live-Line" show on Radio Botswana. The talk show was to discuss the scope of reporting expected from the public service media in Botswana, but was pulled 30 minutes before its scheduled time. When the show's producer was questioned, he referred all queries to the Director of Information and Broadcasting. Ironically, the national director of the Botswana chapter of the Media Institute of Southern Africa (MISA-Botswana), Modise Maphanyane, was to be a panellist on the programme.

It is quite evident that within the ruling BDP there is a disdain for opposing views and a lack of tolerance for such opinions to be aired. The Minister of Presidential Affairs and Public Administration, Daniel Kwelagobe, recently castigated Botswana Television (already government-owned and widely perceived as being under government editorial control) for broadcasting "insults" spoken by an opposition leader against the government. Kwelagobe asserted that BTV should have cut the "offensive" parts of the news item and he demanded that BTV sanitise what they broadcast to the public (*Mmegi* May 6, 2002). Such outbursts came on top of an earlier spat with BTV which saw the editor of news and current affairs, Christopher Bishop, resign after the Director of Information and Broadcasting, Andrew Sesinyi, forbade Bishop from broadcasting a documentary on Mariette Bosch, the South African who had been convicted of murder and executed. The instruction for this allegedly came straight from the vice-president, Ian Khama (*The Botswana Guardian* July 13, 2001).

Government intentions regarding the media in Botswana were expressed in the draft Mass Media Communications Bill of 2001 (which has still not made its way into legislation). The Bill, if passed without amendment, would have profound implications for media freedom and democracy in Botswana. Among its strictures is the need for the registration of publications as well as for the accreditation of local and foreign journalists. The recommendation that a media council be established, to be chaired by government-appointed persons, and the stated aim to introduce fines for every offence and prosecution (and up to three years in jail for convicted journalists) was also within the proposed Bill, as was the right of senior police officers to seize any publication. Currently, the draft is with the government and has not yet been introduced. Its intention, though, seems crystal clear, particularly as the draft is identical, apart from a number of omissions on broadcasting issues, with another Bill which was withdrawn in 1997 after a major outcry over its threat to media freedom. The seriousness of this for the credibility of Botswana's democracy is profound, particularly as:

> The media [in Botswana] is the last line of defence against excesses committed by the government, NGOs and the business community. Botswana ... is a one-party dominant state. The political opposition is fragmented and weak. The parliamentary watchdog role has been eroded ... [and] the civil society is small and still developing. (*The Botswana Guardian* January 21, 2000)

It is the situation of this "small and developing" civil society we now turn to.

Weak Civil Society

Threats to media independence and media surveillance of the government and elites are profoundly amplified in the context of a polity such as Botswana where civil society is very weak. Comparatively speaking, civil society groups in Botswana are not as fully developed as in other African countries. This reality may be partly attributable to the political and economic stability that has prevailed since independence. Furthermore, the lack of any meaningful "struggle" for independence and the concomitant absence of a tradition of questioning – combined with an essentially top-down traditional culture of acquiescence before one's superiors – may explain the relative weakness and disorganised nature of civil society (Holm, Molutsi and Somolekae 1996).

Just as the BDP is adept at co-option, the government in Botswana has also been active in initiating the formation of organisations within "civil society". As a result, "through the corporate strategy, the state has appropriately defined the role and functions of each organisation and circumscribed these such that it becomes easy to label and isolate others as political ... the effect of this strategy was that the state systematically denied itself a chance to hear the voice of the people" (Molutsi 1998). Furthermore, the government has exhibited highly undemocratic tendencies to portray those organs of civil society it deems beyond its control as foreign stooges, and has not been shy to play the race card against any foreign supporters of civil society in an adversarial relationship with Gaborone. The Basarwa issue (discussed below) is a classic example. At the height of the controversy, the Presidential Affairs and Public Administration Minister, Daniel Kwelagobe, charged that those NGOs defending the Basarwa were "racists" who wanted to keep them "chasing wildlife and dressing in hides" (*Mmegi/The Reporter* February 22–28, 2002). An outrageous allegation by the leader of the official opposition Kenneth Koma that "racist whites" were involved in the production of pornographic films starring Basarwa was allowed to pass without comment from the government (*The Botswana Guardian* March 1, 2002).[2]

In addition, if its own citizens stand up to the government then they are quickly regarded as traitors and foreign agents – enemies of the state. Gaborone's Foreign Minister, Mompati Merafhe, was quoted as describing Survival International as "our enemy, and an enemy of Botswana" (*The Midweek Sun* February 20, 2002), whilst the Director of the Remote Area Dweller Programme (in charge of providing services to the Basarwa in the Central Kalahari Game Reserve) declared that by enlisting the help of international NGOs the Basarwa were "highly seditious" and that "someone is going to have to answer" (*Mmegi/The Reporter* February 22–28, 2002). When it was discovered that some Basarwa had been given satellite phones to be in contact with Survival International this was seen as categorical proof that the Basarwa were indeed something akin to an indigenous fifth column. Yet as Otlhogile (1996:57) remarked:

> the law of sedition is not generally used in so-called advanced
> countries. It has no place in a democratic society and multi-party
> system like ours [i.e. Botswanan]. In a multi-party system there is
> bound to be a divergence of views on a public issue. To punish
> such divergent views is a hallmark of authoritarianism and not
> democracy.

Suspicion of foreign involvement, particularly if it involves "sensitive" topics such as the Basarwa situation, readily provokes a clampdown. For example, the Kuru Development Trust, which is a well-known NGO working with the Basarwa around Ghanzi, had their co-ordinator, Bram le Roux, declared a prohibited immigrant in 1993. This was almost certainly due to government hostility to "foreigners" interfering, via civil society, in "controversial" issues.

This demonisation and the smearing of any foreign links is effective. The Botswana Human Rights Centre, also known as Ditshwanelo, had been involved in "the Basarwa issue" for over 10 years prior to the forced removals from the Central Kalahari Game Reserve. In 1992 Alice Mogwe (Director of Ditshwanelo) published a survey on the situation of the Basarwa. Ditshwanelo was one of the very few Botswanan NGOs to exhibit any concern over the government's resettlement project. However, as Survival International stepped up its campaign against the government's plans and as the government responded in ever more vitriolic language, Ditshwanelo began to distance itself from external interests, casting the tactics of Survival International as "confrontational" and against Botswanan culture: "In general, we feel that confrontation and demonstration should be a last resort because Botswana cultures respect discussion and consultation" (press release quoted in Mphinyane 2002:10).

In essence, and the Ditshwanelo case is but one example, civil society in Botswana is readily co-opted into state structures, lacks a strong grassroots base, and is prepared to work within the parameters deemed permissible by the state – and not beyond. Ditshwanelo provides a very good watchdog service and has been critical of the government on a number of occasions. But the Basarwa issue indicated that there are certain limits (staked out by the state) that even they will not cross. Consensus politics and the construction of BDP hegemony post-1966 has created a relatively stable political milieu (Taylor 2002). This has meant that it is fairly easy for the government to de-legitimise any political expression outside the hegemonic agenda (set by the BDP and broadly, "development through unity') as "extremist" or "foreign".

Limitations to Botswana's "Success Story': Poverty amid Plenty

Freed from such diverse pressures emanating from below, the bureaucracy has served a crucial role in fostering development and, in the context of a country starting from nothing at independence, there have been some notable successes. But there are also a number of serious negatives that Botswana has engendered in the post-independence period. These relate to issues of equity, democratic representation and democratic practice. Although Botswana has performed relatively better than other African economies, it faces major problems that take the shine off the country's track record. In particular, the country faces serious problems related to equity within society (Good 1993; Gulbrandsen 1996; Hope 1996; Nteta, Hermans and Jeskova 1997; Jefferis and Kelly 1999). The distribution of disposable income among persons at the last Household Income and Expenditure Survey of 1993/94 indicated high levels of inequality. The poorest 40 per cent earned 11.6 per cent of the total national income; the next 40 per cent earned 29.1 per cent and the richest 20 per cent earned 59.3 per cent. The corresponding figures from the 1985/6 survey were 10.7, 27.8, and 61.5 per cent respectively for the three categories. The GINI coefficient of 0.537 indicated that income is unevenly distributed (Central Statistics Office 1994).[3]

It is quite clear that not everyone has benefited meaningfully from raised incomes or higher standards of living, setting aside for one moment the extensive provision of health and education facilities as well as access to water and a decent transport infrastructure. As Picard has pointed out: "the primary beneficiaries of government policy in the areas of economic and rural development have been the organisational elites, bureaucratic, professional and political, who dominate the system" (1987:264). These factions have most certainly benefited since 1966. Yet despite Botswana's mineral wealth, four out of five rural households survive on the income of a family member in town or abroad. "That still leaves a significant number of rural households, usually female-headed, with no source of income known to statisticians" (Parsons 2000). Indeed, after 30 years of independence and a sustained growth rate comparable to the Asian Tigers, 47 per cent of the population live below the poverty line (*The Mirror* February 20–March 5, 2002).

At present, most analyses of the poverty levels in Botswana are based on the 1996 *Study of Poverty and Poverty Alleviation* by the Ministry of Finance and Development Planning, which reported a significant proportion of the country's population still living below the poverty datum line (Republic of Botswana 1996). The report indicated that the national poverty rate has declined from 59 per cent of the population to 47 per cent between 1985 and 1994 and that 55 per cent of the rural population was found to be below the poverty datum line compared to 46 per cent in urban villages and 29 per cent in urban areas. There had, however, been a sharp fall between the two surveys in the level of extreme poverty in rural areas. The 1996 poverty study found that national poverty levels had declined by 12 per cent (individual) or 11 per cent (household) between the years 1985/86 and 1993/94. However, a study on the impact of HIV/AIDS on poverty in Botswana predicts that between one-third and one-half of that progress will be lost in the coming decade as a result of HIV/AIDS (Botswana Institute for Development Policy Analysis 2000). Poverty was also found to be higher among female-headed households (50 per cent) as compared with male-headed households (44 per cent).

Poverty reduction programmes were seen as being weak. An analysis conducted by the Botswana Institute for Development Policy Analysis argued that there was inadequate popular participation in programme design; implementation; and monitoring and evaluation. These inadequacies resulted in poor targeting and under-utilisation of programmes. In addition, inadequate co-ordination of poverty programmes led to a failure to bring together central and local/district level administrations, whilst inadequate monitoring and evaluation produced a situation where programme outputs were not adequately reconciled with targets and gaps were not identified early enough (Ditlhong 1997).

The Situation of the Basarwa

Compounding the levels of inequality is the democratic deficit that exists in Botswana vis-à-vis the indigenous minority, the Basarwa (San/Bushmen). This was most recently exemplified by their forced removal from the Central Kalahari Game Reserve (CKGR). This event has excited a great deal of world opinion.

The treatment of the Basarwa in Botswana has long been a controversial topic (Mogwe 1992; American Anthropological Association 1996; Gall 2001). Botswana's most famous novelist, Bessie Head, dealt with the widespread racial prejudice against the Basarwa in the country in her book *Maru* (1971). The story is about the treatment of a Mosarwa woman who had been brought up in a white-run mission. The woman (Margaret) tries to integrate herself into the (black) Batswana society in a rural village. But in this village, as in many rural parts of Botswana, the Basarwa are effectively "the slaves and downtrodden dogs of the Batswana" (Head 1971:14), reflecting the discrimination and disenfranchisement of the Basarwa in Botswana. It is noteworthy that Botswana's only internationally recognised novelist chose to talk of such issues in one of her books. The "inconvenient indigenous" (Saugestad 2001) of Botswana remain one of the country's most controversial topics.

The move by Gaborone to terminate supplies of water and other basic social services to the remaining Basarwa in the CKGR must be seen in this context. It has excited profound international interest. Indeed, at the beginning of February 2002, rolling mass protests against the Botswanan government were announced in London, Paris, Madrid and Milan by a London-based NGO, Survival International (*The Botswana Guardian* February 8, 2002). At the same time, questions were being asked in the British House of Lords over the treatment of the Basarwa in Botswana.

All this was excruciatingly embarrassing for a country which has prided itself on being one of the few "shining beacons of democracy and good governance" in Africa. A local newspaper has urgently pointed out, in a plea to the government, that:

> We [Botswana] are already a leading diamond producer. And it shall remain so for many years, even without CKGR diamonds. It is therefore unwise for government to trigger an unnecessary negative global campaign that is set to portray us as a despotic and cruel nation that takes pride persecuting one of the most disadvantaged and powerless people on earth. (*Mmegi/The Reporter* February 15–21, 2002)

The issue surrounds a decision made in August 2001 to cut off services to the Basarwa located in a remote area of the CKGR from January 31, 2002. The twin goals of the CKGR (established by the British in 1961) were to protect the human inhabitants of the central Kalahari and also to protect the fauna and flora (Bishop 1998). However, over the past 16 years or so, Gaborone has sought to remove the Basarwa, relocating many to "resettlement camps" where hunting and gathering is impossible and where the Basarwa have become dependent on government handouts and alcohol – worsening their position at the bottom of the Botswanan social ladder (Good 1999). Those who have thus far chosen to remain in the CKGR have also been dependent on government largesse but, at a total of 55 000 Pula (8 200 dollars) per month the government has said that this is "too expensive" to continue and must now stop (*Mmegi/The Reporter* February 19–25, 2002). The local newspaper *Mmegi* has called the forced removal scheme "one of the most unfortunate courses of action since independence: the banishment of the Basarwa from their ancestral lands to a foreign land, a place with which they have no bond" (February 15–21, 2002). The decision neatly dovetails with the oft-stated wish of the Botswanan state to convince the Basarwa to move out of the CKGR as part of its policy to develop tourism – and possibly diamonds – in the area (Survival International 1997). In October 1986 Moutlakgola Nkwako, Minister of Commerce and Industry, announced the government's determination to have the Basarwa communities leave the CKGR. It was from that point on that sustained pressure was brought to bear on people to leave the reserve and move to relocation camps (Survival International 1989). This has intensified since 1996 (Hitchcock 1999).

Gaborone has asserted that over the last few years 2 200 Basarwa have "voluntarily" left the reserve to take advantage of a number of incentives such as free settlement, grazing land, and compensation for loss of possessions. According to the permanent secretary for political affairs in the Office of the President, Tuelonya Oliphant: "those that want to stay can do so. But the services will be cut off and if they want old age pensions, destitute rations and other services, they must get them from the nearest settlement outside of the reserve" (*Reuters* February 3, 2002). The removal of such provision from point of delivery to a site far from their location has thus left the remaining Basarwa with but one choice if they wish to continue to receive these government benefits: they must leave. Clearly, in Botswana, democratic rights and access to the fruits of the "African Miracle" are available to some more than others.

Workers' Rights and the Limitation on Working-Class Organisation

The situation of the Basarwa, attracting widespread international opinion, is but one manifestation of the authoritarian liberalism of the state in Botswana. The treatment of organised working class bodies, however, is another example of the less-than-benign attitude by the entrenched party in power to democratic rights. In the context of the working class, where opposition to the BDP might be expected to emerge, this is particularly clear. Most of this takes the form of structural limitations against manifestations of workers' power (through the medium of trade unions) rather than outright oppression. In Botswana, the law does not permit trade union officials to be employed on a full-time basis. Elected union officials must, by law, work full-time in whatever industry they represent. As a result, Botswana lacks full-time elected union leaders – seriously limiting existing union leaders' professionalism and capability to do anything other than ad hoc part-time organising.

Strikes are severely constrained and new unions are very hard to register (a legal requirement). The Insolvency Act has not been amended in over two decades. This has meant that if a company were to be liquidated, the workers would receive only 100 Pula: a pathetic amount, now less than 20 per cent of a month's wage at the minimum wage rate. Due to the fly-by-night manner in which many "investors" operate in Botswana (Good and Hughes 2002), companies frequently close overnight. Workers employed by such companies thus find themselves without income at a very short notice. To make matters worse, the law states that employers need pay their employees severance pay only if they have worked for the same company for 60 months. It is common for "investors" to shut up shop after government subsidies and incentives cease which is – perhaps coincidentally – just under five years of operation.

In Botswana, working-class militancy is dissipated by the complexities surrounding the (legal) organisation of strikes. Legal strikes are theoretically feasible but only after an exhaustive arbitration process, and sympathy strikes are illegal: a general strike is thus categorically impossible in Botswana. Incredibly, there has never been a legal strike in Botswana and this is not because the workers are all contented. Instead, "illegal" (as defined by the restrictive laws) strikes occur, opening up workers to the threat of an over-exuberant police force not afraid or reluctant to crack heads in the service of "stability" and "legality". It is true that the Botswanan government has ratified all the International Labour Organisation (ILO) conventions, but this achievement is lessened somewhat by the fact that the Botswanan labour code has not been aligned to these conventions. Of major importance is that ILO conventions oblige the employers to discuss with the unions before liquidating a company – something which even the current Employment Act does not require. Clearly, profound restrictions – enshrined in law – limit the potential of workers to organise effectively and exercise their democratic right to withhold their labour power.

Conclusions

The executive secretary of the Southern African Development Community (SADC), Prega Ramsamy, has argued that Botswana will have reduced poverty by half by the year 2012 if it continues to sustain current economic performance (*Daily News* July 19, 2001). But this calls for determined policy to ensure this occurs. In fact, the creation of a more equitable society and the fairer distribution of resources remains Botswana's greatest developmental challenge and one which will define the success or otherwise of the post-independence project. A less elitist and more egalitarian Botswanan state is urgently required, particularly if the "beacon of democracy" is to be taken seriously. Whilst gross inequality remains and if sections of the population such as the rural poor and the Basarwa are left out of the equation, Gaborone's claims to be a "model" for a democratic Africa remain profoundly suspect.

Indeed, this suggests a rethink of our understanding of what exactly constitutes Botswana's democracy. Orthodox definitions restrict themselves to the procedural realm, meaning that there is no intrinsic contradiction between a "democracy", with all its free elections, free press, free debate and so on, and a social order marked by inequity and elite control. Certainly, such democracies can quite happily effect a democratic appearance without any real democratic content or, crucially, consequence (Robinson 1996:625). The separation of the political from the economic is vital for this definition. As Meiksins Wood (1995:235) asserts:

> The very condition that makes it possible to define democracy as we do in modern liberal capitalist societies is the separation and enclosure of the economic sphere and its invulnerability to democratic power. Protecting that invulnerability has even become an essential criterion of democracy. This definition allows us to invoke democracy against the empowerment of the people in the economic sphere. It even makes it possible to invoke democracy in defence of a *curtailment* of democratic rights in other parts of "civil society" or even in the political domain, if that is what is need to protect property and the market against democratic power.

It is apparent that this logic works itself out within the current Botswana polity. Upon being sworn in as the new president, Festus Mogae was quoted as saying that "one cannot strengthen the weak by weakening the strong and enrich the poor by simply impoverishing the rich" (*The Botswana Gazette* April 8, 1998). Any analysis of why poverty existed amidst such plenty, and how and in what ways Botswana's democracy was impoverished by such scenarios was glossed over, unmentioned, and probably unrecognised.

The state apparatus in Botswana has been commonly deployed to promote political and economic goals which reflect the BDP leadership's understanding of the limitations and opportunities presented by the national, regional and international economy. At the same time, this has reified existing structures of power and privilege within the country. Having said that, a note of caution regarding criticism of Botswana's democracy should be noted. Though ruling for nearly 40 years, the BDP has *not* subverted the constitution, it has *not* outlawed opposition parties or declared the country a one-party state. There are no political prisoners. Despite the handicaps the media faces, the press in the country is flourishing and is critical. The material benefits accrued through diamond sales have been dispersed, and evidence exists that poverty levels are falling. There are, however, things in Botswana that clearly could be done much better.

In Botswana, the state is inclined to behave more rationally in a developmental fashion (but still essentially for the benefit of privileged interest) than elsewhere in Africa. This certainly grants space to the government, but it also benefits significant sections of society. Rewards and social patronage in the context of a virtually non-existent opposition and the absence of any counter-hegemonic project mean that the state acts without any effective challenge to governmental authority or even its legitimacy. This, coupled with the cultural emphasis on consensus and non-confrontation in Batswanan socio-political structures as well as the inherent limited nature of democracy within a capitalist system, has largely precluded a living, dynamic form of democracy in Botswana. To quote the now-unfashionable, Lenin once wrote that "owing to the conditions of capitalist exploitation, the modern wage slaves are so crushed by want and poverty that they "cannot be bothered with democracy", "cannot be bothered with politics'" (Lenin 1977:323). In a country with such gross inequality and where only 460 000 out of an estimated 900 000 eligible voters bothered to register in the last (1999) general election, how apposite Lenin's remarks sound! With such actualities staking out Botswana's democracy, and with no real alternative project to hold the elites accountable, authoritarian tendencies as outlined above and the absence of any "true" competitive democratic discourse in Botswana take the shine off any attempt to ask whether Botswana is really an "African Miracle". This, it seems, is as good as it gets.

Notes

1   Mogoditshane is a suburb of Gaborone. There were serious abuses in the distribution of land in the area involving some cabinet ministers, who subsequently resigned. The Botswana Housing Corporation is a parastatal that was set up to provide housing for the public sector. The chief executive and his deputy were involved in corruption on a grand scale. The National Development Bank (NDB) is also a parastatal, set up to assist the public with loans for developing projects. By 1993 the NDB was virtually bankrupt as top politicians, including a number of cabinet ministers, had been given huge amounts of loans and had interests in arrears totalling millions.

2   The alleged source of this information – Roy Sesana of the First People of the Kalahari – pointedly denied Koma's claims, saying such statements were "not true". Koma was unable to provide any support for his allegations. Racism and xenophobia have been on the rise in Botswana recently. For a treatment of this, see Nyamnjoh 2001.

3   The GINI coefficient lies between zero and one. A value of one corresponds to the opposite extreme where one person has all of the national income and everyone else has zero income. Thus a higher value of the GINI coefficient indicates a higher degree of income inequality.

References

Acemoglu, D., Johnson, S. and Robinson, J. 2001. "How Botswana Did It: Comparative Development in Sub-Saharan Africa". Unpublished paper.

American Anthropological Association. 1996. *Population Relocation and Survival: The Botswana Government's Decision to Relocate the People of the Central Kgalagadi Game Reserve.* Washington, DC: Committee for Human Rights and American Anthropological Association.

Bishop, K. 1998. "Squatters on Their Own Land: Khwe Territoriality in Western Botswana", *Comparative and International Law Journal of Southern Africa*, 31.

Botswana Institute for Development Policy Analysis (BIDPA). 1996. *Study of Poverty and Poverty Alleviation in Botswana.* Gaborone: BIDPA and Ministry of Finance and Development Planning.

_____ 2000. *Impact of HIV/AIDS on Poverty and Inequality in Botswana.* Gaborone: BIDPA.

Chabal, P. 1994. *Power in Africa: An Essay in Political Interpretation.* New York: St Martin's Press.

Dale, R. 1995. *Botswana's Search for Autonomy in Southern Africa.* Westport: Greenwood Press.

Danevad, A. 1993. *Development Planning and the Importance of Democratic Institutions in Botswana.* Bergen: Christen Michelsen Institute.

Ditlhong, M. 1997. "Poverty Assessment and Poverty Alleviation in Botswana", BIDPA Working Paper 12.

Ditshwanelo. 1996. *When Will This Moving Stop? Report on a Fact-Finding Mission of the Central Kgalagadi Game Reserve, April 10–14, 1996.* Gaborone: Ditshwanelo, The Botswana Centre for Human Rights.

Edge, W. and Lekorwe, M. (eds.) 1998. *Botswana: Politics and Society.* Pretoria: Van Schaik.

Gall, S. 2001. *The Bushmen of Southern Africa: Slaughter of the Innocent.* London: Chatto and Windus.

Good, K. 1993. "At the Ends of the Ladder: Radical Inequalities in Botswana", *Journal of Modern African Studies*, 31,2.

_____ 1999. "The State and Extreme Poverty in Botswana: The San and Destitutes", *Journal of Modern African Studies*, 37, June.

_____ 2002. *The Liberal Model and Africa: Elites Against Democracy.* London: Palgrave.

_____ and Hughes, S. 2002. "Globalisation and Diversification: Two Cases in Southern Africa", *African Affairs*, 101,402. January.

Gulbrandsen, O. 1996. *Poverty in the Midst of Plenty.* Bergen: Norse Publications.

Harvey, C. and Lewis, S. 1990. *Policy Choice and Development Performance in Botswana.* London: Macmillan.

Head, B. 1971. *Maru.* Portsmouth, NJ: Heinemann.

Hitchcock, R. 1999. "A Chronology of Major Events Relating to the Central Kalahari Game Reserve", *Botswana Notes and Records*, 31.

Holm, J., Molutsi, P. and Somolekae, G. 1996. "The Development of Civil Society in a Democratic State: The Botswana Model", *African Studies Review*, 39,2.

Holm, J. and Molutsi, P. (eds.) 1989. *Democracy in Botswana.* Gaborone: Macmillan.

Hope, K. 1996. "Growth, Unemployment and Poverty in Botswana", *Journal of Contemporary African Studies*, 14,1.

Jefferis, K. and Kelly, T. 1999. "Botswana: Poverty amid Plenty", *Oxford Development Studies*, 27,2.

Leepile, M. 1996. *Botswana's Media and Democracy.* Gaborone: Mmegi Publishing House.

Lenin, V. 1977. "The State and Revolution". In *Lenin: Selected Works.* Moscow: Progress Publishers.

Media Institute of Southern Africa. n.d. "Botswana". http://www.misanet.org/samd/BOTSWANA.html.

Meiksins Wood, E. 1995. *Democracy Against Capitalism: Renewing Historical Materialism.* Cambridge: Cambridge University Press.

Mhone, G. 1996. "Botswana Economy Still an Enclave", *Africa Development*, 21,2 and 3.

Mogwe, A. 1992. *Who Was (T)here First? An Assessment of the Human Rights Situation of Basarwa in Selected Communities in the Gantsi District, Botswana.* Gaborone: Botswana Christian Council.

Mokopakgosi, B. and Molomo, M. 2000. "Democracy in the Face of a Weak Opposition in Botswana", *Pula: Botswana Journal of African Studies*, 14,1.

Molutsi, P. and Holm, J. 1990. "Developing Democracy when Civil Society Is Weak: The Case of Botswana", *African Affairs*, 89,356.

Molutsi, P. 1998. "Elections and Election Experience in Botswana". In Edge, W. and Lekorwe, M. (eds.) *Botswana: Politics and Society*. Pretoria: Van Schaik.

Mosha, A. 1998. "The Impact of Urbanisation on the Society, Economy and Environment of Botswana". In Edge and Lekorwe.

Mphinyane, S. 2002. "Power and Powerlessness: When Support Becomes Overbearing: The Case of Outsider Activism on the Resettlement Issue of the Basarwa of the CKGR". Paper presented to Department of Sociology, University of Botswana, March 28, 2002.

Nteta, D., Hermans, J. and Jeskova, P. (eds.) 1997. *Poverty and Plenty: The Botswana Experience*. Gaborone: Botswana Society.

Nyamnjoh, F. 2001. "Local Attitudes Towards Citizenship and Foreigners in Botswana: An Appraisal of Recent Press Stories". Unpublished paper, Department of Sociology, University of Botswana.

Osei-Hwedie, B. 2001. "The Political Opposition in Botswana: The Politics of Factionalism and Fragmentation", *Transformation*, 45.

Otlhogile, B. 1996. "The Constitutional Rights of the Mass Media in Botswana: An Academic's View". In Leepile.

Parsons, N. 2000. *Botswana History Pages*. "Economy", October, http://ubh.tripod.com/bw/bhp13.htm#.

Picard, L. 1987. *The Politics of Development in Botswana: A Model for Success?* Boulder: Lynne Rienner.

_____ (ed.) 1985. *The Evolution of Modern Botswana*. Lincoln: University of Nebraska Press.

Republic of Botswana. 1996. *Study of Poverty and Poverty Alleviation*. Ministry of Finance and Development Planning. Gaborone: Government Printer.

_____ 1999. "Statistics Update December 1994". Central Statistics Office. Gaborone: Government Printer.

_____ 2001. "Economic Snapshot". http://www.gov.bw/economy/index.html.

Robinson, W. 1996. "Globalisation: Nine These on Our Epoch", *Race and Class*, 38,2.

Samatar, A. 1999. *An African Miracle: State and Class Leadership and Colonial Legacy in Botswana's Development*. Portsmouth: Heinemann.

Saugestad, S. 2001. *The Inconvenient Indigenous: Remote Area Development in Botswana, Donor Assistance, and the First People of the Kalahari*. Uppsala: Nordic Africa Institute.

Selolwane, O. 2001. "Monopoly Politikos: How Botswana's Opposition Parties Have Helped Sustain One-Party Dominance". Paper presented to the Department of Sociology, University of Botswana, September 27.

Siwawa-Ndai, P. 1997. "Some Facts and Figures about the Quality of Life in Botswana". In Nteta *et al.*

Stedman, S. (ed.) 1993. *Botswana: The Political Economy of Democratic Development.* Boulder: Lynne Rienner.

Survival International. 1989. "Botswana: Kalahari Peoples Threatened with Expulsion from Game Reserve". Urgent Action Bulletin. London: Survival International.

_____ 1997. "Botswana Squeezes Kalahari Peoples Out". Urgent Action Bulletin. London: Survival International.

Taylor, I. 2002. "Hegemony and Post-Colonial Africa: Botswana's Developmental State and the Politics of Legitimacy". Paper presented to conference on "Towards a New Political Economy of Development: Globalisation and Governance", University of Sheffield, United Kingdom, July 4–6.

Thumberg-Hartland, P. 1978. *Botswana: An African Growth Economy.* Boulder: Westview.

Chieftaincy and the Negotiation of Might and Right in Botswana's Democracy

Francis B. Nyamnjoh

Studies of agency are sorely needed if we are to avoid overemphasising structures and essentialist perceptions on chieftaincy and the cultural communities that claim and are claimed by it. Using Botswana as a case in point, this chapter argues that Africans are far from giving up chieftaincy or from making completely modern institutions of it. No one, it seems, is too "citizen" to be "subject" as well, not even in southern Africa where there have been the most "expectatations of modernity" (see Ferguson 1999:1–81), nor in Botswana as Africa's best example of liberal democracy (see Mazonde 2002; Werbner 2002a). Invented, distorted, appropriated or not, chieftaincy remains part of the cultural and political landscapes, but is constantly negotiating and renegotiating with new encounters and changing material realities. The results are chiefs and chiefdoms that are neither completely traditional nor completely modern. Being African is neither exclusively a matter of tradition and culture, nor exclusively a matter of modernity and citizenship. It is being a melting pot of multiple identities. Hence, an idea of democracy too narrowly confined to the cosmetics of "the liberal model" (see Good 2002) would hardly accommodate and account for the reality of conviviality between individual and community interests that emphasises negotiation between rules and processes, subjection and citizenship, might and right in any democracy in action. Real democracy means much more than the right to vote or to be voted for, especially as these rights do not always deliver the recognition, representation and entitlements that individuals and groups seek in any given context.

In Africa, chieftaincy is either of precolonial origins or a colonial and post-colonial creation (Harneit-Sievers 1998; Geschiere 1993). Prominent among the approaches in chieftaincy studies have been partial theories raised to meta-narratives of expectation of "the passing of traditional society" in favour of modernity along the unilinear lines predicted by Daniel Lerner (1958). In tune with their evolutionary and homogenising persuasions, modernisation theorists expected such "passing" as a natural course of things. On their part, even the most progressive or revolutionary theorists have tended to be critical of all traditional institutions, chieftaincy in particular, for having been appropriated or created by colonial, apartheid and post-colonial states for various purposes, including repression and the confection of bifurcation into "citizens" and "subjects" (Mamdani 1996).

Consequently, they have tended to write chieftaincy, tradition or custom out of their radical liberation agenda. Both partial theories have tended to see in chieftaincy more "might" than "right", and consequently have wanted chieftaincy abolished or ignored in favour of citizenship based on the individual as an autonomous agent. These theoretical approaches are prescriptively modernist in their insensitivities to the cultural structures of African societies, and the future they envisage for the continent has little room for institutions and traditions *assumed* to be primitive, repressive and unchanging in character. Chieftaincy, these theories suggest, would always look to the past or depend on a frozen idea of custom for inspiration in the service of exploitation and marginalisation by the highhandedness of African states. Within these frameworks, chieftaincy is seldom credited with the ability to liberate or to work in tune with popular expectations. The tendency to focus analysis "almost exclusively upon institutional and constitutional arrangements" assumes "the classical dichotomy between ascription and achievement" and "takes as given that stated rules should actually determine the careers of actors in the public arena" (Comaroff 1978:1). Pregnant with teleological assumptions, these approaches have been insensitive to the relationship between rules and processes, and have thus inadequately attended to how Africans constantly appropriate and transform their culturally inscribed normative repertoires through their social activities (Comaroff and Roberts 1981).

In accordance with such thinking, modernisation scholarship in the 1950s and 1960s predicted that chiefs and chieftaincy would soon become outmoded, replaced by "modern" bureaucratic offices and institutions (Warnier 1993:318; Harneit-Sievers 1998:57). Even underdevelopment and dependency theorists did not seem to give chieftaincy much of a chance (Harneit-Sievers 1998), which they saw as lacking in mobilisational ability for social and political change. This view has not entirely disappeared, as some continue to argue for a common political and legal regime that guarantees equal citizenship for all, and for abolishing the bifurcation into "citizens" and "subjects" that the invented customs and appropriation of chieftaincy by colonialism brought about (Mamdani 1996). However, scholars acknowledge the resilience of chieftaincy institutions (Fisiy 1995; Goheen 1992; Fisiy and Goheen 1998), and even a "renewed boom" in chieftaincy has been observed in countries like Mozambique where Marxism-inspired radical liberation movements were initially hostile to the institution's role as handmaiden of colonialism (O'Laughlin 2000; Harrison 2002; Gonçalves 2002). Almost everywhere on the continent, many chiefs are taking up central roles in contemporary politics (Harneit-Sievers 1998; Linchwe II 1989:99–102; Van Rouveroy van Nieuwaal and Van Dijk 1999; Van Rouveroy van Nieuwaal 2000). In post-apartheid South Africa, where modernisation is usually credited with its greatest success, active "retraditionalisation" has occurred among historically marginalised cultural communities seeking recognition and representation through claims to chieftaincy (Oomen 2000). Chiefs and chiefdoms, instead of being pushed "into the position of impoverished relics of a glorious past" (Warnier 1993:318), have functioned as auxiliaries or administrative extensions of many a post-colonial government, and as "vote banks" for politicians keen on cashing in on the imagined or real status of chiefs as the legitimate representatives of their communities (Fisiy 1995; Harrison 2002; Gonçalves 2002). Although the presumed representativity and accountability of chiefs to their populations have been questioned, this does not seem to have affected the political importance of chiefs in a significant way (Ribot 1999:30–7).

There is need to counter the insensitivities or caricatures of the modernist discourses of mainstream theories and analysts that have tended, for teleological reasons, to rationalise away chieftaincy and its dynamism. It is important to develop approaches that are sensitive to the reality of intermediary communities between the individual and the state, and to the agency of chiefs and chiefdoms as individuals and cultural communities seeking "right and might" both as "citizens" and "subjects" in the modern nation-state as a reality not an ideal. Almost everywhere, chiefs and chiefdoms have become active agents in the quest by the "the modern big men and women" of politics, business, popular entertainment, bureaucracy and the intellect for traditional cultural symbols as a way of maximising opportunities at the centre of bureaucratic and state power (Geschiere 1993; Miaffo and Warnier 1993; Fisiy 1995; Goheen 1992; Fisiy and

Goheen 1998; Harneit-Sievers 1998). It is in this connection that some scholars have understood the growing interest in the new elite in investing in neo-traditional titles and maintaining strong links with their home villages through kin and client patronage networks.

In Nigeria, for example, investment in chiefship has become a steady source of symbolic capital for individuals who have made it in "the world out there", and also of development revenue by cultural communities who would otherwise count for little as players in their own right in the national and global scenes (Harneit-Sievers 1998). Granted their persistence and influence in Africa, chieftaincy institutions need to be "understood not only, and not even primarily, as belonging to a pre-modern, pre-capitalist past; but rather as institutions which have either (been) adapted to the contemporary socio-political setting, or even have been specifically created for or by it" (Harneit-Sievers 1998:57). There is hardly any justification to label and dismiss chieftaincy, *a priori*, when even the most touristic of observations would point to a fascinating inherent dynamism and negotiability that guarantees both resilience and renewal of its institutions. Such ability to adapt and survive is not confined to chieftaincy in Africa. Monarchies the world over have demonstrated this resilience and adaptability of might in the face of clamours for rights.

Chieftaincy and Democracy as Dynamic Realities in Botswana

Botswana is part of a southern Africa where modernisation is believed to have had its greatest impact in sub-Saharan Africa. Also, Botswana is generally hailed as Africa's best example of liberal democracy. Hence my argument: if chieftaincy remains relevant even in countries that have made the most advances in modernisation and liberal democracy, then the assumption that the institution is incompatible with modernity and democracy has no empirical foundation.

Chieftaincy and chiefs in Botswana have displayed similar agency to that noted among their counterparts elsewhere in Africa, siding with forces that best guarantee their interests as communities and individuals, while hostile to those that radically threaten their might (Morton and Ramsay 1987:11–160; Parsons, Henderson and Tlou 1995; Makgala 1999). Makgala traces this agency back to the colonial period when *dikgosi* [chiefs] were able to reshape to their advantage through insistence on the need to respect "local political conditions", a blanket model of "indirect rule" that was introduced in 1935 (Makgala 1999:11–97). In 1948 Seretse Khama, prince of the Bangwato chiefdom who had gone to read law at Oxford, married Ruth Williams, daughter of an Anglican English family. The marriage was opposed by Khama's uncle Tshekedi and by Ruth's parents, by the apartheid regime in South Africa, and by the British colonial authorities. This resulted in Seretse Khama's banishment from Bechuanaland in 1950. Patient explaining and negotiation between might and right at various *dikgotla*[1] meetings brought reconciliation eventually, and the couple were finally accepted both by the Bangwato and the British government, who in 1955 allowed them to come home (Parsons *et al* 1995:75–149). Khama used his position as a lawyer, a devout liberal and a chief to work towards independence and nation-building in Botswana, which he served as first president until his death in 1980. These factors combined remarkably to guarantee his ruling Botswana Democractic Party (BDP) regular electoral victories in the Central District occupied by his chiefdom, and also in the country as a whole following independence in 1966. Khama's agency, which has been well documented (Parsons *et al* 1995), and other examples provided below are an indication that as scholars of chieftaincy and democracy in Africa or elsewhere we must avoid the tendency to mistake labels for substance, and to prescribe rather than observe.

The Khama factor in Botswana politics and democracy remains strong even after his death. In April 1998 when Festus Mogae took over as president from Sir Ketumile Masire, Lieutenant-General Ian Khama retired as commander of the Botswana Defence Force to deploy his might as *kgosi* of the Bangwato in keeping the BDP of his late father together, and in maximising its fortunes at the 1999 general elections (Molomo 2000). The party's landslide victory was largely attributed to his appeal as *kgosi*, and his appointment as vice-president after the election was viewed as a sign of gratitude by President Mogae. Similarly explained was a decision giving him supervisory powers over other ministers shortly after he returned from a controversial year-long sabbatical from politics. Like his father, Ian Khama is able to negotiate and manipulate might and right in responding to competing claims on him as *kgosi*, MP and vice-president by Batswana as "citizens", "subjects" or both. Other *dikgosi* have demonstrated similar agency and negotiability in their various chiefdoms and nationally. The popularity of the Botswana National Front (BNF) in the Bangwaketse chiefdom, for example, is generally attributed to the traditional support the party has received from successive *dikgosi* – Bathoen Gaseitsiwe II and Seepapitso Gaseitsewe, who in turn have attracted special attention and ambivalence from the BDP government keen to improve its image in the chiefdom and constituency. *Kgosi* Seepapitso Gaseitsewe's appointment as Botswana's ambassador to the United Nations in 2001 was seen by some as an attempt by government to keep the outspoken and critical chief out of the way.

Despite their relative economic success and advances in modernisation, most Batswana continue to be attracted to customary ideas of leadership in the face of the contradictions of liberal democracy, and realise that pursuing undomesticated autonomy is a rather risky business. There is an ever-looming possibility – even for the most successful and cosmopolitan of Batswana, confident in the future of their diamonds and cattle as they may be – of sudden unexplained failure, and of having to cope alone; hence, nearly everyone's eagerness to maintain kin networks they can turn to in times of need and misfortunes such as death – insurance schemes notwithstanding (Ngwenya 2000). The long arm of custom and chieftaincy has refused to leave migrants alone, just as migration has failed to provoke a permanent severing of relations with the home village and its institutions. Civil servants, politicians, chiefs, intellectuals, and academics are all part of this quest for cultural recognition even as they clamour for the entrenchment of their rights as "citizens" in a Botswanan state. Continued interest in chieftaincy by various elites and elite associations is a good indication of such commitment to community and cultural identities beyond the voluntary associations of the liberal democratic type. Elites from majority and minority ethnic groups alike have created associations such as the Society for the Promotion of Ikalanga Language, Pitso Ya Batswana, and Kamanakao to articulate their claims to chiefs, paramountcy and cultural representation, even as the logic of modernisation theorists would portray them uniquely as "citizens" of "a liberal democracy" (Nyati-Ramahobo 2002; Nyamnjoh 2002b; Werbner 2002a, 2002b; Mazonde 2002).

The following examples further illustrate the dynamism of chieftaincy and democracy in Botswana.

Case One: Dikgosi and Marriage

In Tswana chiefdoms, the politics, management, flexibility and negotiability of marriage are well documented (Comaroff 1981). Chieftaincy has conservative and progressive forces within its ranks on various issues, and its survival depends a lot more on negotiation and conviviality between the forces than on revolutions or insensitivities to the interests of one another. There is a generational dimension to how various chiefs perceive the importance of marriage. The older chiefs see marriage as duty to the chiefdom, while the younger generation see marriage as a personal matter to be realised by the individual chief only when he has found the right woman to make him happy as a husband. Yet despite the public display of difference between the older and youthful chiefs, the very fact that the institution tolerates and provides for both married and unmarried chiefs is evidence of how conciliatory towards custom and innovation, age and youth, chieftaincy actually is. It guarantees survival for itself by posing as a melting pot for competing perspectives on marriage and its role in present-day Botswana.

It is Saturday, February 23, 2002 at Goodhope. The occasion is the enthronement of 25-year-old Lotlamoreng II Montshioa as *kgosi* of the Barolong. With his enthronement Lotlamoreng will become one of the youngest paramount chiefs in Botswana. Other young *dikgosi* include Moremi Tawana II of the Batawana, who – his youth notwithstanding – is also chairperson of the House of Chiefs. Lotlamoreng is not married, just like Tawana II, Kgari Sechele of the Bakwena, and Ian Khama of the Bangwato. *Kgosi* Linchwe II of the Bakgatla, oldest paramount chief, revered custodian of culture, and president of the Customary Court of Appeal in Botswana, expresses concern over rapid transformations and loss of dignity in chieftaincy. He claims that the onus of restoring the dignity of chieftainship lies with the chiefs themselves, especially with the young breed of chiefs who have lost respect by staying unmarried. He says that in their days, a young *kgosi*-to-be had to be married "so that your tribe can respect you". Turning to *Kgosi* Tawana II, who was also present, Linchwe says:

> You have to marry. We must know where *dikgosi* wake up each morning, not to be emerging from shacks all over the village. You must be flanked by your wife on occasions like this one. ... This way, you have dignity with your people and they respect you. [He adds] I am touched, *Kgosi ga e a tshwanela mo morafeng* [A Chief should not be coming in the company of a girlfriend in a public place].

Kgosi Linchwe's reputation is such that few would dare to contradict him. But *Kgosi* Tawana is used to talking back. Turning to Lotlamoreng, he says: "Take your time before getting married so that when you marry you do so for your own benefit and the benefit of your family, not for Barolong and other people". He stresses that *dikgosi* must separate their lives from their duties, and drawing from his own experience, adds:

> Life is yours and live it the way you feel comfortable. Don't allow yourself to be under pressure from anybody. You live for yourself, your mother and your family and not your tribe. I made that mistake six years ago when I became chief. I thought my life was inseparable from the Batawana, but suddenly I realised that I had my own life to live. When it is time for you to settle, then you will have chosen the woman who will make you a happy husband – and not one you would leave for other women and schoolgirls. Six years ago, I would not have liked to bring a woman into the Moremi poverty, that is why I am ready to do so now.

Also critical of unmarried *dikgosi* was the Minister of Local Government, Dr Margaret Nasha: "I am pleading with you to go out there and find a wife to wed. I will be waiting anxiously to get news that you are getting married; that is when I will bring you a present, not today".

Kgosi Lotlamoreng replies: "I have been listening to Minister Nasha and *Kgosi* Linchwe attentively, but while I respect them I agree with my chairman, *Kgosi* Tawana. As you all know I have been chief for a short time only and I think it won't be wise for me to wed before some of the elders" (*The Botswana Gazette* March 27, 2002).

Commenting after the ceremony, *Kgosi* Linchwe says he was taken by surprise by the remarks made by *Kgosi* Tawana, claiming that these were not in order.

> A chief should lead by example, if he marries, the tribe will follow suit and the nation will be kept. *Kgosi* Tawana should know that when a chief is given royal counselling, it is abominable for him or anybody to answer back. If you answer back or engage in the game of theorising on the merits and demerits of the advice given, you run the risk of defeating the advice and the sacred exercise. I do not think many would share Tawana's sentiments because it is a given in our culture that adults, let alone chiefs, should marry.

Tawana continues to be equally adamant after the ceremony, claiming his conscience is clear. "A *Kgosi* should not just marry because he is *Kgosi*, he should marry only when he is ready and not because there is pressure." He denies he had problems with *Kgosi* Linchwe, claiming instead that "*Kgosi* Linchwe has always been a father figure to me and he will remain so. He is a very close family friend."[2] The difference of perception between them on the issue of marriage could perhaps be the result of "a generation gap", he speculates.[3]

Shortly after the incident *Kgosi* Tawana reportedly announced his intention to marry Tsitsi Orapeleng of Palapye, his girlfriend since 1998, with whom he has a two-year-old son, in January 2003 (*Mmegi* March 29, 2002). Around the same period, the press reported that preparations were under way for Lieutenant-General Ian Khama to marry his South African girlfriend Nomsa Mbere, a practising dentist in Gaborone.[4]

Case Two: First Female Paramount Kgosi

One of the arguments advanced against chieftaincy in Africa is the assumption that this is a predominantly male institution. The preponderance of male chiefs has been used as proof of the undemocratic nature of the institution (Harrison 2002:125), often in total disregard of subtle and overt examination of mechanisms against autocratic tendencies on the part of chiefs and males. If one were to take this caricature for reality, the following case would seem to suggest that even this pillar (male-centredness) of chieftaincy is not beyond re-negotiation. In other words, the fact that chieftaincy has been dominated by men in the past does not imply that it cannot be reformed to accommodate women. Here again, we see an institution that is adaptable and negotiating with changing political and social realities in Botswana. A woman claiming her "birthright" as a "citizen" as provided for in Botswana's constitution, and stressing her leadership skills within the "modern" service industry, is able to access a position customarily defined by "might" and traced predominantly through the male descent line. The outcome, once again, is victory neither for "tradition" nor "modernity", but for Batswana as individuals and groups for whom "right and might" taken together offer the best protection against the dangers of unmitigated dependence on either. It is victory for democracy not as an insensitive prescription, but rather as a negotiated process.

Mosadi Muriel Seboko was born in Ratmostwa in 1950 as first child of the late Paramount *Kgosi* Mokgosi III. She was educated at Moedin College, where she completed her Cambridge Overseas School Certificate in 1969. She joined

Barclays Bank in 1971, where she later became department manager and administrator. In 1995 she retired from Barclays after 24 years of service. In 2001 she worked as floor manager with Century Office Supplies in Broadhurst, Gaborone. Mosadi is mother of four grown-up children, who are currently pursuing their own careers.

In an interview with Gary Wills, Mosadi Seboko explained why she wanted to be the paramount *kgosi* of the Balete:

> The main reason is that as the eldest child in the family of ... *Kgosi* Mokgosi III this is my birthright. Thus, it's only fair that I inherit what I strongly believe belongs to me. Secondly, I also do not doubt my capacity to lead my tribe and I believe I'm fit in all respects for such a demanding post. I have no criminal record and certainly there are no skeletons in my cupboard! (*The Botswana Gazette* November 28, 2001)

Asked why she, a woman, wanted to become chief in a country where this was considered the prerogative or birthright of men, she replied:

> Because of the rather patriarchal system practised in Botswana, culturally, people believe a woman cannot lead her tribe as a paramount chief. However, the constitution of Botswana does not discriminate against women due to their sex. My understanding of the Bill of Rights in the constitution suggests that actually we have equal rights as men and women, to such positions. (ibid)

And to prove that she would make an excellent chief, she was bringing some important skills and experience to the position:

> In my previous jobs I've had the opportunity to handle, manage and supervise people. This has given me the capacity to discharge and develop my human resource management skills. ... I've also brought up children, including, of course, helping my mother with my younger sisters and brother (the late *Kgosi* Seboko) that is, after my father *Kgosi* Mokgosi III, died rather prematurely. (ibid)

Mosadi Seboko felt that her appointment would have a positive impact on women in Botswana and beyond:

> As regards the impact on other women I do feel this will be a plus, especially concerning the empowerment of women. ... Women's NGOs have, for a long time, lobbied government to look at all sectors with respect to gender neutrality, and this must include the chieftainship. (ibid)

Among her supporters was the women's movement represented by organisations such as Emang Basadi. Mosadi Seboko blamed delays in her appointment on

> the fact that the acting chief, and his team, appear not to accept my wish to become the next paramount chief of the Balete. Actually, they have not taken this issue very well and are not affording it the neutrality that it needs. Obviously, their campaign has been brought to my notice, both from various newspaper articles and through comments I hear from other people. For example, the acting chief Tumelo Seboko stated recently that he would be putting forward Tsimane Mokgosi's name (who is my young cousin) as the "chief designate". I assume that this is simply because he is male? What other reason could there be? However, he has promised to inform the tribe that I have expressed a desire to become the chief, and a meeting is planned this coming Saturday [December 1, 2001] at the main *kgotla* in Ramotswa. (ibid)

Reacting to discontent among "tribal male chauvinists" *Kgosi* Mosadi said:

> What Balete need is a leader. Whether the leader is a man or a woman is immaterial. The key thing is education. People need to be educated to understand that a woman is capable of being a *kgosi*. Other than the unwritten customary rites and practices, *bogosi* [chieftainship] is mainly administrative. As a former administrator, I do not anticipate problems in my new profession as *kgosi*. (*Mmegi* January 11, 2002)

On January 7, 2002 *Kgosi* Mosadi Seboko officially took up duty as paramount *kgosi* of the Balete, following approval of her appointment by the Minister of Local Government, Dr Margaret Nasha. The minister praised the Balete "for being progressive and breaking with tradition by allowing a woman to take the reins of traditional power", and called upon other tribes to emulate the example. At a well-attended *kogtla* meeting in Ratmotswa in December 2001 during which Mosadi was elected to succeed her brother, *Kgosi* Seboko, who died earlier the same year, the minister confirmed the choice made by the people of Balete. The minister's approval made of Mosadi Seboko the first woman substantive paramount *kgosi* in the history of Botswana (*The Botswana Gazette* January 9, 2002), and the first female paramount *kgosi* to be sworn into the House of Chiefs (*The Midweek Sun* January 30, 2002).

Case Three: Succession Disputes

Although succession disputes and competition for power "have occurred with remarkable frequency" in Tswana and other southern African chiefdoms, scholars have tended not to view this "as sufficiently important to warrant a re-assessment of underlying assumptions" (Comaroff 1978:1) about chieftaincy as all might and no right.

Determined not to see democracy in chieftaincy – because of too narrow a focus on the right, in principle, to vote and be voted for – the scholarship of dichotomies has branded such negotiability or manipulability of rules and legitimacy "anomalies" and continued with its sterile prescriptiveness, divorced from real-life experiences. In his study of the Barolong boo Ratshidi of South Africa, a sister chiefdom to the Barolong of Botswana, John Comaroff observed that not only was "competition for power ... a ubiquitous feature of everyday politics and ... neither precluded by rule nor limited to interregna", rules could not "be assumed to determine the outcome of indigenous political processes". Indeed, were succession to be exactly according to prescription, Comaroff estimated that 80 per cent of all cases of accession to the Barolong boo Ratshidi chiefship would have represented anomalies. He also noted that "while access to authority is determined by birth, political power depends upon individual ability", and a significant amount of power in practice is wielded by recruited "talented office-holders". Thus, "although entitled to formal respect and ceremonial precedence", the chief "is regarded as a fallible human being who may or may not be powerful, and who may rule efficiently or ineptly". Placing "a high value upon consultation and participatory politics", as the chiefdom does, would ensure that even an incompetent chief benefits from "the advice of his subjects, whether it be proffered informally or in public" (Comaroff 1978:2–6). Hence, just as power by vote does not preclude resort to might, power by birth does not obviate participation by right.

Similar negotiation and manipulation of legitimacy are frequent among the Tswana of Botswana, almost 30 years since Comaroff's remarkable insights on the Barolong boo Ratshidi of South Africa. Present-day Botswana is characterised by numerous disputes over succession among majority and minority "tribes" alike. This points not only to chieftaincy as an institution that marries might and right in fascinating ways, but also highlights its continued importance in Botswana. Of the eight Tswana chiefdoms with permanent representation in the House of Chiefs, it is not only among the Balete that there have been disputes over succession to the throne.

The Bakwena have for instance been plagued by such disputes, recently epitomised by a bitter legal wrangle between Kgari Sechele and his cousin Kealeboga Sechele, over who should be *kgosi* of the Bakwena. As the story goes, Kealeboga's grandfather *Kgosi* Sebele II was deposed by British colonialists and replaced by his younger brother *Kgosi* Sechele III, who was more agreeable to them. Sebele was banished from Bakwena territory and he died in exile (Morton and Ramsay 1987:30–44). In 1962 Sebele's son, Moruakgomo, made an effort to regain the throne for his family but failed. Upon his death, *Kgosi* Sechele III was succeeded by Bonewamang Sechele whose four-year-old son, Kgari Sechele was designated heir apparent following his own death in 1978. Kgosikwena Sebele, uncle to Kgari Sechele, was appointed regent while waiting for Kgari to come of age, and served in that capacity for 16 years. The descendants of deposed *Kgosi* Sebele II have never given up their struggle to regain the throne. After Moruakgomo's abortive attempt in 1962, his younger brother Mokgaladi instituted fresh legal proceedings to reclaim the throne in 1999. When the latter died in 2000, his son Kealeboga Sechele continued with the claim, describing Kgari Sechele's designation as "irregular and accordingly null and void", and thus arguing that he is the rightful heir following the death of his father Mokgalagadi (*The Midweek Sun* July 3, 2002).

In March 2002, however, Kgari Sechele III was sworn in at the House of Chiefs, taking over from Kgosikwena Sebele who resigned in January 2002. Kealeboga tried in vain through his lawyer to stop the swearing in (*Mmegi* March 29, 2002; *The Botswana Guardian* December 21, 2001; *The Botswana Gazette* January 30, 2002), and Kgosikwena was not happy with initiatives taken by Kgari supporters without consulting him. In 2000 he was instructed by the Ministry of Local Government to make arrangements for Kgari Sechele's assession to the throne. He disobeyed the instructions on the grounds that another Bakwena royal,

Mokgalagadi, was also a claimant to the throne on behalf of his son Kealeboga. Instead, he called upon the Minister of Local Government to appoint a judicial commission of enquiry, as provided for in the law. The minister refused, insisting that Kgosikwena make way for Kgari's enthronement. Kgosikwena took the matter to court, which ruled against him, seeing no credible doubt to Kgari's legitimacy as heir to the throne. The court did not understand "why the applicant was so stubborn as to consult the very tribe upon which his power must largely depend". The court also wondered why Kgosikwena, in full knowledge, had delayed for 21 years before raising his doubts about Kgari's legitimacy as heir apparent. Kgosikwena resigned as regent following the court decision, which he appealed (*The Botswana Guardian* April 19, 2002).

Kgosikwena was opposed to the enthronement of Kgari before the court had decided on the dispute over succession. "When the high court rules, either in Kgari or in Kealeboga's favour, it is only then that we can start talking about installing the next Bakwena paramount chief and sending delegations to other tribes" (*The Midweek Sun* April 17, 2002). Amid this controversy, Kgari's enthronement was scheduled for August 17, 2002. In July 2002, however, Kgosikwena reportedly withdrew his appeal from the court, because he could not raise the P15 000 as security (*Mmegi Monitor* July 2, 2002), thereby clearing the way for Kgari's enthronement to proceed as planned.

Struggles for legimation are also common among subchiefs and headmen of the minority tribes, sometimes not unconnected with the fact that these are paid positions in the civil service (Dingake 1995:171–79).

Case Four: Minority Tribes Fighting for Dikgosi and Representation

If chieftaincy is unpopular and outmoded, this is hardly reflected in the growing clamours by minority tribes for recognition and representation through chiefs of their own. As recently as June 15, 2002, the remains of Bakalanga *She* (Chief) John Madawu Mswazwi, who died in exile in Zimbabwe in 1960, were reburied with pomp and ceremony in the Central District, in the presence of Botswana Television and Vice-President Ian Khama, whose grand-uncle Tshekedi Khama, as regent of the Bangwato chiefdom under which the Bakalanga are a minority ethnic group, had instigated his banishment by the colonial government. While Khama called for reconciliation in the interest of national unity, Bakalanga elite celebrated a milestone in their struggles for recognition and representation, even if this was short of the apology they wanted from Khama "for the wrongful banishment of their chief".[5] The Bakalanga are one of the leading minority groups claiming cultural recognition and representation in Botswana (Werbner 2002b, 2002c). Chiefdom remains the ultimate symbol of identity and freedom in the plural context of modern Botswana, making difference and belonging to given cultural communities a more convincing indicator of citizenship than the illusion of a unifying national culture that, in effect, thrives on inequalities and thinly disguised hierarchies among Batswana. As if to unmask the "unifying" Tswana culture for what it really is – an imposition on ethnic minorities – struggles for representation by the latter have been countered by majoritarian efforts to maintain the status quo of an inherited colonial hierarchy of ethnic groupings (Nyamnjoh 2002b).

Since the late 1980s, minority groups have been seeking equal recognition as "ethnic" or "tribal" entities with paramount chiefs of their own, and with a right to representation in the House of Chiefs on equal terms with the Tswana *dikgosi*. They have taken issue with aspects of the constitution unfavourable to them as cultural minorities (Mazonde 2002; Durham 2002; Solway 2002; Werbner 2002b). Recently, their focus has been on sections 77, 78 and 79 of Botswana's constitution, which they have criticised for mentioning only the eight Setswana-speaking "tribes", thereby relegating all other tribes to a minority status, and providing a basis for discrimination along ethnic lines. Evidence of such discrimination includes: inequalities of access to tribal land and administration; an educational and administrative policy that privileges the use of Setswana to the detriment of 20 minority languages, thereby denying the latter the opportunity to develop and enrich Botswana culturally; unequal representation of cultural interests in the House of Chiefs, which is responsible for advising government on matters of tradition, custom and culture. Critics of the constitution on these aspects have argued that such discrimination is contrary to the spirit of democracy and equality of citizenship (Mazonde 2002; Nyati-Ramahobo 2002).

Another minority group at the forefront of the struggle for representation is the Bayei,[6] who have long resisted their subjugation by the Batawana and have sought recognition for a paramount chief of their own (Murray 1990; Nyati-Ramahobo 2002; Durham 2002). In the words of their leader *Shikati*

Calvin Kamanakao I:[7] "We all deserve to be recognised as different tribal groupings who together make a whole called Botswana. We cannot achieve unity by denying other groups their identity, the age of serfdom and domination has long passed" (*Mmegi Monitor* April 16, 2002).

In November 2001, the Bayei Kamanakao elite association won a partial victory when the high court ruled in favour of its challenge that section 2 of the Chieftaincy Act, which mentions only "eight tribes", discriminated against minority ethnic groups such as the Bayei and needed amendment "to afford equal treatment and equal protection by the law" to all chiefdoms or tribes. In the words of the presiding chief justice, the Chieftaincy Act had "serious consequences, when it is remembered that this Act is one of the laws that define which tribal community can be regarded as a tribe, with the result that such a community can have a chief who can get to the House of Chiefs and that only a tribe can have land referred to as tribal territory." Following the ruling, Dr Lydia Nyati-Ramahobo, chairperson of Kamanako Association, reportedly remarked: "We are now equal to the Batawana; we are no longer a minority group" (*The Botswana Gazette* November 28, 2001; *The Midweek Sun* November 28, 2001).

The ruling in this case should be regarded within the framework of ongoing debates on discriminatory sections of the constitution, which Kamanako had also challenged but on which the court declined to rule. Previously, in July 2000, President Festus Mogae had appointed the Balopi Commission to investigate discriminatory articles of the constitution, and in March 2001 the commission reported its findings (Republic of Botswana 2000:93–110).

A subsequent draft White Paper, based on the commission's findings, argued that: "it makes sense to remove the ex-officio status in the membership of the House and subject each member of the House to a process of designation by *morafe* [tribe]. The same individual may be redesignated for another term if *morafe* so wishes". A central concern of the White Paper was to ensure that "territoriality rather than actual or perceived membership of a tribal or ethnic group should form the fundamental basis for representation in the House of Chiefs". The discriminatory sections of the constitution were to be replaced with new sections "cast in terms calculated to ensure that no "reasonable" interpretation can be made that they discriminate against any citizen or tribe in Botswana". The draft White Paper also endorsed the creation of new regional constituencies, "which are neutral and bear no tribal or ethnic sounding names". Regions were to have electoral colleges of Headmen of Record up to Head of Tribal Administration to designated members, and each region was to be entitled to one member of the House. The president would appoint three special members, "for the purpose of injecting special skills and obtaining a balance in representation".

The draft White Paper met with approbation from the minority tribes and resistance from the Tswana majority, and pushed President Mogae, who himself is from a minority tribe – Batalaote – to embark on a nationwide explanation tour of different *kgotla* (*The Botswana Gazette* April 3 and 10, 2002; *Mmegi Monitor* March 26, 2002). Under pressure from the major tribes, however, President Mogae reportedly "backtracked" on some key aspects of the draft White Paper. In a "war of words" with the majority "tribe" the Bangwato, the president was told, among other things: "It is of course fair that some [minor] tribes should be represented at the House of Chiefs, but their chiefs should still take orders from Sediegeng Kgamane [acting paramount chief of the Bangwato]. We do not want chiefs who will disobey the paramount chief and even oppose him while there [in the House of Chiefs]" (*The Midweek Sun* May 1, 2002; *Mmegi Monitor* April 2, 2002).

President Mogae subsequently appointed a panel to redraft some of the White Paper's more relevant sections, such as more equal representation in the House of Chiefs and change of names of some regions, in time for submission to parliament (*Mmegi Monitor* March 26, 2002; *The Botswana Gazette* April 10, 2002). The revised White Paper, which was eventually adopted by parliament in May 2002, reintroduced four chiefs ex-officio as "permanent" members, raised the number from eight to 12, and increased the total membership of the House to 35 members. It was provided that the four additional ex-officio members will be chiefs from the districts of Chobe, Gantsi, North East and Kgalagadi, elevated to paramount status, while the traditional eight from the Tswana tribes would be maintained (*The Botswana Guardian* May 3, 2002).

The adopted revised White Paper was rejected by most minority tribes, some of whose elite petitioned President Mogae, claiming that the changes were "cosmetic" and accusing the government of having succumbed to pressure from Tswana tribes to ignore the findings of the Balopi Commission. The petition accused the government, *inter alia*, of having betrayed its original intention to move from ethnicity to territoriality as a basis for representation. It called for "the repeal of tribalistic names of landboards, which promote the entrenchment of Tswana domination over the rest of the tribes", and insisted that the so-called lack of land of the minorities must not "stand in the way of the recognition of our paramount chiefs, as we the tribes have and live on our own land" (*The Midweek Sun* May 22, 2002). It was clear, they argued, that "the discrimination complained of has not been addressed", as "the White Paper fails to make a constitutional commitment to the liberty and recognition of, and the development and preservation of the languages and cultures of the non-Tswana-speaking tribes in the country, other than the ethnic Tswana" (*Mmegi Monitor* May 21, 2002). Other voices critical of the revised White Paper claimed it had left unresolved the fundamental issue of tribal inequality, and had actually brought things "back to square one". The ruling Botswana Democratic Party and government had demonstrated that they were for the interests of the eight principal tribes and chosen few, making it difficult for the minority tribes to "trust a government like this one" (*Mmegi* May 24, 2002).

What is important in the above case of minority tribes is the fact that these groups see paramount chieftaincy as a solution to their marginalisation. Through paramount chieftaincy they believe they could have the recognition and representation they seek as citizens of modern Botswana with a given cultural heritage. In other words, while they appreciate their political rights as individual citizens in modern Botswana, they lament their perceived collective subjection to Tswana culture. Hence the clamour for paramount chiefs of their own, and the refusal to endorse the argument that chieftaincy is an outmoded institution in a modern context of rights.

Conclusion

This chapter has argued that instead of being pushed aside by the modern power elites, chieftaincy has displayed remarkable dynamism, adaptiveness and adaptability to new socio-economic and political developments. Chiefdoms and chiefs have become active agents in the quest by the new elites for ethnic cultural symbols as a way of maximising opportunities at the centre of bureaucratic and state power, and also at the home village where control over land and labour often require both financial and symbolic capital. Chieftaincy, in other words, remains central to ongoing efforts at harnessing democracy to the expectations of Batswana as individual "citizens" and also as "subjects" of various cultural and ethnic communities.

The chapter provides evidence to challenge perspectives that present chiefs and chieftaincy as an institution trapped in tradition and fundamentally undemocratic. The idea that chieftaincy and chiefs are either compressors of individual rights with infinite might, or helpless "zombies" co-optable by custom or by the modern state, denies chiefdoms and chiefs community or individual agency. The empirical reality of actual chiefdoms and chiefs in Botswana suggests that these are, and have always been, active agents even in the face of the most overwhelming structures of repression. Chieftaincy is also a dynamic institution, constantly reinventing itself to accommodate and be accommodated by new exigencies, and has proved phenomenal in its ability to seek conviviality between competing and often conflicting influences.

In the realm of democracy, chieftaincy in Botswana has influenced and been influenced by modern state institutions and liberalism. The result of this intercourse is a victory neither for "tradition" nor "modernity", "chieftaincy" nor "liberal democracy", citizenship nor subjection, "might" nor "right", but a richer reality produced and shaped by both. Chieftaincy may be subjected to the whims and caprices of the power elite, but such whims and caprices are not frozen in time and space, nor are the elite a homogenous and immutable entity. Changing political and material realities determine what claims are made on chieftaincy, by whom and with what implications for democracy. The adaptability and continuous appeal of chieftaincy makes of democracy in Botswana an unending project, an aspiration that is subject to renegotiation with changing circumstances and growing claims by individuals and communities for recognition and representation.

Acknowledgement

I am grateful to the Wenner Gren Foundation for a grant that kindled my interest in chieftaincy research, and to the Research and Publications Committee of the Faculty of Social Sciences at the University of Botswana, for funds to research chieftaincy in Botswana.

Notes

1   In the singular *kgotla* — chiefs' council, assembly or parliament.
2   Linchwe knew Tawana's father well, and was friends with him during their school days in England. He considers Tawana his son and is always ready to give him advice.

3   Put together from: *The Midweek Sun* February 27, 2002, p.3; *The Botswana Gazette* February 27, 2002, p.3; *Mmegi Monitor* February 26, 2002, p.9; *Mmegi* March 1, 2002, p.10.

4   See *Mmegi Monitor* April 2, 2002, p.2 and April 9, 2002, p.2: "Bangwato Ask for Khama's Wife".

5   See editorial in *Mmegi Monitor* June 25, 2002, p.10.

6   Also known as *Wayeyi*.

7   It is noteworthy that Calvin Kamanakao's leadership has not been uncontested. See *Mmegi Monitor* April 16, 2002, p.4.

References

Comaroff, J. 1978. "Rules and Rulers: Political Processes in a Tswana Chiefdom", *Man*, 13:1–20.

_____ 1981. "The Management of Marriage in a Tswana Chiefdom". In Krige, E. and Comaroff, J. (eds.) *Essays on African Marriage in Southern Africa*. Cape Town and Johannesburg: Juta: 29–49.

_____ and Roberts, S. 1981. *Rules and Processes: The Cultural Logic of Dispute in an African Context*. Chicago: University of Chicago.

Dingake, O. 1995. *Administrative Law in Botswana: Cases, Materials and Commentaries*. Gaborone: University of Botswana.

Durham, D. 2002. "Uncertain Citizens: Herero and the New Intercalary Subject in Postcolonial Botswana". In Werbner, R. (ed.) *Postcolonial Subjectivities in Africa*. London: Zed: 139–70.

Ferguson, J. 1999. *Expectations of Modernity: Myths and Meanings of Urban Life on the Zambian Copperbelt*. Berkeley: University of California Press.

Fisiy, F. 1995. "Chieftaincy in the Modern State: An Institution at the Crossroads of Democratic Change", *Paideuma*, 41:49–62.

_____ and Goheen, M. 1998. "Power and the Quest for Recognition: Neo-Traditional Titles Among the New Elite in Nso, Cameroon", *Africa*, 683:383–402.

Geschiere, P. 1993. "Chiefs and Colonial Rule in Cameroon: Inventing Chieftaincy, French and British Style", *Africa*, 632:151–75.

Goheen, M. 1992. "Chiefs, Sub-chiefs and Local Control: Negotiations over Land, Struggles over Meaning", *Africa*, 623:389–412.

Gonçalves, E. 2002. "Perceptions of Traditional Authority in Southern Mozambique, 1992–2002: A Case Study in Mocumbi District, Inhambane". BA (Hons) dissertation. University of Cape Town.

Good, K. 2002. *The Liberal Model and Africa: Elites Against Democracy*. Basingstoke: Palgrave.

Harneit-Sievers, A. 1998 "Igbo "Traditional Rulers': Chieftaincy and the State in Southeastern Nigeria", *Afrika Spectrum*, 33:57–79.

Harrison, G. 2002. "Traditional Power and its Absence in Mecúfi, Mozambique", *Journal of Contemporary African Studies*, 20:107–30.

Lerner, D. 1958. *The Passing of Traditional Society: Modernising the Middle East.* New York: The Free Press.

Linchwe II, K. 1989 "The Role a Chief Can Play in Botswana's Democracy". In Holm, J. and Molutsi, P. (eds.) *Democracy in Botswana.* Gaborone: Macmillan Botswana: 99–102.

Makgala, C. 1999. "The Introduction of the Policy of Indirect Rule into Bechuanaland Protectorate, 1926–43". M.Phil. research dissertation. University of Cambridge.

Mamdani, M. 1996. *Citizen and Subject: Contemporary Africa and the Legacy of Late Colonialism.* Cape Town: David Philip.

Mazonde, I. (ed.) 2002. *Minorities in the Millennium: Perspectives from Botswana.* Gaborone: Lightbooks.

Mbembe, A. 2001. *On the Postcolony.* Berkeley: University of California Press.

Miaffo, D. and Warnier, J.-P. 1993. "Accumulation et ethos de la notabilité chez les Bamiléké". In Geschiere, P. and Konings, P. (eds.) *Pathways to Accumulation in Cameroon.* Paris: Karthala: 33–69.

Molomo, M. (ed.) 2000. *Pula,* (special issue on: *Elections and Democracy in Botswana),* 14,1.

Morton, F. and Ramsay, J. (eds.) 1987. *The Birth of Botswana: A History of the Bechuanaland Protectorate from 1910 to 1966.* Gaborone: Longman Botswana.

Murray, A. 1990. *Peoples' Rights: The Case of BaYei Separatism.* Human and Peoples' Rights Project Monograph No.9. Maseru: National University of Lesotho.

Ngwenya, B. 2000. "Gender and Social Transformation through Burial Societies in a Contemporary Southern African Society: The Case of Botswana" Ph.D dissertation. Michigan State University.

Nyamnjoh, F. 2001. "Review Article: Expectations of Modernity in Africa or a Future in the Rear-view Mirror?" *Journal of Southern African Studies*, 27:363–9.

———— 2002a. " "A Child Is One Person's Only in the Womb': Domestication, Agency and Subjectivity in the Cameroonian Grassfields". In Werbner, R. (ed.) *Postcolonial Subjectivities in Africa.* London: Zed: 111–38.

———— 2002b. "Local Attitudes Towards Citizenship and Foreigners in Botswana: An Appraisal of Recent Press Stories", *Journal of Southern African Studies*, 28:755–76.

Nyati-Ramahobo, L. 2002. "From a Phonecall to the High Court: Wayeyi Visibility and the Kamanakao Association's Campaign for Linguistic and Cultural Rights in Botswana", *Journal of Southern African Studies*, 28:685–710.

O'Laughlin, B. 2000. "Class and the Customary: The Ambiguous Legacy of the Indigenato in Mozambique", *African Affairs*, 99:5–42.

Oomen, B. 2000. ""We Must Now Go Back to Our History': Retraditionalisation in a Northern Province Chieftaincy", *African Studies*, 59:71–95.

Parsons, N., Henderson, W. and Tlou, T. 1995. *Seretse Khama: 1921–1980*. Gaborone: The Botswana Society.

Republic of Botswana. 2000. *Report of the Presidential Commission of Inquiry into Sections 77, 78 and 79 of the Constitution of Botswana*. Gaborone: Government Printer.

Ribot, J. 1999. "Decentralisation, Participation and Accountability in Sahelian Forestry: Legal Instruments of Political-Administrative Control", *Africa*, 691:23–66.

Solway, J. 2002. "Navigating the "Neutral" State: "Minority" Rights in Botswana", *Journal of Southern African Studies*, 28:711–30.

Van Rouveroy van Nieuwaal, E. and Van Dijk, R. (eds.) 1999, *African Chieftaincy in a New Socio-political Landscape*. Hamburg and Münster: LIT Verlag.

Van Rouveroy van Nieuwaal, E. 2000. *L'état en Afrique face à la chefferie: Le cas du Togo*. Paris: ASC-Karthala.

Warnier, J.-P. 1993. "The King as a Container in the Cameroon Grassfields", *Paideuma*, 39:303–19.

Werbner, R. 2002a. "Challenging Minorities, Difference and Tribal Citizenship in Botswana", *Journal of Southern African Studies*, 28:671–84.

_____ 2002b. "Conclusion: Citizenship and the Politics of Recognition in Botswana". In Mazonde, I. (ed.) *Minorities in the Millennium: Perspectives from Botswana*, Gaborone: Lightbooks: 117–35.

_____ 2002c. "Cosmopolitan Ethnicity, Entrepreneursip and the Nation: Minority Elites in Botswana", *Journal of Southern African Studies*, 28:731–54.

Newspapers

The Botswana Gazette, Gaborone.

The Botswana Guardian, Gaborone.

The Midweek Sun, Gaborone.

Mmegi, Gaborone.

Mmegi Monitor, Gaborone.

Between Competing Paradigms: Post-Colonial Legitimacy in Lesotho

Roger Southall[1]

The "liberated" states of southern Africa have typically assumed liberal democratic forms, yet the underlying reality is one of authoritarianism exercised by national liberation movements which have transformed themselves into dominant political parties (Good 2002:1–19). To be sure, the contradictions are far more pronounced in some states (such as Zimbabwe) than others, notably South Africa, where a higher state of industrialisation and societal complexity than elsewhere in the region may serve to counter potentially authoritarian trends displayed by the now ruling African National Congress (ANC). Even so, whilst the liberation movements have quite clearly left numerous emancipatory hopes unfulfilled, the liberation movements themselves remain overwhelmingly unselfcritical and also acutely reluctant to criticise the obvious failings of their fellow movements, which are viewed as historically progressive organisations which successfully fought colonialism and oppression. Hence it is that the Southern African Development Community (SADC) is dominated by a core group of countries (South Africa, Zimbabwe, Angola, Mozambique and Tanzania) whose current ruling parties are deemed to have been integrally involved in the struggle for liberation. In contrast, there are other countries where the original "progressive" movements have been defeated at the polls (Zambia) or where the present rulers played a more ambiguous role during "the struggle" (for example, Botswana, Lesotho, Malawi and Swaziland).

This division points to competing paradigms of legitimacy in southern Africa (Southall 2003a). On the one hand, the paradigm of "national liberation" celebrates past leadership of, and involvement in, the nationalist armed struggle against colonialism and apartheid. It stresses the ruling party as the embodiment of the national will, its historic right to rule for and on behalf of the people, and critically, it effectively prioritises the past over the present. This set of assumptions serves to delegitimise competitors to power, even if they operate within state-defined rules. On the other hand, the paradigm of "democracy" stresses the right of rulers to hold state power by reference to their enjoying the active support of the people, as demonstrated most notably by their having secured victories in cleanly fought and run popular elections. It therefore prioritises the present over the past, for under this paradigm ruling parties which lose elections are expected to stand down and allow their more popular competitors to take their place.

Now of course, these competing paradigms overlap massively, thereby allowing for enormous ambiguity and nuance. For instance, "liberated" states typically assume democratic forms and rules, even though the underlying reality may be one of authoritarianism exercised by former national liberation movements which have transformed themselves into dominant political parties which (like the ANC and Namibia's South West African People's Organisation, SWAPO) genuinely win successive popular elections. In contrast, the Botswana Democratic Party (BDP) appears to found its right to rule principally upon its successes in promoting economic growth and in constructing Africa's longest-standing democracy, yet most certainly does not seek to deny its anti-colonial credentials. Nor indeed should it be forgotten that many radical critics claim that "liberal" or "representative" democracy (the contemporary hegemonic form from which all self-proclaimed southern African democracies are derived) so fatally compromises the original ideal of democracy as direct rule by "the demos" that it habitually produces rule by an elite at the expense of popular participation (Good 2002:69–88, 165–94). None the less, it remains the case that ultimately the two paradigms clash. Hence liberal democratic commentators now constantly bewail the tyranny installed by the Mugabe regime in Zimbabwe, citing highly convincing evidence that the ruling Zimbabwe African National Union–Patriotic Front (ZANU-PF) has stolen successive elections at the expense of the opposition Movement for Democratic Change (MDC). In contrast, ZANU-PF's fellow liberation movements have closed their eyes to its electoral malfeasance, have endorsed its victories and actively deny the MDC legitimacy.

The two paradigms may clash, yet they necessarily co-exist. Former national liberation movements such as the ANC deploy the competing sets of ideas situationally. When dealing with the West, the ANC will stress South Africa's liberal democracy. But when operating in southern Africa, or in the wider continent beyond, it is the language of anti-colonialism and anti-imperialism which typically sounds the most sympathetic chords. Hence it is that far more weight is attached to the core group within SADC being composed of fellow national liberation movements than it is to their constituting a collegial gathering of liberal democracies. When the cards are down, "national liberation" is prioritised. Yet where does this leave non-core political parties which cannot claim full membership of the "national liberation" club? And what are the longer-term implications of this prioritisation regionally?

This chapter attempts a partial answer to these questions by reference to the highly ambiguous post-colonial experience of Lesotho.

From Defensive Nationalism to Dependent Democracy

Lesotho's Defensive Nationalism

The existence of Lesotho, a predominantly mountainous and small territory entirely surrounded by South Africa, is predicated upon the historical resistance of the Basotho to subjugation to their neighbours, combined with shrewd diplomatic exploitation of differences between materially and militarily stronger outsiders. Originally forged as a people by the great Moshoeshoe I from diverse sets of refugees fleeing the depradations of Shaka's Zulu expansionism, conquest of the Basothos' mountainous refuge by the Boer Republic of the Orange Free State was avoided when Moshoeshoe I secured protection for Basutoland under the British Crown in 1868. Annexation of the territory to the Cape Colony by the British in 1872 and the impositions that it entailed were effectively repudiated by the Gun War of 1880–81, which resulted in the reimposition of direct rule by the British in 1884. Resistance to incorporation into the Union of South Africa translated into continuing preference for British protection against total subjection to segregation and apartheid from 1910 until the early 1960s (Eldredge 1993).

In these circumstances, the anti-colonial demand for self-determination, which first took explicitly political form with the establishment of the Basutoland African Congress (BAC) under the leadership of Ntsu Mokhehle in 1952, was based upon a defensive nationalism, whereby the Basotho defined themselves as a people in response to external threats (Southall 1999). Initially premised upon resistance to the *difiqane*, this nationalism was for the bulk of Lesotho's history founded upon a negative, the determination *not* to be absorbed into South Africa, *not* to be subjected to white settler domination, and from 1948 on, *not* to fall directly under the rule of apartheid. Hence it was that Lesotho proceeded to a political independence from Britain in 1966 which was widely deemed as scarcely viable: so dependent was the territory upon South Africa economically, and so evident was its weakness in contrast to the apartheid republic's political and military might, that numerous commentators essentially dismissed the country as no more than a bantustan (Halpern 1965). Indeed, this was the initial reaction of black Africa, too, and it was only from the early 1970s, when the then Prime Minister Leabua Jonathan began to curry international support by indulging in anti-apartheid rhetoric, that the Organisation of African Unity (OAU) and others engaged in the struggle against apartheid began to take Lesotho at all seriously (Grundy 1973:135–6; Hirschman 1979).

Lesotho's Twisted Entanglements in Liberation Politics

The celebration of the anti-colonial, anti-apartheid, national liberation struggle lies at the heart of the definition of nationalisms throughout most of southern Africa. In Lesotho, however, this has not been the case, not merely because doubters have chosen to query the reality of the country's political independence, but because the Basotho political heritage has been so severely fractured and bitterly contested. This fracturing of the Basotho body politic is one reason for the survival of Lesotho's monarchy, which despite having come worst off in numerous battles with both ruling parties and military governments, has never been in severe danger of being overthrown, for if adopted as a political agenda, republicanism would strike at what the overwhelming majority of the king's subjects understand what it means to be a Mosotho. Whatever the personal flaws of the individual monarch, the monarchy remains one of the few undisputed symbols of Basotho nationalism, and serves as a unifying force which, ultimately, no government has thought it wise to disrespect (Weisfelder 1977). Hence it is that "Moshoeshoe Day", a public holiday which celebrates the original construction of the nation by its peculiarly wise, diplomatic and humane founder king, is popularly regarded as rather more important than "Independence Day", which marks the country's freedom from colonial oppression.

In contrast to the ideal of the monarchy, any celebration of nationalist struggle proves immediately divisive. This is a result of the Byzantine twists and turns of

Lesotho's post-independence history and the inability of any of the country's major political parties to lay a monopoly claim to have been the vehicle of a convincing Basotho nationalism. Of course, Weisfelder (1999:1–2) is right when he proposes that the behaviour and policies of other political parties have to be defined in relation to the Basutoland Congress Party (BCP) (the successor body to the BAC), for the BCP was the first political party to mobilise anti-colonial sentiment and solicit a mass base, and its victory in the first general election (1960) seemed to render it destined to lead the nation to independence. Other parties' activities were "primarily reactive to the vigorous thrust of Mokhehle's organisation". Had the BCP proceeded to win the second pre-independence election, and thereafter to establish itself in power for a generation in the way, for instance, that Kenneth Kaunda's United National Independence Party did in Zambia, then the construction of a national-liberation mythology might have been relatively uncomplicated. Yet the reality was that the BCP lost out, albeit very narrowly (and controversially), in the second general election (1965), to the socially conservative Basotho National Party (BNP) of Leabua Jonathan. Although there were (and are) minority political traditions,[2] this article will focus on ideological competition between the BCP (and its later offshoots) and the BNP for the simple reason that they are by far the most significant.

In crude summary, the BNP won its mandate through expressing the fears of lesser chiefs and headmen that the BCP would erode their privileges, through the hostility of the influential Catholic Church to the BCP's radical pan-Africanism and alleged "communism", and through the inability of the large majority of migrant workers (the majority of whom inclined to the BCP) to return to Lesotho to cast their votes on polling day. In addition, the BNP may have gained advantage from the fact that it was quietly favoured by the colonial administration and more overtly by the South African government, which in the subsequent election in 1970 actually provided the Jonathan government with food aid at a time of shortage, which was dispensed in key constituencies. The result was that the principal vehicle of Basotho nationalism was outfoxed and displaced in government by a party which had come into existence only to counter and dilute the BCP's message and policies, and whose leader, initially at least, openly ridiculed nationalist leaders to the north and decried their attempts to isolate, boycott and destroy white minority rule in South Africa (Grundy 1973:133–4). Meanwhile, Mokhehle and the BCP never advocated a suicidal strategy of confrontation with South Africa, arguing that progress in

Lesotho would be severely inhibited so long as apartheid survived. The fundamental purpose of Basotho nationalism was therefore to serve as a catalyst for rapid, revolutionary change in South Africa. Yet this commonsensical caution was somewhat obscured by the radicalism of its sloganeering calls for the defeat of "imperialism" and "oppression" (Weisfelder 1999:95–7). In contrast, the BNP argued that economic reality dictated good relations with South Africa, and loudly projected BCP "communism" as a threat to the necessity of ensuring cross-border goodwill in order to ensure national survival. Whereas the BCP condemned collaboration, the BNP initially stressed co-operation over confrontation (Weisfelder 1999:86–97). In political and ideological terms, the overall outcome was that the BNP could not convincingly beat the nationalist drum. On the one hand, it could scarcely highlight the anti-colonial struggle, for to do so would be to celebrate the vision and leadership of Mokhehle; on the other, it could not mobilise around its opposition to racialism and apartheid, for likewise, on this count, it was always outgunned by the more radical message of the BCP (Weisfelder 1999:Part II). Any attempt to project itself as the equivalent of the nationalist parties that had come to power elsewhere in Africa was further negated in 1970, when it confirmed its status as an apartheid quisling by staying in power only by virtue of South African and British assistance in nullifying a general election whose results should by right have provided a victory for the BCP (Macartney 1973). Indeed, the BNP's abrogation of the constitution appeared to confirm allegations that Lesotho was little more than a glorified bantustan.

In this context, the BCP was able to claim a near monopoly of virtue, and to present itself to Africa as the authentic voice of Basotho nationalism. Yet that picture was soon to become clouded by developments that built upon an earlier disjunction between the Basotho and South African streams of Congress politics. As Weisfelder (1999:2–23) elaborates, the genesis of the BAC/BCP had been intimately related to post-war changes in South African political activity. The large numbers of Basotho migrant workers in South African urban centres ensured rank-and-file Basotho involvement in the ANC and other dissident movements. Lekhotla la Bafo, the principal forerunner of the BAC which had expressed commoner concerns, had had loose connections with the South African Communist Party from the 1930s, numerous Basotho attended South African educational institutions which fostered political militancy, and Mokhehle himself was expelled but later graduated (in 1944) from Fort Hare, where he became a member of the ANC Youth League. None the less, despite this fundamental political harmony of outlook, based upon anti-colonialism and opposition to white minority rule, there were difficulties in the relationship, for many ANC activists seemed ambivalent about Mokhehle's establishment of a purely Basotho organisation "which might divert energies from broader African protest activities in South Africa". Furthermore, Basutoland's "identity as an ethnically homogeneous, rural labour reserve also contributed to the emergence of an "Africanist" orientation in the BAC" which resonated more clearly than the ANC's emphasis upon forging a multiracial Congress Alliance of Africans, Indians, "coloureds" and radical whites (Weisfelder 1999:5). Mokhehle's enthusiastic participation in the All-African People's Conference in Accra, and his romantic identification with Kwame Nkrumah's version of radical pan-Africanism not only facilitated cheap BNP jibes that he was "communist" but prepared the way for his further association with Robert Sobukwe and his party's subsequent alignment with the Pan-Africanist Congress (PAC) in South Africa after its foundation in 1959. In so doing, he thrust a minority of BCP dissidents, who feared the excesses of a Mokhehle regime patterned after that of Nkrumah, into the arms of the royalist Marematlou Freedom Party (MFP), which at that time, apart from providing a convenient home for those opposed to both Mokhehle and Jonathan, included a militant minority component of ANC refugees and sported the ANC's own colours of black, gold and green.[3] All this was to have serious consequences in the years that lay ahead, for in allying with the minority stream of the South African liberation movement, the BCP was to leave the way clear for the ANC in later years to forge a relationship of convenience with the BNP.

Following its nullification of the 1970 election, the BNP had suspended the constitution and ruled by fiat. Attempts to broker a compromise with the BCP, whereby in essence the latter would serve as a subordinate partner in government, foundered on Mokhehle's outrage and intransigence and Jonathan's efforts to undermine his rival by cultivating divisions within his party. These were to become manifest after 1974, when a bungled coup attempt by the BCP was put down in blood and violence, and Mokhehle and leading supporters fled into exile (mostly in Botswana). Thereafter, the BCP, ever fractious, was to become divided into external and internal wings, with the latter, led initially by Gerald Ramoreboli, eventually being tempted in 1975 into what Jonathan described as a government of "national reconciliation". Efforts by Mokhehle to entice the OAU into mediating a resolution to Lesotho's political crisis all came to nought (Bardill and Cobbe 1985).

The scene might have been set for Mokhehle's external wing of the BCP to generate extensive international support as the opponent of a quasi-bantustan government which manifestly lacked domestic legitimacy. But things were not that simple. To be sure, the BCP's decision, following the failure of its coup in 1974 to resort to armed struggle through the creation of the LLA, received immediate support from the PAC, which viewed the BCP as not only an ally but a possible source of recruits for its own military wing. LLA recruits were therefore dispatched for training to Libya (and later to Syria and Tanzania). Yet the PAC's star was already fading internationally, not least because it was wracked by internecine divisions. In any case, after Soweto exploded in 1976, the PAC was no longer so short of potential guerrilla recruits. Besides, like the ANC before it, it was becoming increasingly resistant to Mokhehle's insistence on the autonomy of the BCP. By 1978, when the BCP deemed itself ready to launch its armed struggle in earnest, it was effectively isolated. Worse, it had to face the refusal of Botswana to be used as a launch-pad, yet most problematic was the necessity it faced of moving its soldiers across South African territory to QwaQwa, the Basotho ethnic homeland, which bordered Lesotho and amongst whose population the BCP was confident of establishing a popular base. Given other factors such as internal dissension and acute underequipment, it was entirely predictable that early LLA forays ran straight into the tender arms of the awaiting South African police. From as early as 1979, it was becoming clear that the LLA could not hope to launch any serious assault upon the BNP regime without South African connivance (Southall 2002).

For the South Africans, the launch of the LLA's armed struggle was a gift. Pretoria's relations with Maseru had begun to deteriorate precipitately from the mid-1970s for two reasons. First, weakened by his government's declining domestic legitimacy, Jonathan had begun to cultivate both internal and especially African support by widening his international linkages. These included the establishment of diplomatic ties and receipt of foreign aid from various communist countries, including the People's Republic of China, moves which provoked acute anxiety next door. Secondly, especially after Soweto exploded in 1976 and Lesotho began to provide a haven for South African political refugees, Jonathan was increasingly able to present his regime as a plucky David confronting the apartheid Goliath. Aid began to pour in, and extremely rapidly, Lesotho began to acquire a previously unheard-of international respectability (Hirschman 1979). Critically, too, although Jonathan proclaimed publicly that the country was no more than a host for political refugees, his government began to firm its links with the ANC, which increasingly regarded Lesotho as an important listening post and a base for ANC/*Umkhonto we Sizwe* activities. Indeed, Chris Hani had taken up residence in Lesotho as early as 1974 (Ellis and Sechaba 1992:esp.122–7).

In these circumstances, the LLA found itself condemned to operate under the umbrella of South Africa. There is no evidence of any increasing ideological affinity to the apartheid regime. Both sides of the relationship regarded each other with distrust and distaste, yet mutual co-operation was convenient to both. Mokhehle had various meetings with South African military and intelligence personnel who, whilst perhaps not aiding the LLA overtly, certainly facilitated its launch of a series of attacks upon Lesotho's paramilitary unit, police stations and government installations. South African facilitation of these activities appeared to be confirmed after the number of LLA attacks decreased following South African Prime Minister P.W. Botha's meeting with Jonathan in August 1980, when the latter apparently parlayed a withdrawal of South African support for the LLA in exchange for his clamping down on ANC activities. But the resulting peace did not last for long, and the level of LLA incursions increased markedly from early 1981. By 1982, the LLA had clearly gained a greater capacity to engage in conventional military operations, not least because it had now, willy-nilly, been brought closer to the centre of South African "total strategy", whereby South Africa launched a co-ordinated military and political response to an alleged communist "total onslaught". *Inter alia*, this entailed the LLA opening up a second base of operations in Transkei, the Xhosa "homeland" which shared a long border with Lesotho to the latter's south-east. Resentful of Lesotho's independence, which Transkei – "independent" since 1976 – regarded as no more real than its own, and alarmed at MK's penetration of its own security forces, which allegedly came via Lesotho, the homeland government not only provided a base for the LLA but drew it into a working relationship with the Transkei Defence Force, which by this time had fallen under the control of white officers recruited from the former Rhodesian security forces. For the LLA, however, there was to be no triumphant ending. In December 1982 the then South African Defence Force (SADF) launched a major raid upon Maseru, killing some 43 people, justifying its action as an attack upon the ANC, which it said was using Lesotho as a base for terrorism. This culminated in an agreement between the two governments to clamp down on each others' insurgents, and the subsequent airlift of ANC personnel to Mozambique and Tanzania. The number of LLA raids upon

Lesotho then declined drastically, not least because South Africa shifted its tactics to promoting an internal opposition, the Basotho Democratic Alliance, to undermine the Jonathan regime, with which relations remained tense. The saga of distrust was finally to be brought to an abrupt end with South Africa's provocation of a military coup in January 1986, and its effective installation of a puppet regime headed by Major-General Lekhanya. Little more was to be heard of the LLA (Southall 2002).

How the Uneasy Past Challenged Lesotho's Dependent Democracy

In May 2002, Lesotho appeared to put much of its unhappy history behind it. In that month, the Lesotho Congress of Democracy (LCD), led by Prime Minister Pakalitha Mosisili, swept to an outstanding 79 to 41 seat victory over the BNP and an array of minor opposition parties. This was via a new mixed-member proportional electoral system which promised to provide the country with a modicum of badly needed political stability. The road to reach this point had been hard, littered with obstacles largely of Basotho politicians' own making.

The military government of Justin Lekhanya, which had proved oppressive and highly corrupt, had been cajoled by domestic discontent and pre-South African settlement international pressure into leaving office in 1993. The exiled BCP, which had been allowed back into Lesotho after 1990, had then proceeded to secure a comprehensive victory over its old antagonist, the BNP, by winning all 65 seats in the lower house of parliament. At long last, Mokhehle claimed his inheritance and took office as prime minister. Careful dissection of the results indicated that the result was wholly legitimate, that the BCP had benefited from a widespread popular rejection of the BNP's post-1970 dictatorship, and that the BNP failed to secure even a single seat because of the remarkably even division of support for the BCP and BNP throughout all constituencies around the country.

Hence despite obtaining some 25 per cent of the popular vote in the then first-past-the-post election, the BNP was left without representation. It called foul, and dismissed the election as rigged. Subsequently, in 1994, it lent support to King Letsie III's[4] dismissal of the Mokhehle government (provoked by the latter's attempt to establish a commission of inquiry into various aspects of the monarchy and by flawed efforts to impose controls over the BNP-inclined army) before that was reversed under pressure from South Africa working in tandem with Botswana and Zimbabwe (as representatives of SADC) (Southall and Petlane 1995).

Worse disruption of Lesotho's newly installed parliamentary democracy followed in 1998. In 1997, the by now ageing and ill Mokhehle had sought to overcome severe internal fracturing within the BCP by marching the majority of MPs out of his original party into a new one, the LCD. This proceeded to yet another clean-sweep victory in an April 1998 general election under the leadership of Mosisili, Mokhehle's hand-picked successor. Again the BNP could not believe the results, but this time round it was joined by the rump BCP and other minor parties. Disturbances followed as the opposition alliance flooded Maseru with their supporters and, with the army and much of the police choosing to stand on the sidelines, brought the capital and much of the country to a total standstill. Chaos reigned as the LCD government, shorn of the capacity to rule, warned of a "creeping coup" and eventually called for assistance from the SADC. These events culminated in armed intervention by the South African National Defence Force (SANDF) and the Botswana Defence Force in September 1998, which was initially badly bungled. Opposition supporters rioted and burned down much of Maseru and other towns before the SANDF eventually restored order, but not before various controversial armed encounters with the Lesotho Defence Force (LDF) after which the latter succumbed to the inevitable and laid down its arms (Southall and Fox 1998). The situation was fraught, as the LCD stood accused by its opponents and by the bulk of international commentators of having effectively annulled Lesotho's independence by inviting a South African "invasion".

In the event, these deeply etched troubles were to find an apparently happy ending. South African and other international insistence upon, and assistance to, inter-party negotiations which, although hugely difficult and seemingly endlessly protracted, led to the adoption of a new multi-member electoral system, whereby 40 proportionately elected seats were added to the existing 80 constituency seats, which were still to be elected by first-past-the-post, thus guaranteeing the proportional representation of the opposition. Massive international efforts were put into making sure of the neutral administration of an independent electoral commission so as to ensure that the election was free and fair, and when, initially, the BNP – now led by former military strongman Justin Lekhanya – sought to disavow the results, they were quite bluntly told to behave by Lesotho's donors. They fairly swiftly agreed to take their places in parliament, and to play the role of opposition. Meanwhile, the South African umbrella had provided the backing for the LCD to reform the military, which hitherto had retained a close connection to the BNP. In sum, although few were rash enough to predict plain sailing in the years ahead, Lesotho appeared to be emerging from its political troubles: the LCD had established itself as a dominant party which enjoyed undoubted popular and electoral legitimacy; opposition parties had acquiesced to a new, more appropriate electoral system; and the military, which had so long abused its power either on behalf of BNP dictatorship or its own praetorian interests, had been newly subjected to civilian control and a professional code of behaviour. Of course, the critics are right when they object that this has only been achieved at severe cost to Lesotho's sovereignty, for the country has become a dependent democracy, that is, one wherein the legitimacy and viability of its elected governments is ultimately guaranteed by South Africa. None the less, for a country whose survival options are so limited, it can be claimed that this is remarkably beneficent outcome (Southall 2003b). Even so, that achievement remains threatened by the failure of major political actors in the drama to confront their past.

Let us look first at the LCD as the inheritor of the anti-colonial, nationalist tradition. From this perspective, the massive victory of the BCP in the 1993 election constituted the delayed moment of national liberation, the realisation of hopes that were cruelly denied in 1965 and smashed in 1970. It was a triumph of good over evil, and punishment of the BNP's dictatorship. Mokhehle had been led by Fate in his earlier years to the pinnacle of Mount Sinai, but unlike Moses had eventually reached the promised land. Historical justice had been done. Yet it was not long before this nationalist nirvana began to unravel. Critically, it was not just that the BCP fell victim to factionalism, internal battles for limited spoils in a country where resources are so desperately few, but rather that the party leadership, and Mokhehle in particular, declined to disclose the skeletons in its cupboard, preferring to maintain a myth of uncomplicated nationalist triumph over adversity.

In this reconstructed historiography, the LLA was quietly relegated to the margins of history, and its human remnants dispersed as unfussily as possible, some taking jobs in the private security industry, but probably more being left to languish at home in the mountains. It was not just that any serious attempt to integrate them into the police or army was likely to render the latter even more unruly than they were. It was rather that a serious interrogation of the role of the LLA would pose too many awkward questions about how Mokhehle, the youthful scourge of colonialism and apartheid, had later sat down to sup with the devil. Unfortunately for him, many of the stories of how he had been brought into collaboration with the SADF were to be revealed before the South African Truth and Reconcilation Commission, and then to be repeated verbatim in the local Sesotho press, where they provided ample ammunition about how he had betrayed the true BCP to his enemies within the party. Given the immense detail which was laid bare, his outright denials of any connection at all with the South African regime were utterly unconvincing, whereas his presentation of his actions as those of a man who had to make unsavoury choices in pursuit of a justifiable cause, the overthrow of a domestic dictatorship, might well have quietened his adversaries. Of course, Mokhehle was subsequently to dish his opposition by forming the LCD and to use the undoubted magic of his name throughout countryside to hand a massive victory to his successor as prime minister. Yet it was to be at the cost of some fragmentation of the popular support base for the Congress tradition, and for preparing the ground for challenges to the LCD's legitimacy after the 1998 election. Never disposed to examining their own faults, the opposition were genuinely nonplussed as to how such a newly born party could have swept the board so clean without having rigged the election. It may also be argued that it was the very success of the LCD in vanquishing the BCP in 1998 which encouraged Mosisili's former deputy, Kelebone Maope, to lead a dissident faction of MPs out of the LCD in 2001 into a Lesotho Congress Party, which then challenged for power in the 2002 election. Even though it received a bloody nose for its pains, it had contributed to the steady reduction of the popular vote for Mokhehle's party from 75 per cent in 1993 to just over 55 per cent in 2002 (Southall 2003b).

Not that the BNP was any better at examining its past. Indeed, if anything, it was worse. For a start, the party was never really able to overcome the trauma of its ejection from power by its own military in 1986. Since assuming office two decades earlier, the BNP had elaborated its belief in its own right to rule. The myth had been inculcated that it had not lost the 1970 election; that the election had been suspended because of the electoral malfeasance of the BCP; that the BCP and Mokhehle had subsequently shown their treachery by the attempted coup of 1974; that the BNP had extended the hand of reconciliation out to its opponents thereafter; and that the stern measures it took to face down the threat posed by the LLA were a necessary response to an attempted armed uprising. But most of all, in the context of the 1990s, the BNP came to believe its own propaganda, that it had forged a close relationship with the ANC and that under its leadership Lesotho had played an integral role in the struggle for the liberation of southern Africa from racism and apartheid. Hence it was that the BNP greeted the results of the 1993 general election with total disbelief: with the ANC clearly destined to take power in South Africa in the very near future, it seemed thoroughly perverse that its close ally in Lesotho should fail to win a single seat in parliament, whilst its pan-Africanist rival, the BCP, should sweep the board. The only possible answer to this absurdity was that the election result, pilloried as "robotic", had been rigged. Nor could the courts which repudiated BNP appeals be trusted, for they were clearly part of a conspiracy hatched up against the party, although why and by whom (even if international electoral monitoring organisations were clearly in on the plot) it was difficult to say (Sekatle 1993). Despite the fact that by 1998 the BNP elite was deeply divided (with an old guard furious that Lekhanya, who had ejected them from power, had now returned to lead them), the same set of beliefs governed the party's response to the similar election result of that year, even if by now its actions were also governed by a far more cynical attempt to annul the electoral process by manipulating its still strong links to the military and police. Yet in all this, and again in 2002, what the party was never able to admit to itself was that the reversal in its fortunes was overwhelmingly because of popular memories about the brutality of its dictatorship.

The third actor whose miscomprehension of the past contributed to the making of Lesotho's crisis was the ANC. To be sure, South Africa's rebirth as an electoral democracy required diplomatic endorsement of Lesotho's own renaissance when King Letsie attempted to reverse the 1993 election result in August 1994. Yet there was no warmth in the relationship with Mokhehle and the BCP, which was remembered as having identified from the earliest days with the PAC, and worse, which was seen as having allowed itself to be used against the ANC as part of South African total strategy in the late 1970s and early 1980s. The LLA, it was felt, was less a liberation army like MK or even the PAC's Azanian People's Liberation Army, than a counter-revolutionary terrorist force like RENAMO in Mozambique. Hence it was that the ANC read the result of the 1998 election in terms of the history of the South African liberation struggle rather than that of the struggle against colonialism in

Lesotho. Despite the unanimous endorsement of the election as free and fair by domestic and international electoral monitoring teams, the ANC was skeptical about the result, not least because it was almost certainly fed BNP propaganda by the South African High Commissioner in Lesotho, Japhet Ndlovu, a strong party man who had been in exile in Maseru during the 1980s. Ultimately, the South African government had no option but to accept the report of a SADC commission, led by South African judge Pius Langa, which in early September 1998 concluded that it could find no evidence of electoral malpractice and fraud. It was only then, perhaps, that the penny began to drop, that the LCD genuinely enjoyed popular legitimacy, and that its own historic ally, the BNP, was an emperor without clothes. South Africa's subsequent successful transformation into an honest broker in Lesotho's politics was founded not just on this reassessment, but upon the hard fact of the SANDF's confrontation with the LDF.

As a result of the 2002 election, the ANC now endorses the LCD's legitimacy. What is peculiarly significant, however, is that this acceptance is based upon democratic rather than liberationist criteria.

Towards the Democratic Paradigm in Lesotho?

"Liberation" and "democracy" are competing yet coexisting paradigms in southern African politics, yet the former one is dominant. This paradigm prioritises the past over the present in the sense that the national liberation experience is deemed to have marked out the now dominant parties as the legitimate inheritors of the past. Yet such a perspective necessarily cultivates a deliberately heroic past, a past which glorifies the party and justifies its present leaders as embodying continuity with their predecessors, ideological correctness and accumulated wisdom. It also views the past in terms of right overcoming wrong, of history as the fulfilment of justice, and in terms of black and white rather than the shades of grey which in actuality compose "real" history in all its messiness, and as a pottage of contested arguments and never finalised alternative "truths". Crucially, however, what this also implies is that the demands of the present, of justifying the party as the vehicle of historic progress, actively encourage the obfuscation of past errors, of deviations from the "correct" path, of "struggles within the struggle" and most particularly, of examination of the circumstances and details of incidents where the national liberation movement has fallen short of the standards of human rights and justice which it purports to represent. Hence it is that the ANC has sidelined the findings of the Truth and Reconciliation Commission, which found that it had been guilty of human rights abuses in its military camps whilst in exile, and SWAPO has likewise built a "wall of silence" around indications that it similarly misused its own internal dissidents in its liberation past. In this respect, it would seem that the national liberation paradigm actually rests upon at least a degree of untruth and self-delusion. The particular contrast with the democracy paradigm is that the latter rests upon the demonstrable and regularly demonstrated right of rulers to rule. This is not to say that democratic legitimation will not regularly be claimed by those who misuse it, and in particular to justify elite rather than mass participatory rule. None the less, it is integral to the logic of the paradigm that both unintended failings and intended obstacles to the realisation of the system should be exposed and amended.

Lesotho's most significant political parties have faced peculiar problems of legitimation, and in effect they have fallen between the two competing paradigms. Indeed, it has been argued that the BNP has faced particular difficulties of self-justification because it has been unable to lay any serious claim to either. As a chiefs' party, its origins lie in a social conservatism which runs contrary to the radical and populist messages of anti-colonial nationalism; as a party of government, its involvement with the national liberation struggle of the ANC was overwhelmingly opportunistic; and as a party of opposition it has been wholly unable to come to terms with the requirements, mechanics and verdicts of electoral democracy. Riven by internal disputes which still focus largely on the past, it clearly has a long way to go to reinvent itself and to make itself electable. Meanwhile, the Congress tradition in Lesotho has had its own problems. According to the national liberation paradigm it should have swept to power at independence, but after losing the election in 1965 and being ruthlessly denied its victory in 1970, it not only became victim to factionalism but, in effect, sold out its birthright by its association, via the LLA, with the SANDF. In retrospect, whilst the 1993 election may have delivered a delayed "liberation", it was to be severely flawed not just by the organs of state that the BNP era left behind (notably an unsatisfied monarchy and an unruly, politically hostile army) but also by its own severe internal divisions, centred on personal battles left over from its chequered past. Most certainly, a heavy measure of responsibility for this factionalism lies with Mokhehle, who, like so many dominant nationalist leaders, personalised power and was either unable or unwilling to prepare the ground for the succession that age makes inevitable. Although, in the event, he was to confirm his hold on power by creating the LCD, it was at some considerable cost to the integrity and unity of the Congress tradition.

Despite this muddied past, it is possible that this story might have a happy ending for the simple reason that the birth and successive triumphs of the LCD may have provided Lesotho's party system with a new beginning in the sense that its legitimation now relies almost exclusively upon the logic of democracy. To be sure, the LCD can and will lay claim to be the embodiment of the Congress tradition, and to be the creation of Mokhehle, whose complicated legacy it has yet to interrogate. Yet the difference now is that, with the Congress tradition split four ways, it has no monopoly on those claims, which increasingly become disputes between various sets of old men fighting for control over an increasingly distant legacy. If the LCD is to win this ideological battle, it will have to do so, not by pointing out how Lesotho's Congress tradition was always right, but how it was often wrong. Indeed, in that way, it might be able to firm its relationship with the ANC by demonstrating how it is descended from the same broad stream of Congress politics from which the latter draws its own strength.

For the moment, however, what is much more to the point is the fact that the LCD owes its current legitimation to its undisputed electoral prowess, which it has had to justify not just once but thrice in turbulent circumstances. Most particularly, however, the LCD now rules by virtue of a reformed (mixed, proportional) electoral system which was extensively canvassed and neutrally implemented, its outcome accepted – albeit reluctantly by the losers – by all. Meanwhile, the LCD's shift from what was, in any case a deeply flawed national liberation tradition, is also a generational one, which bodes well for the future. If the 1993 general election was really "about 1970", that of 2002 was fought about Lesotho's present and future. The challenge to the other political parties (especially the BNP) will now be to meet the LCD on this new turf.

Lesotho's may now be a "dependent democracy", its existence and maintenance effectively guaranteed by South Africa. Even so, the prospects for its survival would appear to have been significantly enhanced by the accidental yet now unambiguous adoption of the democracy paradigm as the underlying legitimacy of its party system. A wider perspective suggested by the extinction of basic human right and freedoms by the Mugabe regime in Zimbabwe and by authoritarian trends elsewhere suggests that, whilst the democracy and national liberation paradigms can and do coexist, the long term consolidation of democracy in southern Africa will eventually require the triumph of the former over the latter.

Notes

1   I would like to acknowledge with thanks valuable comments made upon a draft of this article by Professor Richard Weisfelder of the University of Toledo.

2   The only minority tradition of any significance is that of the Marematlou Freedom Party (MFP), formed in a merger from predecessor parties in 1962, which had its origin in early breakaways from the BCP around attempts to secure and promote the position of the then Bereng Seeiso (later Moshoeshoe II), as an effective and politically influential monarch and bulwark of a competitive democratic system against potential political excesses of rule by either the BCP or BNP (Weisfelder 1999:37–50). This attempted assertion of the interests of the traditional hierarchy (the senior chiefs) suited neither of the major parties, and although the MFP has remained a constant presence, it has never enjoyed more than minimal popular support. Not for nothing was its leader throughout the 1990s, Mr Vincent Malebo, derisively referred to in some quarters as "Mr one per cent!".

3   Personal communication from Richard Weisfelder, who also notes that at this time the BCP supported people like TT Letlaka of the PAC when the colonial administration tried the PAC leadership in Lesotho for subversive acts against South Africa under the "Prevention of Violence Abroad Act". Letlaka was subsequently to return from exile to South Africa at the time of Transkei "independence" in 1976, when he became Minister of Finance in the Bantustan cabinet. It is interesting to speculate that Letlaka's old BCP connections may have proved instrumental in facilitating the use of Transkei as a base for the BCP's Lesotho Liberation Army from the late 1970s on.

4   Moshoeshoe had been deposed as king in favour of his son, subsequently known as Letsie III, in 1992. He was reinstalled as king by the BCP government in 1995 before his tragic death in a car crash in early 1996 once more brought Letsie to the throne.

References

Bardill, J. and Cobbe, J. 1985. *Lesotho: Dilemmas of Dependence in Southern Africa*. Boulder: Westview Press.

Eldredge, E. 1993. *A South African Kingdom: The Pursuit of Security in Nineteenth-Century Lesotho*. Cambridge: Cambridge University Press.

Ellis, S. and Sechaba, T. 1992. *Comrades Against Apartheid: The ANC and the South African Communist Party in Exile*. London: James Currey; Bloomington and Indianopolis: Indiana University Press.

Good, K. 2002. *The Liberal Model and Africa: Elites Against Democracy*. Basingstoke and New York: Palgrave.

Grundy, K. 1973. *Confrontation and Accommodation in Southern Africa*. Berkeley, Los Angeles and London: California University Press.

Halpern, J. 1965. *South Africa's Hostages*. Harmondsworth: Penguin.

Hirschman, D. 1979. "Changes in Lesotho's Policy Towards South Africa", *African Affairs*, 78,311:177–96.

Macartney, W. 1973. "The Lesotho General Election of 1970", *Government and Opposition*, 8,4:473–94.

Sekatle, P. 1993. "Disputing Electoral Legitimacy: The BNP's Challenge to the Result". In Southall and Petlane (eds.): 105–17.

Southall, R. 1999. "Is Lesotho South Africa's Tenth Province?" In Lambrecht, K. (ed.) *Crisis in Lesotho: The Challenge of Managing Conflict in Southern Africa"*. Braamfontein: Foundation for Global Dialogue: Series 2:19–25.

Southall, R. and Fox, R. 1998. "Lesotho's General Election of 1998: Rigged or *De Rigeur*?" *The Journal of Modern African Studies*, 37,4:669–96.

Southall, R. 2002. "The Lesotho Liberation Army: A Synopsis and Challenge to Research", *NUL Journal of Research*, 9:57–82.

_____ 2003a. "Democracy in Southern Africa: Overcoming a Difficult Legacy", *Review of African Political Economy*, 96, forthcoming.

_____ 2003b. "An Unlikely Success: South Africa and Lesotho's Election of 2002", *The Journal of Modern African Studies*, 41,2:1–28.

_____ and Petlane, T. (eds.) 1995. *Democratisation and Demilitarisation in Lesotho*. Pretoria: Africa Institute.

Weisfelder, R. 1977. "The Basotho Monarchy". In Lemarchand, R. (ed.) *African Kingships in Perspective: Political Change and Modernisation in Monarchical Settings*. London: Frank Cass.

_____ 1999. *Political Contention in Lesotho 1952–1965*. Lesotho: Institute of Southern African Studies.

From Controlled Change to Changed Control: The Case of Namibia

Henning Melber

Fundamental socio-political changes took place towards the end of the twentieth century in southern Africa with the mediated and controlled decolonisation processes of the previously settler-dominated societies. The spectre of prolonged civil war and the need to keep the economies running prompted policies of compromise. This came also as a result of pressure exercised by international actors on both the colonial powers and the liberation movements. Hence the transition to independence negotiated and implemented for Namibia under the initiative of the United Nations was a process of controlled change, which finally resulted in changed control. As a result of a negotiated settlement, the national liberation movement, SWAPO reconstituted itself as a political party composing the government, and took over state structures and subsequently exercised increasing control over the political sphere within Namibian society. However, in so doing, SWAPO found itself inevitably engaged in compromise in that, although it formally acceded to power, it did so without securing adequate control over wide swathes of society and the economy. Instead, the structural legacy of settler colonialism remained alive. Consequently, the project of effecting social transformation was always going to be a long drawn out process at best. The same applies to profound changes of political culture towards the consolidation of democracy. Apart from the fact that there are lasting structural and psychological effects resulting from the colonial legacy (Melber 2000, 2001, 2002a), vested interests are re-established, and originally formulated goals of social transformation are either compromised or even totally abandoned in favour of the interests of a new elite mainly rooted in the sphere of a new nationalism and its power of definition. It is the complexity of these interrelated processes that this analysis seeks to document.

Decolonisation and Democracy

SWAPO's armed liberation struggle, launched in the mid-1960s, had a major impact on the further course of decolonisation. Yet Namibian independence was as much the result of a negotiated settlement which, eventuating after the end of the Cold War, was none the less also guided by the strategic interests of the two formerly competing global power blocs. It paved the way for a legitimate government led by the victorious liberation movement, SWAPO, albeit after far too many delays and sacrifices by its supporters. The goal of the struggle was national liberation. This was defined as political independence in a sovereign state under a government representing the majority of the people, who hitherto had been excluded from full participation in society on racial grounds through the imposition of apartheid. The power of definition concerning the post-colonial system of political governance was exercised during this process mainly by the national liberation movement in interaction with the international system represented by a variety of competing actors under the polarised conditions of superpower rivalry during the 1970s and 80s. The emphasis of the struggle was thus on exile politics and couched in terms of international diplomacy.

Dobell (1998:23) proposes that:

> Namibia provides a particularly fascinating case study of the gradual dismantling of a century of colonial rule, and its ultimate replacement – through democratic means, and monitored by external powers – by a movement which, some would argue, had in certain respects come to resemble the forces against which it had originally struggled.

Her study indicates that the easy assumption that the liberation of Namibia from illegal occupation by a colonial minority regime would imply more or less automatically the installation of a democratic society is sadly misleading.

SWAPO's agenda was first and foremost shaped by the goal of establishing a formally legitimate and internationally recognised sovereign Namibian state. By implication, the expectation among many of the forces involved in this struggle was that this would entrench a lasting democracy. Explicit evidence for this, however, remains scarce and scattered. Throughout the 1970s and 1980s the liberation struggle was overwhelmingly interpreted in terms of the right to self-determination of the Namibian population. Once achieved, the task of formulating further specifications was left to those policy-makers who emerged as representatives of the Namibian demos as a result of free and fair general elections. It was therefore not democratisation which was foremost on SWAPO's agenda for Namibia, but decolonisation.[1] From a liberationist perspective, this is understandable, since there can by definition be no democracy under colonialism. Only a decolonisation process provides the necessary framework for democratisation. Even so, liberation and democratisation are neither identical nor necessarily congruent.

The mandate implemented by the United Nations Transitional Assistance Group (UNTAG) under UN Security Council Resolution 435 (1978) provided for the supervision of free and fair general elections for a Constituent Assembly. These regulated competition between all those political parties which were registered under the transitional authority, which was composed jointly by the South African Administrator-General and the United Nations Special Representative. Even so, the competing parties were not operating from a basis of equal opportunities. While the one side, the allies of South Africa, could rely on massive support from the departing de facto colonial power, SWAPO had the privilege and advantage of being the only recognised representative of the Namibian people internationally. The possibility of any similar support to other forces not aligned to either the liberation movement or South Africa was basically eliminated by the political polarisation which had occurred since the early 1970s. Hence Martti Ahtisaari, previously head of the United Nations Council for Namibia and UNTAG Special Representative counterpart to the South African Administrator-General during 1989/1990, subsequently summarised the intrinsic contradiction of this constellation with regard to the selective and exclusive recognition of liberation movements both in South Africa and Namibia:

> I don't think it was the most democratic way of going about it but I think the justification for that was to concentrate the efforts vis-à-vis the occupying power. That was the fact, which we had to deal with. But it obviously didn't make life easier and the solution of the problem either. Because in the end, I think, the mere armed struggle would never have solved the problem; and if you go for a democratic solution, then you have to give everybody the chance to participate and agree conditions so that they would be starting on a fairly equal basis. As a result (the political forces not affiliated to

SWAPO) were eliminated from that political opportunity and that of course diminished plurality and complicated matters. (1999:185)

The Namibian independence process therefore resulted, first and foremost, in an internationally supervised and legitimated transfer of political power. That this met the definitions and expectations of democracy was a desired result but not the main goal. After all, so the argument went, the democratically elected representatives of the Namibian people should themselves have the discretion and power to decide upon the character of their own political system. However, what has been maintained with reference to the subsequent changes in South Africa applies as much to Namibia:

> South African society, with its massive inequalities, racial and ethnic sensitivities and authoritarian legacies, is hardly an ideal environment for textbook liberal democracy. However although South Africa may not have the democracy it deserves, it may well have the democracy that it can sustain. (Schrire 2001:148)

Initially, at least, the processes of liberation and democracy in Namibia produced remarkable results. Yet the warning of Goran Hyden (2000:19) is apposite: "applying the principles of good governance to post-conflict situations is taking them to a new frontier, where the unknowns prevail". He therefore urges caution and prudence as salient attributes of any approach by the international community to promoting reconciliation and democratisation in post-conflict situations. This touches upon democratisation as "a transitional phenomenon involving a gradual, mainly elite-driven transformation of the formal rules that govern a political system" (Gros 1998:2).

Democracy at Independence

The remarkable introductory and concluding passages of the preamble to "The Constitution of the Republic of Namibia" represent symbolically and materially the end of an era of colonial oppression and popular resistance against foreign rule, drafted and adopted by consensus of the members of the country's Constituent Assembly. The 66 men and six women who drafted the constitution represented a total of seven parties, were elected under the United Nations-supervised general elections in November 1989 and were thereby authorised to undertake this important mission.[2]

The constitutional democracy that was formally institutionalised as a last preliminary step towards formal sovereignty confirmed in both its contents and drafting procedures a negotiated compromise. Since the constitutional document had to be adopted by a two-thirds majority, none of the parties involved in the negotiations had the power to impose a unilateral decision upon the other interest groups represented in the Constituent Assembly. SWAPO, with 41 seats (57 per cent of the votes) had missed out on securing a two-thirds majority in the 1989 pre-independence elections. Meanwhile, the Democratic Turnhalle Alliance (DTA), which was representative of settler, South African and conservative interests, failed to emerge as a really powerful opposition, having gained just 21 seats via 28 per cent of the votes. In this constellation, both parties preferred a negotiated settlement to continued conflict. The emerging process has been qualified as "an impressive example of successful bargaining by opposing political elites in a transitional democratic context" (Forrest 1998:43). Available first-hand statements of actors involved in the transition likewise confirm that the negotiated settlement in Namibia resembled an "elite pact" (Dobell 1998:38).[3]

The constitutional negotiations were the final chapter of a decolonisation process "closely supervised by international forces, and facilitated by a "transitional pact" (which) alongside at least an instrumental commitment to democracy on the part of opposing forces ... surely ... made a difference" (Bauer 2001:36). As Erasmus (2000:80) points out, the international settlement plan as laid down in Security Council Resolution 435 (1978) "gained an important additional element when it was decided to determine the basic content of Namibia's constitution in advance. Constitution-making became part of the international peace-making operation".[4] From the outset, SWAPO

> formally proposed the incorporation of the 1982 constitutional principles, a proposal that was adopted to resounding applause. These 1982 principles laid down ground rules for a multiparty democracy with regular elections by secret ballot, an independent judiciary, and a declaration of fundamental human rights, including recognition of property rights. The reassertion of these principles laid to rest the spectre of a one-party state that had worried some of SWAPO's opponents. (Cliffe *et al* 1994:199ff)

In other words, the negotiated settlement, started under United Nations supervision, continued to acknowledge the externally defined rules of the game, and the parties involved were "eager to seize the reins of power" (1994:213). Given these various constraints, "the 80-day miracle" (Diescho 1994:29–38) consequently received rather mixed appraisals. Most observers agree, however, that the internal drive to conclude colonial rule was hugely complemented by external factors which helped shape the particular style of independence.

> The Namibian Constitution is a lengthy and detailed document. ... It was the product of a complex political compromise between a right-wing, racist South African government and a leftist, nationalist SWAPO government in exile, brokered by the United Nations. As such it sets out a number of political relationships in a very detailed way. (Harring 1995:31)

As Cliffe (1994:205, 214) noted, at this particular defining moment, "land and property rights were never the subject of public debate" and the "aspect of the Bill of Fundamental Human Rights that gave guarantees to existing property owners received surprisingly little attention".

The package which paved the way for a sovereign Namibia under a SWAPO government therefore implied a socio-economic and political regulatory framework which had emerged as a compromise between basically antagonistic social forces. The independence process under UN auspices "profoundly influenced the form of the new Namibian democracy" (Saunders 2001:10). The constitutional rooting of formal political liberties and human rights secured a "yardstick for good governance" (Erasmus 2000:98), and to that extent it constitutes a valuable instrument contributing towards democracy. Even so, the *ground norm* which it has introduced still requires societal acceptance and, in practice, there remains a "discrepancy between the acclamation of the constitution as the symbol of liberation and independence, and the translation of the constitution into daily life" (Hinz 2001:91).

Meanwhile, the under-secretary for legal affairs at the Ministry of Foreign Affairs has had another important warning to offer:

> To instil democratic and human rights values ... is not enough, however; we also need to insist that institutions themselves become more democratic ... [It is ironic] that although we have a widely admired constitution, the organisations which are supposed to provide the officials who will protect this constitution, namely our

political parties, are the most undemocratic institutions in the country. (Pickering 1995:107)

Political Culture Since Independence

The most striking phenomenon in terms of political development during Namibia's first decade of independence has been the constant consolidation of political power and control by the former liberation movement. From election to election during the first 10 years it has managed to add further strength to its dominant role. While SWAPO had originally failed to obtain the aspired two-third majority of votes in the elections for the Constituent Assembly in November 1989, it managed to grasp exclusive control over the parliamentary decision-making process with the national elections in December 1994.

The election figures over the first 10 years (Table 7.1) indicate only a small absolute increase of votes for SWAPO. In fact, while SWAPO expanded its representation in the National Assembly by 17 per cent in 1994, obtaining with 73.9 per cent the two-third majority, the number of votes received had actually dropped by 22 767. Due to a total decrease of all votes (almost 28 per cent less), the loss (5.9 per cent) was more than compensated for. With a total of 408 174 votes in the 1999 national elections, SWAPO received 23 607 votes (6.1 per cent) more than in 1989. Due to the lower number of total votes cast (151 751 or 22.1 per cent less than in 1989) the party increased its representation by another almost 2.3 per cent to 76.15 per cent.

Another characteristic of the first decade was the failure of any single opposition party to establish itself as a relevant political factor. Nor was the situation to be significantly changed with the founding of the Congress of Democrats (CoD) as a new political party in early 1999. Given that CoD counted various defectors from SWAPO amongst its leading figures and activists, many observers originally expected it to attract a significant number of frustrated SWAPO followers, thereby perhaps challenging that party's two-thirds majority. In practice, however, CoD established itself as the second largest party, at the expense of the DTA, albeit by a marginal number of votes. Its principal impact was to split the forces of opposition. In the process, the already rather modest share of the United Democratic Front, previously the third force within the political map of Namibia, became even less meaningful.[5]

Table 7.1 Election results 1989–1999 for the larger political parties

Election Votes	Total	SWAPO	DTA	UDF	CoD
1989	687 787	384 567	191 532	37 874	—
Constituent		56.90%	28.34%	5.60%	—
1992	381 041	256 778	103 359	9285	—
Regional		68.76%	27.68%	2.49%	—
1992	128 973	73 736	42 278	7473	—
Local		58.02%	33.26%	5.88%	—
1994	497 499	361 800	101 748	13 309	—
National		73.89%	20.78%	2.72%	—
1998	63 545	37 954	15 039	4191	—
Local		60.35%	23.91%	6.66%	—
1999	536 036	408 174	50 824	15 685	53 289
National		76.15%	9.48%	2.93%	9.94%

Source Keulder 1998:63 and official figures by Directorate of Elections for 1999.

Opposition parties never managed to obtain enough weight to seriously challenge the dominance of SWAPO. For this reason, the hostile reception given by SWAPO to the emergence of CoD is disturbing. While this could have been interpreted prior to the 1999 elections as a sign of uncertainty and lack of self-confidence, the post-electoral reaction was positively paranoid. This applies also to the election post-mortems conducted by SWAPO's party organ, *Namibia Today*, and the continued smear campaigns and character assassinations it has pursued since then with ever increasing vigour against private or public disagreement with the official party line.

> Given the steady consolidation of political power in the hands of SWAPO's top leadership ... it seems odd that it should appear increasingly insecure, as evinced by the ever more draconian measures employed against political opponents, and the lashing out against a broad range of "unpatriotic" elements perceived as unsupportive or unduly critical of the government. (Dobell 2000)

This and other developments point to the emergence of autocracy under SWAPO's de facto one-party rule. Based on its reputation as the liberating force and in the absence of serious political alternatives, SWAPO initially managed to entrench its political dominance by means of obtaining a continuously higher proportion of votes in a fairly legitimate way.[6] However, an increasingly repressive atmosphere during the election campaign in late 1999 might in contrast be perceived as a "lack of consolidation of Namibian democracy" (Glover 2000:147). The far-reaching mandate that SWAPO had received had encouraged the misperception that the government is supposed to serve the party and that the state is the property of the government.[7] While a slogan in the days of the liberation struggle claimed that "SWAPO is the people", the adjusted slogan for today might be that "SWAPO is the government and the government is the state". As a result, "the social forces that control the state are also capable of using the state organisations to pursue their interests in an arena characterised by domination and opposition" (Salih 2000:19). This tendency towards abuse of state power fails to acknowledge the difference between a formal democratic legitimacy (obtained via a majority of votes in a free and fair general election) and the moral and ethical dimensions and responsibilities of such legitimacy. As a result, "the state often uses democracy to perpetuate hegemony rather than to advance rights, liberty and democracy. The adoption of non-democratic measures is often justified against the backdrop of achieving "national" objectives through a democratic mandate" (Salih 2000:24).

Subsequently, the constitution was changed for the first time in 1998 for the sole purpose of securing President Sam Nujoma a third term in office. Despite strong objections from opposition political parties and civil society, SWAPO's politically elected representatives in both houses (the National Assembly and the National Council) adopted the constitutional amendment allowing the president a third term as head of state with the required two-thirds majority. From a formal point of view, this was wholly legal and based on a mandate received through general elections by secret vote of all registered citizens. In practice, however, the move sent out the wrong signal, as it suggested that Namibia had not yet accepted democratic norms, according to which "the consolidation of institutional, social and legal frameworks" would have been "independent of the persons who happen to be in power" (Abbink 2000:7).

That same year (1998), Namibia joined a war in the Democratic Republic of Congo as a result of a personally ordered intervention by the head of state. He is constitutionally entitled by the power vested in his office to order such a far-reaching single-handed initiative in protection of national security. But its execution in this particular case posed the question of whether it was in fact necessitated by the stipulated urgent state of emergency. Neither cabinet nor parliament was consulted, and the decision to go to war was taken with total disregard of any need for consultation with elected political office-bearers and society at large. Yet this was only one instance of the authoritarian deployment of force. During 1999, an attempt at secession by various forces within the Caprivi region provoked a peculiarly repressive response by the state and led to a new stage of national chauvinism (Hopwood 2000). And later in that year, Namibian army forces were to become involved in military conflict with the UNITA movement in Angola until its collapse after the death of Savimbi, again without public debate. It turned parts of Namibia's own border areas into a low-key war zone with high sacrifices for the local civilian population.[8]

Critical voices on these and other issues were labelled as unpatriotic. Loyalty to Namibia is equated with loyalty to SWAPO's policy and in particular the party's president. Dissenting views are marginalised. Nation-building efforts take place at the expense of minorities. Gay-bashing and xenophobic sentiments are among the repertoire of high political office-bearers, often combined with an "anti-white" slant.[9] The independence of the judiciary is openly questioned when it takes unpopular decisions not in favour of the government's political will. SWAPO's newspaper disseminates hate speech and party officials articulate unconstitutional demands without being corrected by the leadership.[10] Self-enrichment by higher-ranking officials and politicians utilising their access to the state apparatus is tolerated at the expense of public morale (Kössler and Melber 2001) and illustrates the emergence of a new post-colonial class interest among the political elite (Tapscott 1995 and 2001).[11]

The Limits to Liberation

Each decolonisation process can claim a degree of uniqueness. Premature generalisations should therefore be avoided. Nonetheless, it would appear that there are certain common features between the liberation movements in southern Africa which obtained political power.

The emphasis on free elections and an agreed constitutional framework for a controlled transition in Zimbabwe, Namibia and South Africa suggests important similarities in the shaping of the post-colonial environment. Their cases represent examples of liberation movements turning into parties to occupy political power in a formally independent, sovereign post-colonial state (see Melber 2002a). These parties have managed to consolidate their dominant position and have so far maintained control over the state apparatus. In all cases, legitimacy is based on the claim of the liberation movements being representative of the majority of the people. Simultaneously, however, democracy is contested territory. Post-colonial policies in these countries display a lack of commitment to democratic principles and/or practices.[12] There are visible trends towards autocratic rule, nepotism and patron–client relations. The "national interest" serves as an instrumental concept, which is subject to highly biased and selective interpretations by those in control.

John Saul (1999) characterises these developments as "liberation without democracy". The track records of the liberation movements with regard to their internal practices during the wars of liberation as well as their lack of democratic virtues and respect towards the protection of human rights once in power are far from positive examples. Victims were as liberators often also perpetrators. While these movements – supported by international solidarity based on moral and ethical categories – were fighting against systems of institutionalised violation of basic human rights, they were at the same time far from sensitive to human rights issues within their own ranks. The fact that they were fighting against unjust systems of oppression, which were rooted in the totalitarian practices of colonial, minority rule, did not prevent them from resorting to internal oppression of the worst kind.[13] Dobell (1998) argues, in concert with Leys and Saul (1995), that there has been a lack of democratic conviction within the ranks of the organised social forces seizing political power. The organisation of a serious liberation struggle had much in common with the authoritarianism and hierarchical organisation which was inherent in the colonial system being opposed. Features of the colonial character are reproduced in the fight for their abolition and the emerging concepts of power applied during the era of post-colonial reconstruction.

The result of such constraints is at best, a restricted permissiveness. In practice, there is a highly unreceptive attitude towards criticism, especially when it is articulated within a public discourse. Non-conformity is associated with disloyalty if not betrayal. The marginalisation, if not suppression of dissent, therefore limits the capacity of the political system to reproduce itself through constant modifications based on corrective innovations, and hence ultimately undermines the polity's credibility and legitimacy. The circle of political office-bearers tends to be restricted to those comrades who gained reputation within a command-and-obey system, but not for their democratic convictions as independent-minded, autonomous individuals. As Ellis (2000:70) observes, "there has for some years been a growing perception ... that many self-proclaimed liberators in Africa have achieved rather little of what they promised".

In the context of an appeasement strategy towards the southern African region, Namibia was the laboratory for testing the scope of controlled change for South Africa too. The overt policy of national reconciliation was the reflection of such an approach, yet it was to be compromised by the self-interest of the new government, for the liberators blocked any meaningful dialogue concerning the violation of human rights within their own ranks during the years of exile (Leys and Saul 1994, 2003; Groth 1996; Dobell 1997; Lombard 2001).[14] By doing so, they unintentionally – and in contrast to the approach adopted later by the ANC in South Africa – gave away their comparative advantage of being able to claim moral superiority over those who committed (much greater) atrocities on behalf of the apartheid regime.

Hence it is that, more than a decade after independence, Namibia's political culture reveals some truly disturbing features.[15] A survey conducted at the turn of the century among six African countries (Mattes *et al* 2000) ranks Namibia last in terms of public awareness of democracy. A summary of the report concludes with reference to Namibia and Nigeria, "the consolidation of democracy is a distant prospect in both these countries" (Bratton and Mattes 2001:120). A survey among six southern African states by the Helen Suzman Foundation produced a similarly sobering result: Namibia was the only country in which a large majority would not accept defeat of its party. It diagnosed "a complete collapse of confidence in the future", while finally "not much more than one-third of respondents felt confident of democracy's future" (Johnson 1998). The most recent survey among Namibians aged 18 to 32 concludes: "Namibia does not have sufficient young democrats to make the consolidation of democracy a foregone conclusion" (Keulder and Spilker 2002:28).

"The Pitfalls of National Consciousness"

The official responses of SWAPO and the Namibian government to the rigged presidential elections in Zimbabwe in early 2002 are revealing. The secretary-general of SWAPO conveyed the following congratulatory message to the administrative secretary of ZANU-PF:

on behalf of the leadership and the entire membership of SWAPO party ... our elation over the resounding victory scored. ... Your party's triumph is indeed victory for southern Africa in particular and the African continent at large. It is victory over neo-colonialism, imperialism and foreign-sponsored puppetry. We in SWAPO party knew quite well that despite imperialist intransigence and all round attempts by enemies of peace, democracy and the rule of law to influence the outcome of the elections in favour of neck-chained political stooges, people of Zimbabwe would not succumb an inch to external pressure. They spoke with one overwhelming voice to reject recolonisation. Their verdict should, therefore, be respected unconditionally by both the external perpetrators of your great nation in celebrating this well deserved and indeed well earned victory over the forces of darkness and uncertainty, we wish to call upon the people of Zimbabwe to prove to the prophets of doom that they can do without their unholy blessing, through hard work. In the same vein, we call for unity of purpose among the African people as the only viable weapon to ward off outside influence.[16]

The head of the Namibian election observer mission had already dismissed allegations of manipulations by ZANU-PF, by declaring that the system was "water-tight without room for rigging" and that they "are satisfied that an environment existed that enabled the people of Zimbabwe to exercise their democratic right to elect a leader of their choice".[17] Such a selective view, which contrasts with the reports presented by independent observer groups, seems to express an inner logic shared by all the former liberation movements. For them, the seizure of power signals "the end of history". Hence "Mugabe's struggle to stay in power became a struggle for their own survival too. Supporting ZANU-PF was no longer just a matter of solidarity but of fundamental self-interest" (Johnson 2002). From this understanding follows the view that a liberation movement should stay in power forever once it has succeeded in its anti-colonial struggle:

> The NLMs (national liberation movements) share what can only be termed a common theology. National liberation is both the just and historically necessary conclusion of the struggle between the people and the forces of racism and colonialism. This has two

implications. First, the NLMs – whatever venial sins they may commit – are the righteous. They not merely represent the masses but in a sense they are the masses, and as such they cannot really be wrong. Secondly, according to the theology, their coming to power represents the end of a process. No further group can succeed them for that would mean that the masses, the forces of righteousness, had been overthrown. That, in turn, could only mean that the forces of racism and colonialism, after sulking in defeat and biding their time, had regrouped and launched a counter-attack. (Johnson 2002)

Namibia's head of state confirmed such a suggested perception attributed to him and others, when he addressed the congress of the Namibia Public Workers Union (NAPWU) and lectured the delegates about the necessity to fight Western imperialism and decay at all fronts:

Today it is Zimbabwe, tomorrow it is Namibia or any other country. We must unite and support Zimbabwe. We cannot allow imperialism to take over our continent again. We must defend ourselves. ... In Namibia, we will not allow these lesbians and gays. We fought the liberation struggle without that. We do not need it in our country. We have whites who are Namibians, but they must remember they have no right to force their culture on anyone. If they are lesbian, they can do it at home, but not show it in public. I warn you as workers not to allow homosexuality. Africa will be destroyed.[18]

At the World Summit for Sustainable Development in Johannesburg in early September 2002 he blamed the British prime minister personally for the situation in Zimbabwe and went on: "We are equal to Europe and if you don't think that, then to hell with you. You can keep your money. We will develop our Africa without your money." On his return from Johannesburg he told his newly appointed prime minister and foreign minister:[19]

I told them off. We are tired of insults [from] these people. I told them they can keep their money ... that these political good governance, human rights, lesbians, etc., that they want to impose on our culture, they must keep those things in Europe.[20]

Several weeks later, in an exclusive interview with a journalist representing a widely read newspaper in Germany, he declared:

> If you whites continue with arrogance, surely we will hit you! We will have the capacity to deal with you. Don't rubbish our situation, we have the capacity to deal with you. You killed our people in this country – do you think we will just forget? And you write nonsense! If you don't stop that, we will deal with you directly.[21]

Such pseudo-revolutionary rhetoric is in direct line with the mindset also articulated in the president's biography (Nujoma 2001). Its analysis prompted a respected historian to conclude that the reading "will bring no comfort to those concerned about the future of democracy in Namibia today" (Saunders 2003).

More than 40 years ago Frantz Fanon expressed his disgust about the emerging new elites he witnessed in independent (West) African countries:

> During the struggle for liberation the leader awakened the people and promised them a forward march, heroic and unmitigated. Today, he uses every means to put them to sleep, and three or four times a year asks them to remember the colonial period and to look back on the long way they have come since then. Now it must be said that the masses show themselves totally incapable of appreciating the long way they have come. The peasant who goes on scratching out a living from the soil, and the unemployed man who never finds employment do not manage, in spite of public holidays and flags, new and brightly-coloured though they may be, to convince themselves that anything has really changed in their lives. (2000:136)

Fanon's warnings concerning "the pitfalls of national consciousness" ring all too true in relation to post-colonial Namibia.

Notes

1   It can be argued that the Constitutional Principles which were drafted in the early 1980s by the Western Contact Group and adopted by the conflict parties (SWAPO and South Africa) as prerequisite for the implementation of Resolution 435 (1978) as an agreed framework for the foundations of an independent Namibian state were characterised by a democratic notion. However, this democratic notion was mainly crafted to maintain a status quo under a controlled change in terms of securing existing property relations and former privileges by those who benefited from minority rule. Dobell (1998:104)

suggests that "the nature of the transition process itself should be treated as an independent variable, which served to institutionalise democratic political structures in Namibia, while simultaneously helping to construct perhaps insurmountable obstacles to the extension of political democracy to social and economic institutions".

2   In marked contrast to all eyewitness accounts by actors in this crucial episode of Namibian contemporary history, one of the protagonists of a radical appropriation of land, to which the Namibian Constitution is an obstacle, Ponhele Ya France, maintained during the late 1990s that "the founding fathers and mothers of our Republic had neither moral or political democratic or legal right to entrench anything in the constitution without consulting the people" and that they "went too far beyond their mandate". They therefore committed an "illegal" act.

3   The pragmatic give and take approach is documented by Namibia's first head of state, who plainly states in his biography: "we agreed without argument that Namibia would be a multiparty democracy with an independent judiciary and a strong bill of rights" (Nujoma 2001:424). Similar views, stressing the general consensus among the main parties, were presented by both the then leader of the DTA and Namibia's first foreign minister during a conference which retrospectively reflected upon the Namibian decolonisation process (see Weiland and Braham 1994). And a local politician involved in the drafting process explained to Dobell (1998:101): "everybody wanted to be seen as a democrat during these negotiations".

4   He refers to the impact of the UN Security Council's adoption of Document S/15287 of July 12, 1982 ("Principles concerning the Constitutent Assembly and the constitution for an independent Namibia"), introducing several "constitutional principles" next to procedural rules for the planned election under UN supervision.

5   CoD obtained 2465 votes (or 0.46 per cent of the total votes cast) more than the DTA but the same number of seats in the National Assembly. It therefore should have had no difficulty in qualifying as the official opposition. Notwithstanding this, efforts were made to bypass its claim. The DTA and the United Democratic Front (UDF) were prepared to assist SWAPO in this effort by entering a parliamentary coalition which was used to award them the status of official opposition.

6   See among the numerous reports on the different elections, Commonwealth Secretariat (1995), Keulder (1998 and 1999), Keulder, Nord and Emminghaus (2000), Kössler (1993), Lodge (2000), Simon (2000), Soiri (2001), and The Electoral Commissions Forum of SADC Countries (1999).

7   This equation is supported by the three complementing analyses of Tapscott, Weiland and Du Pisani presented to and summarised in "Forum for the Future" (1999). See also Kössler and Melber (2001), Tapscott (1995 and 2001) and Du Pisani (2001).

8   See Lamb (2002:35–7) for a summary on human rights abuses by state security forces in both Caprivi and Kavango between 1998 and 2000.

9   Åfreds (2000); Brynjúlfsdóttir (1998); Melber (2003a).

10 Quite the opposite, SWAPO conducted its election campaign during 1999 with a brochure which declared that "saving democracy, or more appropriately saving the opposition, is the latest version of Europe's burden to civilise the natives" (SWAPO Party Department of Information and Publicity 1999:24).

11 The current rent-seeking activities under the guise of a Namibianisation of the fisheries sector is a particular case, which illustrates the point that national wealth is privatised for the benefit of a few privileged instead of utilised for the general good of the impoverished majority (see Melber 2003b). The issue of land redistribution (Melber 2002b) is similarly exploited for self-enrichment by high-ranking state officials and political office-bearers (see reports in *The Namibian*, November 21, 2002). An editorial on the matter critically concluded that certain officials "in accordance with the unofficial policy of entitlement and cronyism, will ensure they get their farm, in addition to generous monthly salaries, and the other perks and benefits of affirmative action and black empowerment, such as fishing quotas and mining concessions" (Lister 2002).

12 This does not imply that the people of these countries are less democratically minded than anywhere else (see Mattes *et al* 2000; Bratton and Mattes 2001).

13 As Lamb (2001:33) has put it with regard to SWAPO's violation of human rights in exile: "The international community turned a blind eye to human rights abuses, viewing the goal of Namibian independence as of greater importance. In particular, SWAPO had to be seen as morally superior to the South African security forces. This contributed to an environment in which human rights violators continued to act with impunity". For a detailed account by one of the victims of the mid-1970s wave of internal repression, see Nathanael (2002).

14 A media statement by SWAPO "on the so-called detainee issue" had been issued on March 12, 1996 in reaction to the book by Groth, which a prominent SWAPO politician in a public speech suggested should be burnt. As the statement argued, SWAPO "cannot allow this country to be made ungovernable and be turned into a chaotic and lawless society by irresponsible, unpatriotic elements and foreign remainents (*sic*!) of fascism and apartheid".

15 According to a recent survey among citizens in Lesotho, Mozambique, Namibia and Zimbabwe, only 57 per cent among interviewed Namibians (less than in the other countries) disagree with the opinion that freedom of movement should, as a basic human right, transcend national boundaries. Eighty per cent (more than in the other countries) shared the opinion that it is important for a country to draw borders which make it different from other states (Frayne and Pendleton 2000:16).

16 SWAPO, Office of the Secretary-General, Windhoek, March 14, 2002.

17 Quoted from *This Day*, Lagos, March 15, 2002 (http://allafrica.com/stories/200203150013.html). Kaire Mbuende, the head of the Namibian observer mission, has previously been SADC Executive Secretary and has since then been promoted to

Deputy Minister of Foreign Affairs. The editorial of *The Zimbabwe Independent*, Harare, March 15, 2002, qualified his statement as "manifestly deceitful opinion" (http://allafrica.com/stories/200203150187.html).

18 Quoted from *The Namibian*, Windhoek, August 19, 2002.

19 The head of state at the end of August 2002 removed the prime minister from office and used the subsequent reshuffle to appoint himself as Minister of Information and Broadcasting (*The Namibian*, Windhoek, August 28, 2002). His later actions included instructions to the Namibian Broadcasting Company to stop broadcasting foreign films and series that have a bad influence and to show films that portray Namibia in a positive light instead (*The Namibian*, Windhoek, October 1, 2002).

20 Quoted from reports in *The Namibian*, Windhoek, September 3 and 4, 2002.

21 Published in full in *The Namibian*, December 9, 2002. The interview appeared in a German version in *Die Welt*, December 2, 2002.

References

Abbink, J. 2000. "Introduction: Rethinking Democratization and Election Observation". In Abbink, J. and Hesseling, G. (eds.) *Election Observation and Democratisation in Africa*. London: Macmillan: 1–17.

Åfreds, J. 2000. *History and Nation-Building: The Political Uses of History in Post-Colonial Namibia*. Uppsala: Department of Economic History, Uppsala University.

Ahtisaari, M. 1999. "Interview with the President of the Republic of Finland: Martti Ahtisaari, 29.1.1966". In Soiri, I. and Peltola, P. *Finland and National Liberation in Southern Africa*. Uppsala: The Nordic Africa Institute: 181–8.

Bauer, G. 1999. "Challenges to Democratic Consolidation in Namibia". In Joseph, R. (ed.) *State, Conflict and Democracy in Africa*. Boulder and London: Lynne Rienner: 429–48.

_____ 2001. "Namibia in the First Decade of Independence: How Democratic?" *Journal of Southern African Studies*, 27,1:33–55.

Bratton, M. and Mattes, R. 2001. "How People View Democracy: Africans' Surprising Universalism", *Journal of Democracy*, 12,1:107–21.

Brynjúlfsdóttir, O. 1998. *Tolerance for Non-Conformity: A Study of the Namibian Political Elite*. Uppsala: Department of Government, Uppsala University.

Cliffe, L., Bush, R., Lindsay, J., Mokopakgosi, B., Pankhurst, D. and Tsie, B. 1994. *The Transition to Independence in Namibia*. Boulder and London: Lynne Rienner.

Commonwealth Secretariat. 1995. *The Presidential and National Assembly Elections in Namibia, 7–8 December 1994. The Report of the Commonwealth Observer Group*. London: Commonwealth Secretariat.

Constitution of the Republic of Namibia, The. 1990. Windhoek: Government Printer.

Diescho, J. 1994. *The Namibian Constitution in Perspective*. Windhoek: Namibia Institute for Democracy.

Dobell, L. 1997. "Silence in Context: Truth and/or Reconciliation in Namibia", *Journal of Southern African Studies*, 23,2:371–82.

_____ 1998. *Swapo's Struggle for Namibia 1960–1991: War by Other Means*. Basel: P. Schlettwein.

_____ 2000. "An Historic Past, An Uncertain Future", *Namibia At Ten!* Supplement to *The Namibian*, March 16.

Du Pisani, A. 2001. "Non-Emancipatory Politics", *The Namibian*, May 3.

Electoral Commissions Forum of SADC Countries, The. 1999. *The Namibian Elections Report December 1999*. Compiled by Tom Lodge. Auckland Park: Electoral Institute of Southern Africa.

Ellis, S. 2000. "Africa's Wars of Liberation: Some Historiographical Reflections". In Konings, P., Van Binsbergen, W. and Hesseling, G. (eds.) *Trajectoires de libération en Afrique contemporaine*. Paris: Karthala and Leiden: African Studies Centre: 69–91.

Erasmus, G. 2000. "The Constitution: Its Impact on Namibian Statehood and Politics". In Keulder, C. (ed.) *State, Society and Democracy: A Reader in Namibian Politics*. Windhoek: Gamsberg Macmillan: 77–104.

Fanon, F. 2002. *The Wretched of the Earth*. London: Penguin (reprint; French original 1961).

Forum for the Future. 1999. *Conference Report: Namibia After Nine Years – Past and Future*. Windhoek: Forum for the Future.

Forrest, J. 1998. *Namibia's Post-Apartheid Regional Institutions: The Founding Year*. Rochester: Rochester University Press.

Frayne, B. and Pendleton. W. 2000. "Namibians on South Africa: Attitudes Towards Cross-border Migration and Immigration Policy". In McDonald, D. (ed.) *On Borders: Perspectives on International Migration in Southern Africa*. New York: St. Martin's Press: 86–118.

Glover, S. 2000. "Namibia's Recent Elections: Something New or Same Old Story?" *South African Journal of International Affairs*, 7,2:141–8.

Gros, J-G. 1998. "Introduction: Understanding Democracy". In Gros, J-G. (ed.) *Democratisation in Late Twentieth- Century Africa: Coping with Uncertainty*. Westport and London: Greenwood: 1–20.

Groth, S. 1996. *Breaking the Wall of Silence*. Wuppertal: Peter Hammer.

Harring, S. 1995. "The Constitution of Namibia and the Land Question: The Inconsistency of Schedule 5 and Article 100 as Applied to Communal Lands with the "Rights and Freedoms' Guaranteed Communal Land Holders". Paper presented to a Workshop on "Traditional Authorities in the Nineties: Democratic Aspects of Traditional Government in Southern Africa". Centre for Applied Social Sciences, Faculty of Law at the University of Namibia, November 15–16.

Hinz, M. 2001. "To Achieve Freedom and Equality: Namibia's New Legal Order". In Diener, I. and Graefe, O. (eds.) *Contemporary Namibia: The First Landmarks of a Post-Apartheid Society*. Windhoek: Gamsberg Macmillan: 75–91.

Hopwood, G. 2000. "Caprivi: A Year After", *The Namibian*, August 2.

Hyden, G. 2000. *Post-War Reconciliation and Democratisation: Concepts, Goals and Lessons Learnt*. Working Paper 2000:8. Bergen: Chr. Michelsen Institute.

Johnson, R. 1998. "Six Countries in Search of Democracy". Focus 9. Johannesburg: Helen Suzman Foundation.

_____ 2002. "The Final Struggle Is to Stay in Power". Focus 25. Johannesburg: Helen Suzman Foundation. (http://www.hsf.org.za/focus25johnson_print.html).

Keulder, C. 1998. *Voting Behaviour in Namibia I: Local Authority Elections 1998*. Windhoek: Friedrich Ebert Stiftung.

_____ 1999. *Voting Behaviour in Namibia II: Regional Council Elections 1998*. Windhoek: Friedrich Ebert Stiftung.

Keulder, C.; Nord, A. and Emminghaus, C. 2000. "Namibia's Emerging Political Culture". In Keulder, C. (ed.) *State, Society and Democracy: A Reader in Namibian Politics*. Windhoek: Gamsberg Macmillan: 237–63.

Keulder, C. and Spilker, D. 2002. "In Search of Democrats in Namibia: Attitudes Among the Youth". In Melber, H. (comp.) *Measuring Democracy and Human Rights in Southern Africa*. Discussion Paper 18:19–28. Uppsala: The Nordic Africa Institute.

Kössler, R. 1993. *Towards Greater Participation and Equality? Some Findings on the 1992 Regional and Local Elections in Namibia*. Windhoek: The Namibian Economic Policy Research Unit.

Kössler, R. and Melber, H. 2001. "Political Culture and Civil Society: On the State of the Namibian State" In Diener, I. and Graefe, O. (eds.) *Contemporary Namibia: The First Landmarks of a Post-Apartheid Society*. Windhoek: Gamsberg Macmillan: 147–60.

Lamb, G. 2001. "Putting Belligerents in Context: The Cases of Namibia and Angola". In Chesterman, S. (ed.) *Civilians in War*. Boulder and London: Lynne Rienner: 25–39.

_____ 2002. "Debasing Democracy: Security Forces and Human Rights Abuses in Post-Liberation Namibia and South Africa". In Melber, H. (comp.) *Measuring Democracy and Human Rights in Southern Africa*. Discussion Paper 18:30–49. Uppsala: The Nordic Africa Institute.

Leys, C. and Saul, J. 1994. "Liberation Without Democracy? The SWAPO Crisis of 1976", *Journal of Southern African Studies*, 20,1:123–47.

_____ 1995. *Namibia's Liberation Struggle: The Two-Edged Sword*. London: James Currey. Athens: Ohio University Press.

Lister, G. 2002. "What About the Have-Nots?" *The Namibian*, November 22. Windhoek.

Lodge, T. 2000. "Heavy-Handed Democracy: SWAPO's Victory in Namibia", *Southern Africa Report*, 15,2:26–9.

Lombard, C. 2001. "The Detainee Issue: An Unresolved Test Case for SWAPO, the Churches and Civil Society". In Diener, I. and Graefe, O. (eds.) *Contemporary Namibia. The First Landmarks of a Post-Apartheid Society*. Windhoek: Gamsberg Macmillan: 161–84.

Mattes, R., Bratton M., Davids, Y. and Africa, C. 2000. *Public Opinion and the Consolidation of Democracy in Southern Africa: An Initial Review of Key Findings of the Southern African Democracy Barometer*. The Southern African Democracy Barometer.

Melber, H. 2000. "The Culture of Politics". In Melber, H. (ed.) *Namibia: A Decade of Independence 1990–2000*. Windhoek: The Namibian Economic Policy Research Unit: 165–90.

_____ 2001. "Liberation and Democracy in Southern Africa: The Case of Namibia". In Melber, H. and Saunders, C. *Transition in Southern Africa: Comparative Aspects. Two Lectures*. Uppsala: The Nordic Africa Institute: 17–28.

_____ 2002a. "From Liberation Movements to Governments: On Political Culture in Southern Africa", *African Sociological Review*, 6,1:161–72.

_____ 2002b. "Contested Territory: Land in Southern Africa. The Case of Namibia", *Journal 50*, Windhoek: Namibia Scientific Society: 77–85.

_____ 2003a. ""Namibia, Land of the Brave': Selective Memories on War and Violence Within Nation Building". In Abbink, J., De Bruijn, M. and Van Walraven, K. (eds.) *Rethinking Resistance: Revolt and Violence in African History*. African Dynamics, 2. Leiden and Boston: Brill: 305–27.

_____ 2003b. "Of Big Fish and Small Fry: Rent-Seeking Capitalism Made in Namibia. The Case of the Fishing Industry", *Review of African Political Economy*, 95 (in print).

Nathanael, K. 2002. *A Journey to Exile: The Story of a Namibian Freedom Fighter*. Aberystwyth: Sosiumi Press.

Nujoma, S. 2001. *Where Others Wavered. The Autobiography of Sam Nujoma*. London: PANAF.

Pickering, A. 1995. "Instilling Democracy and Human Rights Values in Namibian Society". In *Human Rights Education and Advocacy in Namibia in the 1990s: A Tapestry of Perspectives*. Windhoek: Gamsberg Macmillan: 101–7.

Salih, M. 2000. *Majority Tyranny in a World of Minorities*. The Hague: Institute of Social Studies.

Saul, J. 1999. "Liberation Without Democracy? Rethinking the Experiences of the Southern African Liberation Movements". In Hyslop, J. (ed.) *African Democracy in the Era of Globalisation*. Johannesburg: Witwatersrand University Press: 167–78.

Saul, J. and Leys, C. 2003. "Lubango and After: "Forgotten History" as Politics in Contemporary Namibia", *Journal of Southern African Studies*, 29,1 (in print).

Saunders, C. 2001. "From Apartheid to Democracy in Namibia and South Africa: Some Comparisons". In Melber, H. and Saunders, C. *Transition in Southern Africa: Comparative Aspects. Two Lectures.* Uppsala: The Nordic Africa Institute: 5–16.

_____ 2003. "Liberation and Democracy: A Critical Reading of Sam Nujoma's "Autobiography"". In Melber, H. (ed.) *Re-Examining Liberation in Namibia.* Uppsala: The Nordic Africa Institute (in print).

Schrire, R. 2001. "The Realitites of Opposition in South Africa: Legitimacy, Strategies and Consequences". In Southall, R. (ed.) *Opposition and Democracy in South Africa.* London and Portland: Frank Cass: 135–48.

Simon, D. 2000. "Namibian Elections: SWAPO Consolidates its Hold on Power", *Review of African Political Economy,* 27,83:113–15.

Soiri, I. 2001. "SWAPO Wins, Apathy Rules: The Namibian 1998 Local Authority Elections". In Cowen, M. and Laakso, L. (eds.) *Multi-Party Elections in Africa.* London: James Currey: 187–216.

South West African People's Organisation (SWAPO). Department of Information and Publicity. 1999. *SWAPO: The Driving Force for Change.* Windhoek: SWAPO.

Tapscott, C. 1995. "War, Peace and Social Classes". In Leys, C. and Saul, J. *Namibia's Liberation Struggle: The Two-Edged Sword.* London: James Currey. Athens: Ohio University Press: 153–70.

_____ 2001. "Class Formation and Civil Society in Namibia". In Diener, I. and Graefe, O. (eds.) *Contemporary Namibia: The First Landmarks of a Post-Apartheid Society.* Windhoek: Gamsberg Macmillan: 307–25.

Weiland, H. and Braham, M. (eds.) 1994. *The Namibian Peace Process: Implications and Lessons for the Future.* Freiburg: Arnold Bergstraesser Institut.

Armed Struggle in South Africa: Consequences of a Strategy Debate

Martin Legassick

It would be possible to draw a line from the founding leaflet of *Umkhonto We Sizwe* (MK), issued on December 16, 1961 (and from the 1962 South African Communist Party [SACP] programme, *The Road to South African Freedom*) to the Harare Declaration of 1989 – and to the eventual outcome and claim that the strategy of the African National Congress (ANC) was always for a negotiated settlement to achieve democracy in South Africa (*Umkhonto we Sizwe* 1961, 1989a, 1989b). That indeed is the idea which Allister Sparks attributes to Nelson Mandela: "I started *Umkhonto We Sizwe* ... but I never had any illusions that we could win a military victory; its purpose was to focus attention on the resistance movement" (1994:26).[1] However, that standpoint is contradicted by the decisions of the ANC conference at Morogoro (April 25–May 1, 1969) and by countless other ANC documents which insist that the goal was the armed seizure of power by the masses.

This chapter reviews the strategies of MK.[2] It will argue that the political economy of South Africa differed from the other largely peasant societies of southern Africa (Mamdani 1996:27–32).[3] There would have been the possibility of organising the working class at the head of a movement to achieve national and social liberation by ending capitalism and establishing a workers' democracy (which is different from a "people's democracy'). Yet this was not the strategy of MK. This chapter argues, in fact, that MK lacked a realistic strategy for achieving power, despite the heroic sacrifices of its combatants. In the end the negotiated solution in South Africa was not a "choice" by the ANC leaders but forced on them because they had no alternative. Ironically the result in South Africa has been the establishment of a bourgeois democracy which, because of the strength of the working class and hence of civil society, has far greater resilience than in the other countries of southern Africa.[4]

The Strategy Debate 1961–75[5]

In colonial and semi-colonial conditions the commencement of armed activity has not always been related to the moment in time when the guerrilla fighter is a political fighter, a member of an organised revolutionary force, who uses the struggle itself, the actual physical conflict, as an instrument of agitation and mobilisation. He aims to raise the level of popular participation to the point at which revolutionary aims become general.
(Slovo 1974:339)

The background to the decision to turn to armed struggle in South Africa has been described many times and will not be gone into here (see Mandela 1994; ANC 1969; Slovo 1976, 1995; Shubin 1999; Callinicos unpub.). Taking up armed struggle in South Africa was followed by similar decisions by the FNLA (*Frente Nacional de Libertação de Angola*) and MPLA (*Movimento Popular da Libertação de Angola*) in Angola (1962–63), by SWAPO (South West African People's Organisation) in Namibia in 1962, by FRELIMO (*Frente de Libertação de Moçambique*) in Mozambique (1963–64), and by ZAPU (Zimbabwe African People's Union) and ZANU (Zimbabwe African National Union) in 1964. The southward thrust of decolonisation through West and East Africa, and to Zambia and Malawi, had reached its limits by the means of non-violent mass struggle. By 1967 it was possible to describe "a guerrilla front across southern Africa from the Indian Ocean to the Atlantic". This included, of course, members of MK fighting in Rhodesia in alliance with ZAPU (Legassick 1970).[6]

Cuba and Algeria were models for armed struggle in southern Africa. The first operational plan for *rural* guerrilla warfare in South Africa was titled "Operation Mayibuye" (OM) and was captured by police in the raid on Rivonia on July 11, 1963.[7] Apparently drawn up by Joe Slovo and Govan Mbeki, it appears not to have been fully approved by the time it was captured.[8] OM argued that "very little, if any, scope exists for the smashing of white supremacy other than by means of mass revolutionary action, the main content of which is armed resistance leading to victory by military means". "Important ingredients" of a revolutionary situation were present. But the "objective military conditions make the possibility of a general uprising leading to direct military struggle an unlikely one. Rather, as in Cuba, the general uprising must be sparked off by organised and well-prepared guerrilla operations during the course of which the masses of the people will be drawn in and armed". As in Cuba, moreover, it was to be "the rural areas which become the main theatre of guerrilla operations in the initial phase" (Slovo and Mbeki 1963:760–8).

The Marxist Workers' Tendency (MWT) of the ANC, however, argued that in South Africa, with a working-class majority, it was eventually a popular insurrection led by the working class which was the only means of seizing power. They therefore argued that military actions must be subordinated to political action, that military cadres must be absorbed into the mass movement, and that armed action "should in its early stages have mainly the character of organised self-defence by the mass movement against the terror tactics of the state" – armed defence of strikes, demonstrations and squatter camps, and so on. As the movement gained strength, confidence and fighting skills, as the enemy weakened and divided, it would become possible to pass over to the offensive (anon. 1979:34–5).

The Morogoro conference document *Strategy and Tactics* was, according to Mzala, "obviously a development. Unlike Operation Mayibuye, it clearly saw the military strategy as forming part of, and being guided by, a broader political strategy to ensure that revolutionary battles were fought on all possible fronts, involving not just an army but the whole masses of the oppressed people" (1986:23; cf.. Saeboe unpub.). However, the attempt in *Strategy and Tactics* to articulate and summarise both sides of the questions posed in the Cuban struggle was very uneasy. It referred to the "danger of the thesis which regards the creation of military areas as the generator of mass resistance" and insisted that

> the primacy of the political leadership is unchallenged and supreme
> and all revolutionary formations and levels (whether armed or not)
> are subordinate to this leadership ... the involvement of the masses
> is unlikely to be the result of a sudden natural and automatic
> consequence of military clashes. It has to be won in all-round
> political mobilisation which must accompany the military
> activities. (ANC 1969:6, 8–9)

Military (guerrilla) action, in other words, *could* hasten the development of a revolutionary situation, yet political mobilisation was necessary to lay the groundwork for military action. How much politics was necessary was uncertain! This would have been a conundrum even in a rising tide of mass mobilisation. In a period of defeat and counter-revolution, as in South Africa in the latter part of the 1960s, the way out was even more problematic.

In addition, this strategy was flawed because it was a strategy for *rural* guerrilla warfare. In 1971 Slovo continued to insist that initially at least the struggle must be fought in *rural* areas:

> Because of the imbalance of military strength the guerrilla group, in order to survive and maintain its cohesion and mobility, has in general to operate *away from the urban complexes* in which the enemy is strongest and is most highly organised and centralised. It has to operate in terrain in which the basic population from whom it draws its strength is in the overwhelming majority". (Dubula [Slovo] 1971:32–3)

In 1981 Mzala appeared to take a different position, stating that "any strategic perspective would be moving from insufficient, nay, false, premises if it did not recognise that South Africa is above all else an industrial capitalist society" – apparently, in other words, recognising the need for a struggle based on the working class. But at the same time he tried to justify the emphasis on *rural* guerrilla warfare:

> The fact that the 1969 document (*Strategy and Tactics*), like Operation Mayibuye, saw rural areas as the main theatre of guerrilla operations in the initial phase, did not alter our recognition of the fact that only the industrial proletariat can and should play the role of leader of the South African revolution ... The theory of guerrilla warfare maintains that the enemy has to be attacked where he is weakest. It is this consideration, therefore, that gives the rural areas this strategic role". (1986:24)

What a misuse of dialectics!

In the event there was no armed activity by MK after 1968 until after the Soweto uprising of 1976.[9] Crisis in the ranks of MK after the Wankie and Sipililo campaigns was resolved only by the Morogoro Conference, which was critical of the strategy of the campaigns and put a certain emphasis on building a political underground inside South Africa to prepare to receive guerrillas (Mzala 1987b:21).[10] Turok, however, could write in 1973 that "the view is now growing within the movement itself that solidarity work and international questions have absorbed the exile leadership to the point where internal work has been neglected" (1974:52). But the fundamental difficulty for a guerrilla strategy was the geographical isolation of the ANC, SACP and MK from South Africa. Zambia and Tanzania, moreover, were relatively unreliable as "rear bases". For example, MK cadres were temporarily expelled from Tanzania in 1969 (Shubin 1999:96–100). Together with this, a "dialogue lobby" – for dialogue with the South African regime – periodically raised its head (Slovo 1974:329). In 1972 the ANC headquarters moved from Tanzania to Zambia.

The Strategy Debate 1976–87

> We were clearly not dealing with a defeated enemy and an early
> revolutionary seizure of power by the liberation movement could
> not be realistically posed. (Slovo explaining the negotiated
> settlement 1992)

From the late 1960s, liberated areas had existed in Mozambique and Angola. The outbreak of a revolutionary crisis in Portugal in 1974, in large part a product of its colonial wars, led to the victories of the liberation struggles in Mozambique and Angola (with an ominous invasion of Angola by South Africa in 1975). Within five years, with ZANU able to use Mozambique as a rear base, the Smith regime in Zimbabwe had fallen as well. Thus by the decade of the 1980s, only South Africa and South West Africa/Namibia remained as arenas of the struggle for liberation. In the southern African context, the "unholy alliance" had been broken and white minority rule had lost substantial ground. Mozambique and Angola had won real independence – though the South African invasion of Angola was an attempt to mobilise against a "breakthrough".

The liberation of Angola, moreover, opened up a new base and training area for MK from late 1975 (see anon. 1976:1–6; Saeboe unpub.); and from mid-1976 the Soweto uprising brought a stream of young recruits – perhaps 3 000 to the ANC, tripling the size of MK – to the armed struggle (see Barrell 1993:131 on numbers). Defending its colony of South West Africa, however, and in aggression against the Angolan non-capitalist regime, South Africa, together with its proxy UNITA *(União Nacional para a Independência Total de Angola)*, waged war on and in Angola from 1978 through the 1980s. South African aggression was soon extended to Mozambique and other black-ruled territories of the region, partly against the non-capitalism of the Mozambican regime and partly to deny MK rear bases contiguous to South Africa. In this the South African regime got encouragement from the similar United States support for the counter-revolutionary Contras in Nicaragua. This was also the aim of the Nkomati Accord (March 1984), the similar accord signed with Swaziland, and South African support for the coup which toppled Chief Jonathan in Lesotho in January 1986. Crucial entry routes were cut off. However, these were crucial only to a strategy of protracted guerrilla war. Like China, Cuba and Vietnam, Angola and Mozambique (and Zimbabwe) were peasant countries. Success here through rural guerrilla war was an entirely different question from armed struggle in the urbanised conditions of South Africa. While SWAPO might expect victory by means of rural guerrilla struggle, the South African situation required a strategy of armed self-defence of the workers' movement (as a preparation for insurrection), which would have implied far lower-key re-entry to the country for trained cadres.

In the 1970s the mass movement in South Africa had revived. Mass struggle had ground to a halt in the 1960s after the banning of the ANC and Pan-Africanist Congress (PAC). The revival of the struggle inside the country came about first in the 1972–74 national industrial strike wave encapsulated as the (early 1973) "Durban strikes" and secondly in the national youth "Soweto" revolt and general strikes of half a million and a million workers of 1976. As Mzala wrote later: "The devastating apathy in the oppressed community that followed the Rivonia arrests had come to an end" (1986:26). All this took place independently of the ANC (Mbeki 1996).[11] This mass movement declined through 1977 and 1978 and began to reappear in 1979–81 – through another industrial strike wave and another nation-wide school boycott. Though it declined again through 1982 and 1983, the 1979–81 movement was a herald of a decade of a mass revolutionary upsurge inside South Africa. The balance of forces was shifted from white power to black power: society was democratised from below by the struggle of the working class.

After 1976, MK members were sent back into South Africa for the first time on military operations. Significantly, the targets were almost exclusively *urban*: economic installations, courts, pass offices, police stations in Soweto, and so on (Barrell 1993:220–1).[12] (This confirmed the standpoint of the MWT of the ANC that "lacking any basis for a peasant war, guerrilla struggle in our country can only take the form of urban guerrilla action"). The MWT had added that such action "cannot overthrow the regime. *It is quite simply not a strategy for power.*

There is no force which can make the revolution for the South African workers" (MWT 1982:155). The MWT was concerned that urban guerrillaism would rather *divert* the masses from a struggle for power. Indeed, the masses were already in struggle. MK actions in fact did not divert them from that, and the ANC in the 1980s called for "mass struggle" in addition to "armed struggle". In that sense many of the actions of MK had neutral rather than negative effects on mass consciousness. Moreover, to the extent that many people wrongly believed that MK was a defence organ for the mass movement, MK sustained its popularity. However, an MK leader does also refer critically to the "myth that MK [was the people's] highly trained professional army which would liberate them" – a sign of the disempowering of the masses characteristic of urban guerrilla action (Salojee quoted by Barrell 1993:329). Some have argued that the symbolism of actions by MK infused the masses with the confidence to take on the "Hippos" (armed vehicles) and other embodiments of the state. The problem was that the creativity of the masses in this respect was deprived of arms and skills in the hands of MK.

The requirements of urban guerrilla action kept many potentially excellent political cadres in MK isolated from the mass movement, rather than assisting in developing it. The method employed from the start of armed actions after 1976 did not conform to the precepts of *Strategy and Tactics*: put political mobilisation first. The aim was not principally to stimulate mass activity, which was already present, but to maintain the prestige of the ANC. Houston, in a study of the UDF, goes as far as to claim that "armed propaganda" was guerrilla activity intended not even to mobilise mass struggle but to "popularise the *armed struggle*" [author's emphasis] (Houston 1999:25–6)!! In reality, once the mass struggle revived in the 1970s and 1980s, armed propaganda became irrelevant.

In October 1978 a delegation of the ANC's National Executive Committee (NEC) visited Vietnam. According to Howard Barrell (1992), the insistence on the *primacy of the political* was the main lesson coming from this visit. Slovo (1992) wrote a report on the visit emphasising the primacy of the political and arguing, "much ANC practice hitherto had been militaristic". A joint meeting of the NEC and the Revolutionary Council (RC) was held in Luanda in late December 1978 to hear a report-back. This meeting elected a Politico-Military Strategy Commission consisting of Oliver Tambo, Thabo Mbeki, Joe Slovo, Moses Mabhida, Joe Gqabi and Joe Modise to discuss the lessons of Vietnam. The commission emphasised that the idea of a protracted people's war was "broadly consistent with the thinking of the movement up to now as expressed in the bulk of our basic documents ... with an added emphasis on the possible role of partial and general uprisings". It did not rule out the possibility of a general insurrection in the future but stressed that this could not be "an exclusive perspective" (Tambo *et al* unpub:724–5). As we shall see, however, it was the idea of nation-wide insurrection that was to be picked up in debate on the question in the 1980s, as the result of developments inside the country.

Vietnam had been fought predominantly as a rural struggle. In South Africa the struggle was predominantly urban. The commission, however, made no explicit pronouncement on the question of rural versus urban struggle! But it consciously did not refer to the "peasantry".

> We have restricted ourselves to the expression "landless mass in the countryside" to describe the rural stratum. We concluded that not enough research and analysis have so far been undertaken to enable us to characterise both the size and social significance of what could classically be regarded as the peasant class and the process of differentiation within it. We consider it of vital importance that such a study should be undertaken. (Tambo *et al* unpub:725)[13]

The commission confirmed in words the primacy of the political. A people's war, it stated "can only take root and develop if it grows out of, and is based on, political revolutionary bases amongst the people" (729, 731). It admitted errors in this respect when it concluded that

> *our revolutionary practice* has in the recent past not always conformed to the strategic approaches contained in some of our basic documents, and has ignored key experiences of earlier phases of struggle. This is particularly in the vital areas of our approach to mass mobilisation, the character of our armed struggle, and the way we see it taking root and growing. (ibid:722–3)[14]

According to Mzala, the ANC resolved on the need for *three years* of active political mobilisation and organisation before commencing "people's war" (Mzala 1987a:24; cf. Mzala 1987c). However, it was in precisely these three years that a special operations unit was formed, headed by Slovo, to conduct *military* actions: including the sabotage of SASOL in early June 1980; the rocket attack on Voortrekkerhoogte in 1981; the attack on the coming-on-stream Koeberg nuclear power plant in 1982; and the attack outside the South African

Air Force (SAAF) Pretoria headquarters in which 19 were killed in 1983 (Barrell 1993:236–80, 299–301, 323–4).[15]

The perception created was that a *focoist* strategy of armed propaganda had been replaced by a strategy of "people's war" *à la* Vietnam (with, it is true, no conscious adaptation of this to the urban industrial conditions of South Africa). In reality "armed propaganda" fuelled by the "detonator" idea continued to be the main form of military activity. In Vietnam armed propaganda was conducted in an entirely different way. A group of guerrillas, armed, would board a bus, hold it up, and make a political speech to passengers; or take over a cinema and do the same (Barrell 1993:240). In South Africa, however, armed propaganda simply meant explosions – "propaganda of the deed". A further document drafted by Slovo was adopted by the RC in about April 1980. While this paid lip service to the "primacy of the political" analysis of the Politico- Military Strategic Commission, it claimed that armed activity "had a vital contribution to make towards domestic political mobilisation". As examples of armed propaganda it stated: "every clause in the Freedom Charter pointed to a [military] target which would serve to highlight a particular demand" (quoted in Barrell 1993:247–9). Nothing could be more *focoist* than this!

Slovo's 1980 document argued that armed propaganda was a short-term objective, while the longer-term objective was "developing a sustained armed struggle inside South Africa" (Slovo document quoted in Barrell 1993:248): presumably "protracted people's war". Slovo spoke of the need to be prepared for uprisings inside the country: "a situation in which we [MK?] could enter a region in large numbers relying on the massive and overwhelming mood of militancy to provide cover and protection" and stressed the importance of building up "within the country adequate supplies of ordinance [hand grenades, small arms] which would be protected and adequately preserved for us when such a time came". But these tasks were never undertaken (Slovo interview quoted in Barrell 1993:252, 366). The viewpoint of the machinery responsible for internal organisation was that the continuation of an armed propaganda approach "was not helping to organise an ANC domestic political-military base – the single most important task given that the ANC was unlikely ever to enjoy reliable bases in states adjacent to South Africa" (Barrell 1993:253). As late as February 1986, towards the end of the revolutionary upsurge of 1984–86, *Sechaba* printed a justification of armed propaganda – that is, military predominance – identical in words with what it had printed from Alfred Nzo in September 1980 (*Umkhonto We Sizwe* 1986)!

The rise of the mass movement (together with the lessons of Vietnam) sparked off (to this author's knowledge) the only serious debate during 30 years of exile on the strategy of armed struggle – looking, in the words of Mzala (1987a:2) for "a new approach in our military planning and activities". It reflected serious questioning in the ranks of the activists, and an inability of the leadership to present convincing answers. Mzala launched the debate with an article provocatively titled: "Has the Time Come for Arming the Masses?" This was an implicit critique of "armed propaganda" and pointing to a "people's war" strategy. He pointed out that "retaliatory violence" had become a spontaneous but permanent feature of the 1980 mass upsurge (Mzala 1980b:85).[16] A further article by Khumalo Migwe (1982:89,80) also drew on the lessons of the post-1976 struggle – where "the masses are *themselves* breaking an old pattern of peaceful struggle" (author's emphasis) – and claimed to supplement Mzala's "strategic" considerations with "tactical" ones. This discussion, however, still assumed that it was "guerrilla actions" that were preparing the way for the emergence of a revolutionary situation – and thus remained within the framework of militarism. Though Mzala and Migwe conceived of arming the masses, they did not address the strategy and tactics of this in terms of the need for self-defence of the mass workers' movement rather than the conducting of "guerrilla actions" in separation and isolation from that movement.[17]

As this debate progressed, rural guerrilla struggle was presented as more and more marginal (Shombela 1986). In 1981 Mzala argued that urban struggle needed to be backed up by rural guerrilla operations because of the limitations of actions in the townships. These, he stated, included the distance of townships from city centres (where urban warfare needed to take place), the deliberate isolation of townships, and the inability to use "certain heavy weapons" – which were these, carried by guerrillas? – in townships. "This is not to challenge the feasibility of the urban guerrilla struggle", he added: the need was to combine both and leave it to "concrete reality to determine which one will play the primary role" (1980b:91).[18] Later Cabesa (1986:38–9) maintained that while "armed campaigns will be focused on cities and urban areas", this needed to be combined with rural warfare to force the state to scatter its forces throughout the countryside. In May 1986, Ronnie Kasrils, while "not ruling out" rural guerrilla war, pointed out that it was "only one element, and maybe not even the leading or dominant mode". Instead, he maintained that "urban areas are vital terrain of our struggle ... we should utilise our urban strength, our township strength, our working-class strength as a springboard".[19]

The Kabwe Conference of the ANC (June 16–23, 1985), the second such event to be held in exile, was precipitated by the mutinies in Angola in 1984. It took place, however, in the midst of the biggest upsurge ever of the mass movement inside South Africa. As we have seen, there were deep anxieties and problems among cadres regarding what should be done. Mzala (1987c) was later to argue that the 1969 Morogoro Conference document *Strategy and Tactics* defined an "approach to armed struggle that *confines* our military strategy within a perspective of a purely protracted guerrilla warfare" (author's emphasis). Moreover, *Strategy and Tactics*, in the face of the facts, defined the strategy as one of *rural* guerrilla warfare. It was clearly outmoded. Yet no new strategy and tactics document was drawn up beforehand to present to the conference, nor was such a document passed by the conference.[20] Barrell (1993) concludes:

> At the most crucial moment in its history, in the midst of the most serious uprisings in South Africa in which its name was being widely proclaimed a leader of a revolution, the ANC had held a conference and concluded it with no generally agreed formulation of strategy.

The result, according to him, was "deepening strategic confusion". By the end of 1986 the ANC was "stuck in a profound strategic hiatus, if not crisis" (Houston 1999:384, 388, 442).

The failure of the Kabwe Conference to provide a clear strategy, coupled with the intensity of the struggle inside the country, sharpened the debate, which took place in the pages of the movement's publications. Towards the start of the upsurge, Mzala (1985:26), this time in *Sechaba* rather than the *African Communist*, remarked how "events throughout the country and in the Vaal Triangle in particular demonstrate in no uncertain terms that the masses have definitely resolved to change the situation by organised violent means".[21] He defined the task as:

> To continue ... to form the nuclei of armed guerrilla units, operating both in the towns and countryside, which should exist not merely to fight to destroy the enemy's military strength, but also to shoulder such important tasks as mobilising the masses,

organising them, arming them, and helping them to form
revolutionary organs of self-government.

In this article, his conception was of developing a guerrilla war of a mass
character, and he mentioned the idea of armed insurrection only in passing.

Up until 1985 armed activity in South Africa still comprised "mainly sporadic
sabotage attacks mounted by hit-and-run units that were usually commanded
and supplied from abroad" (Barrell 1993:260). This was no basis whatever for
the mythical "people's war", let alone preparation, through armed self-defence,
for insurrection. The actual activities of MK escalated during 1985 and 1986.
Operation Zikomo was launched from mid-1985, sending in large numbers of
combatants with hand grenades to participate as "shock troops" in township
uprisings. This led to 136 "incidents" of MK activity in 1985, according to
Barrell (1993:388–92, 440), more than double that of any previous year.
Moreover, the ratio of three guerrillas captured or killed for each 13 attacks was
MK's most favourable casualty rate ever. This campaign was brought to a halt
when state agents (*askaris*) started to give youth booby-trapped grenades,
causing immense suspicions that reacted on genuine MK personnel. In 1986
the number of "incidents" increased to 231 – and more of them directed at
military and police personnel than ever before. But MK's success rate
dropped to four guerrillas captured or killed for every five attacks.[22] Ronnie
Kasrils (1986:6) maintained that "our trained combatants are now able to
merge among our risen people, more and more of whom are being brought
into MK units at home" (*Citizen* March 18, 1986, cited in O'Meara 1996:337).
In similar vein Dan O'Meara wrote "by May 1986 … ANC military operations
had risen dramatically and were increasingly being carried out by locally
trained guerrillas". In contrast, Barrell's study (1993:441, 461) maintains that
by 1986 there had been "no qualititative improvement in the ANC's capacity
to locate an armed presence inside the country" and that the organisation
never achieved "bridging the gap between a largely externally-based MK and
internal militants".

Until the mid-1980s the published material on the strategy of armed struggle
had regarded conditions for victory as emerging simply out of the dispersal of
the state's armed forces as the result of protracted guerrilla struggle – involving
simple application of the maxim that "if the enemy is concentrated, it loses
ground; if it is scattered, it loses strength" (Mzala 1980a:71). However, "havoc
and confusion" are not identical with a revolutionary situation. Moreover the

"stretching" of the enemy's forces could in theory hasten the onset of negotiations, rather than of revolution (Cabesa 1986 on dispersal).

If military confrontation would be necessary, however, the *political line* for splitting the state was crucial. For most participants in the debate, the emphasis was on race. The main concentration, in fact, was on winning the allegiance of *black* troops – who were a marginal minority in the state's forces. In 1979, for example, the Politico-Military Commission had resolved that "we must work systematically to undermine the morale and cohesion of the enemy's forces and their social support base within the country. We must in the first place work to win over or neutralise those amongst the black oppressed who have been recruited into the regime's puppet armed force" – although it did mention in passing the need "to take full advantage of ... secondary contradictions" in order to win over sections of whites. Mzala (1980c:66–77) maintained that blacks in the South African Defence Force (SADF) and bantustan armies were an advantage for the winning of enemy forces – as was the "nonracial" policy of the ANC against "the racial barrier created by colonialism". Mashinini (1985) paid attention to whites, but his conclusion was the need to create "white anti-apartheid movements" with an anti-militarist character – essentially the End Conscription Campaign, with its moral appeal attractive to sections of the white middle class only.

The defeat of the state, in other words, would have required at least a part of the whites to swing to the left behind a consciously anti-capitalist class programme promoted by the ANC (not, by the way, the "pure class" programme often caricatured by Slovo, but a programme combining national and class demands). Together with this it would have required effective organisation by the ANC of armed self-defence of black urban and rural working class struggles. Could this white swing have taken place? It sounds impossible – but the state could have been defeated in no other way. In that case a new and far more democratic state would have come into existence – a workers' democracy on the basis of the organs of "people's power" spread throughout society. Without such a strategy all the proclamations of an armed mass revolution to defeat the state were in fact so much hot air. Indeed, much of the activity of MK only served to cement white support for the state.

The way that in fact the containment of so-called liberated zones to the townships was addressed in practice was through the idea of "taking the struggle into the white areas" (Trevor 1994 97:70).[23] This was a call made, for example, by President Tambo on July 22, 1985, shortly after the Kabwe Conference, and two days after the declaration of the first state of emergency inside South Africa (Barrell 1993:402). This was echoed by others in publications.The call coincided with the onset of a campaign for planting landmines in border areas (particularly in the western and eastern Transvaal), directed at white farmers (Barrell 1993:420–3).[24] It was also followed by such terrorist acts as the bombing of Magoo's Bar in Durban. By the mid-1980s the whites were increasingly splintered, with big swings towards the ultra-right. The "terrorist" strategy that developed merely inflamed and enlarged the white ultra-right. It was totally counter-productive to any aims of creating a split among the whites serious enough to weaken the state.

In April 1987, Mzala (1987c:6) wrote that

> a revolutionary strategist must take cognisance of the developing revolutionary situation, and accommodate it in planning, and not merely cling to a theory of a decade ago, which like all theories was only outlining the general situation of that period.

According to Barrell (1993:427–8), Maharaj and Kasrils maintained in 1986 and 1987 to him that the idea of people's war as a protracted phenomenon was no longer relevant, and that the issue was one of gathering the forces for a national insurrection. They were alone among ANC leaders, he states, in "attempting to incorporate the new forms of struggle being developed on the ground into a strategic scheme". In 1986 the NEC appointed a subcommittee consisting of O.R. Tambo and Joe Slovo to organise the movement of top leadership into the country – from where they would lead a future insurrection. It was to have a blank cheque and would not report to the NEC. Again, according to Barrell (1993:445–6), Operation *Vul'indlela* (Operation *Vula*) was motivated by Maharaj with the intention of bypassing those on the NEC "wedded to crass militarism, the detonator theory and political-military parallelism".[25] In addition, against the onslaught of the state-backed Inkatha in the Transvaal, some ANC/SACP leaders such as Chris Hani were involved in the building of self-defence units on the ground. Was some convergence taking place between some strategists of MK and the ideas of the MWT of the ANC (four of whose members had been expelled at the Kabwe Conference)?

With its social base still intact, from 1985 onwards the state began to support and promote black vigilante groups in the townships – the Black Hundreds of the South African revolution – Inkatha in Natal, and others elsewhere (Haysom 1986).[26] Counter-revolution with a black face came home from outside South Africa (the UNITA and RENAMO (*Resistência Nacional Moçambicana*) movements, for example). MK had no answer to this: a guerrilla strategy was unable to defend the mass movement – not in Natal, where the youth heroically organised self-defence against Inkatha *impis* in the civil war of 1986–90 and beyond; not in Crossroads where there were barely any arms with which to resist the *witdoeke*. Combined with massive numbers placed in detention (25 000 in 1986) "people's power" in the townships was crushed, for the moment. The state went too far, however: its attempted crackdown on organisations such as the UDF and the Congress of South African Trade Unions (COSATU) on February 24, 1988 tried "to exercise a power against us which they do not have" (EB Statement 1988:2–7). The successful boycott of municipal elections in that year, together with the defiance campaign of 1989, were already indications of the revival of the movement – and this continued into the early 1990s, combined with the massive escalation of vicious state-organised counter-revolutionary violence. Eventually (if negotiations had not been taking place), the movement would have swept ahead to overtake the movement of 1984–87 – though, without the adoption by the ANC of a clear strategy for achieving national and social liberation through working-class power, the mass struggle would once again have reached stalemate and been driven back.

Conclusion

Rural guerrilla warfare; armed propaganda; people's war – none of these were strategies in South Africa for the taking of state power by the masses. A strategy of armed insurrection was talked and written about but not seriously implemented. The ANC leaders had to fall back on the only strategy they in fact had: a negotiated settlement. This was not an "alternative" to a mass revolutionary seizure of power, as Tom Lodge and other commentators of the 1980s put it (see Lodge 1989; Phillips 1988). It was the only strategy open to the ANC leadership. It was presaged by the talks between top South African businessmen and the ANC in Lusaka in September 1985 – only months after the Kabwe Conference – by the abortive mission of the Commonwealth Eminent Persons' Group in 1985–86, and by the overtures of Mandela from prison to government at the same time. By the latter part of 1986 writers in *Sechaba* on armed struggle were already looking over their shoulder at the possibilities of a negotiated settlement (see Mandla 1986; Mkwanazi 1989). This, of course, was what transpired in the 1990s, initiated by secret discussions of Mandela and ANC leaders with representatives of the regime in the late 1980s, followed by De Klerk's announcement in February 1990 of the unbanning of the ANC, PAC and SACP and the release of Mandela. Thereafter every compromise was justified by ANC/SACP leaders in the terms that the forces of MK were "too weak" to secure an alternative (see, in particular, Slovo 1992). MK was "too weak", however, simply because of a false political strategy. The assessment did not take into account the strength and consciousness of the working class.

On the one hand, the capitalist ruling class in South Africa saw the dangers of continuing its rule in the old way. In this sense the mass upsurges of the 1980s were crucial to the transition. It was not the ANC's strategy of armed struggle which had helped bring things to this point, though ironically the ANC was to inherit the credit for the transition brought about by the masses. On the other hand, the changed standpoint of the Soviet Union was also critical. Under Gorbachev the Soviet Union began to retreat from its international obligations and commitments. The 1988 accord between South Africa, Cuba and Angola (excluding SWAPO) was a crucial preliminary to South African withdrawal from Namibia and the holding of democratic elections.[27]

Such an accord would not have been possible for Cuba or the Soviet Union to agree to earlier. It was a period of what, in hindsight, was the beginnings of capitalist restoration in the Soviet Union and Eastern Europe (though not in Gorbachev's understanding). At the same time Soviet academics began floating preposterous compromise scenarios for a South African settlement. The key Moscow bureaucrat relating to the ANC leadership, Vladimir Shubin (1999:327, 311–2), has written that the word "armed" set before "struggle" was by 1988 "becoming unfashionable in Moscow".

On February 2, 1990 De Klerk drew attention to the changes in Eastern Europe as a central element in his decision to change course. Among the factors favouring negotiations, he mentioned that the events in the Soviet Union and Eastern Europe "weaken the capability of organisations which were previously supported strongly from those quarters" (Kamsteeg and Van Dijk 1990:93, 104). Patti Waldmeier, *Financial Times* journalist, also wrote at the time that "the convulsions in Eastern Europe have played a big part in bringing about Pretoria's change of heart". On the one hand, she cited the National Party fear of the example of authoritarian regimes being toppled by "people's power". On the other hand, like De Klerk, she referred to the ideological, financial and moral loss suffered by the ANC (Waldmeier 1990). The unbanning of the ANC, PAC and SACP of course prepared the way – again, not in a straight line – for the negotiated settlement and the democratic elections of 1994. The strength that the working class accumulated in the 1980s and early 1990s, even unarmed, even battered by the counter-revolution, has also been the main factor underpinning the democratic nature of the settlement and of the South African constitution. The participatory democracy characteristic of "people's power" has been crushed, by counter-revolution, by parliamentary rule, and to a certain extent by the legacy of guerrillaism in the officials of the new state. But the legacy of democracy still survives in the strength of the working class and of civil society.

Since 1994 the ANC government has voluntarily implemented a neo-liberal policy akin to the structural adjustment programmes advocated by the International Monetary Fund and World Bank. Foreign investment has, however, not been forthcoming, certainly not enough to prevent the loss of half a million to a million jobs since 1994. It is doubtful whether this economic programme can alleviate poverty. In the long run, therefore, it will threaten democracy also. If so, it is the price that will be paid for aborting a worker-led democratic revolution in favour of a negotiated compromise. In 1990 Mzala could still believe that

> the position of the South African Communist Party within the alliance of the ANC, as well as the growing role of the working class within the mass democratic movement, ensures precisely the desire that on achieving national liberation, the South African revolution will proceed uninterruptedly towards the building of socialism.

In reality the Triple Alliance is blocking the road to workers' democracy in South Africa – the precondition for socialism. However, it is conceivable that working-class resistance to worsening economic conditions can lead to the establishment of a mass trade-union-based workers' party and eventually to workers' democratic rule in South Africa.

Notes

1   That this was indeed Mandela's position is supported by Neville Alexander (2002:179–80).

2   This chapter is a drastically shortened version of a paper published as a booklet: Legassick, M. 2002. *Armed Struggle and Democracy: The Case of South Africa*. Nordiska Afrikainstitutet, Discussion Paper 20. Readers are recommended to read the longer version to get the full argument presented by the author.

3   Mahmood Mamdani (1996:27–32) argues against theories of "South African exceptionalism". While agreeing with Mamdani that "apartheid, usually considered the exceptional feature in the South African experience, is actually its one aspect that is uniquely African", I also regard the level of industrialisation and proletarianisation as an "exceptional" feature within Africa.

4   I should declare my own interest in this paper: In 1960 I left to study in Britain. By 1961, to consider whether violence was necessary in the South African struggle, I was reading Mao Tse-Tung and Che Guevara. People subsequently attempted to recruit me to the sabotage organisation African Resistance Movement but I refused because of my support for the ANC. In 1967 I was briefed by Joe Matthews of the ANC on the Wankie campaign and wrote a paper first delivered to the African Studies Association meeting in the United States that year. Che Guevara was a model for me through the 1960s and I was also strongly influenced by William Hinton's account of revolution in the Chinese village of Fanshen. I wrote in *Sechaba* an anonymous review of books on urban armed struggle at a time when ANC policy was confined to rural guerrilla warfare. Subsequently I began to differ with MK's strategy of armed struggle and in 1979 associated myself with a memorandum by Robert Petersen, then editor of SACTU's newspaper *Workers' Unity* produced in London. For this Petersen, myself, Paula Ensor and David Hemson were unconstitutionally and undemocratically suspended from the ANC in 1979 and expelled in 1985. I resigned from my university job in 1981 and worked politically fulltime for the next 10 years, financed by unemployment benefits in Britain. During this time we, along with numerous others, were supporters of the Marxist Workers' Tendency of the ANC, and continued to support the ANC despite our suspension and expulsion.

5   I read Barrell's dissertation, a history of MK (1993) omitting chapter 1, only after forming my own conclusions on these questions, and discover they are similar.

6   During this period, *Sechaba* ran features on all the struggles.

7   I do not deal here with the transitional phase of the 1961–64 sabotage campaign.

8   The political background to it is provided by Mbeki (1964), much of the manuscript written in prison on rolls of toilet paper, and edited in London by Ruth First. See on its approval or not, Frankel (2001:23–4, 26, 107–10, 210, 238, 242, 244–5, 249); Slovo (1976:188); Slovo (1995:146); Callinicos (unpub.); Clingman (1998:407, 414). It was opposed *inter alia* by Roly Arenstein, Rusty Bernstein, Braam Fischer, Ahmed Kathrada, Jack Simons and Walter Sisulu. An insight into Slovo's support for it is provided by his daughter Gillian Slovo (1997:57).

9   See also Slovo (1976:200): "The stark reality is, after more than 10 years of effort, there is as yet no evidence of any form of military engagement inside the country".

10 See also: Suttner 2001; Cronin interview 2001; Holiday interview 2002; Kasrils 1986. This was the period (c. 1969–76) when Raymond Suttner (in Durban), Jeremy Cronin, David and Sue Rabkin (in Cape Town) and Tony Holiday (in Johannesburg) conducted virtually solo propaganda activity.

11 See also Mzala (1987c): "It must be pointed out that the events of June 16 came as a complete surprise for everyone".

12 Between November 1978 and March 1980 MK was probably responsible for 15 out of 17 attacks which involved: nine of sabotage of economic installations, four on police stations or personnel (two in Soweto and one in Soekmekaar), two on civilian targets (one the Silverton siege in a Volkskas bank near Pretoria), one on a court building and one on a building administering the pass laws.

13 There is no evidence such a "study" was ever undertaken.

14 Even at the level of the commission, it admitted, "different interpretations emerged and we found it necessary to debate some very fundamental propositions ... which go to the root of our strategic line".

15 The special operations unit, moreover, from 1979 to early 1983, was responsible only to the president of the ANC, bypassing the military command of MK and the Revolutionary Council.

16 Compare Mzala "Armed Struggle" (1980a:73), where he had praised the militancy of the 1976 youth by referring to their "*suicidal* offensive campaigns" (author's emphasis). Gorm Gunnarsen "Leaders or Organisers Against Apartheid: Cape Town, 1976–84" (2002:149), in contrast, stresses the relative nonviolence of the mass struggle in 1980.

17 Curiously, reference to armed self-defence came in a broadcast by Chris Hani and Mac Maharaj on Radio Freedom, published in *Sechaba* (November 1984).

18 Mzala made similar points in "MK: Part 1" (1986:38–9).

19 See also Kasrils (1998:195): "The Factor Missing in South Africa Was a Massive Peasantry".

20 However Houston (1999:26) refers to an ANC document of 1985 titled *Strategy and Tactics*, which he claims placed "greater emphasis on the mobilisation of various forces in the country to participate in the liberation struggle".

21 Mzala "Cooking the Rice Inside the Pot", *Sechaba*, January 1985. The point of Mzala's title was to insist on the re-establishment of ANC leadership inside the country ("inside the pot") "among our fighting masses" (1985:26).

22 See also Barrell (1993:326–30). Apparently MK attacks peaked at 300 in 1988 (beyond the period of Barrell's thesis). There exists, not presently available to the public, a listing of the targets of every MK attack, which would have been an invaluable research tool for this study.

23 The idea is in a sense foreshadowed when Trevor wrote of the need for wider struggles than those in the townships: "Struggles within the townships and Bantustans must be

linked to wide-scale struggle in the urban areas (at the centre of these areas) and in the 'white farming' areas" (*African Communist* 97:70).

24 This campaign fizzled out by 1987 because of the opposition of the neighbouring states from which it was launched on a plant-and-run basis, with units spending only a few hours inside South Africa.

25 See also, for Slovo's views, interview with Cronin by Helena Sheehan, April 17, 2001 in All Africa House at the University of Cape Town.

26 Vigilantes were operating in Duduza in May 1985, though the main onslaught came from 1986 (see Haysom:1986).

27 However, as in Zimbabwe and Mozambique and Angola, the heritage of guerrillaism produced hierarchical, bureaucratic, and dictatorial tendencies in the post-independence SWAPO government.

References

Alexander, N. 2002. *An Ordinary Country.* Pietermaritzburg: University of Natal Press.

Anon. 1976. "Viva MPLA!" *Sechaba*, 10:1st quarter.

_____ 1979. *South Africa: The Workers' Movement, SACTU and the ANC.* London: Cambridge Heath Press.

African National Congress (ANC). 1969. *Strategy and Tactics.* Johannesburg: ANC.

Barrell, H. 1992. "The Turn to the Masses: The African National Congress' Strategic Review of 1978–79", *Journal of Southern African Studies*, 18,1.

Cabesa, Q. 1986. "From Ungovernability", *African Communist*, 104:37–9.

Clingman, S. 1998. *Bram Fischer: Afrikaner Revolutionary.* Cape Town: David Philip.

Dubula, S. [Slovo, J.] 1971. "10 years of MK", *African Communist*, 47:32–3.

EB Statement. March 15, 1988. "After the Crackdown: How to Advance? Defy the Bans! Build the Locals! Build the ANC!" *Inqaba ya Basebenzi*, 26:2–7.

Frankel, G. 2001. *Rivonia's Children: Three Families and the Costs of Conscience in White South Africa.* New York: Continuum.

Hani, C. and Maharaj, M. 1984. "Radio Freedom Broadcast", *Sechaba*, November.

Haysom, N. 1986. *Mabangalala: The Rise of Right-Wing Vigilantes in South Africa.* Johannesburg: Centre for Applied Legal Studies, University of Witwaterstrand.

Houston, G. 1999. *The National Liberation Struggle in South Africa: A Case Study of the United Democratic Front, 1983–1987.* Aldershot: Ashgate.

Kamsteeg, A. and Van Dijk, E. 1990. *F.W. de Klerk: Man of the Moment.* Cape Town: Vlaeberg.

Kasrils, R. 1986. "People's War", *Sechaba*, May.

_____ 1998. *Armed and Dangerous*. Bellville: Mayibuye Books.

Legassick, M. 1970. "Guerilla Warfare in Southern Africa". In Cartey, W. and Kilson, M. (eds.). *The Africa Reader*. New York: Vintage.

_____ 1971. "Armed Revolution in the City", *Sechaba*, 5,11: November.

_____ 2002. *Armed Struggle and Democracy: The Case of South Africa*. Discussion Paper 20. Uppsala: Nordiska Afrikainstitutet.

Lodge, T. 1989. "People's War or Negotiation? African National Congress Strategies in the 1980s". In Moss, G. and Obery, I (eds.) *South African Review 5*. Johannesburg: Ravan Press.

Mamdani, M. 1996. *Citizen and Subject*. Cape Town: David Philip.

Mandela, N. 1994. *Long Walk to Freedom*. London: Little Brown.

Mandla, C. 1986. "MK: Let Us Move to an All-Out War", *Sechaba*, November.

Mashinini. 1985. "Preparing the Fire", *Sechaba*, April.

Marxist Workers' Tendency of the ANC (MWT). 1982. *South Africa's Impending Socialist Revolution*. London: Inqaba ya Basebenzi.

Mbeki, G. 1964. *The Peasants' Revolt*. London: Penguin.

_____ 1996. *Sunset at Midday*. Braamfontein: Nolwazi.

Migwe, K. 1982. "Further Contribution", *African Communist*, 89:80.

Mkwanazi, S. 1989. "Our Vanguard and the Seizure of Power", *Sechaba*, 1. January.

Mzala. 1980a. "Armed Struggle", *African Communist*, 82:72.

_____ 1980b. "Has the Time Come?" *African Communist*, 86:85,91.

_____ 1980c. "On the Threshold", *African Communist*, 102:66–77.

_____ 1985. "Cooking the Rice Inside the Pot", *Sechaba*, 26. January.

_____ 1986. "MK: Part 1", *Sechaba*, 23–6. December.

_____ 1987a. "MK: Part 2", *Sechaba*, January.

_____ 1987b. "*Umkhonto We Sizwe*: Building People's Forces for Combat War and Insurrection, Part 2", *Sechaba*, 21. January.

_____ 1987c. "Towards People's War and Insurrection", *Sechaba*, April.

_____ 1990. "Is South Africa in a Revolutionary Situation?" *Journal of Southern African Studies*, 16,3:575.

O'Meara, D. 1996. *Forty Lost Years*. Johannesburg: Ravan Press.

Phillips, I. 1988. "Negotiation and Armed Struggle in Contemporary South Africa", *Transformation*, 6.

South African Communist Party (SACP). 1962. *The Road to South African Freedom*. SACP programme.

Shombela, M. 1986. "Our Armed Offensive: Military Strategy in South Africa", *Sechaba*, March.

Shubin, V. 1999. *ANC: A View from Moscow.* Cape Town: Mayibuye Books.

Slovo, G. 1997. *Every Secret Thing: My Family, My Country.* London: Little Brown.

Slovo, J. 1974. "Southern Africa: Problems of Armed Struggle", *Socialist Register, 1973,* 339.

_____ 1976. "South Africa: No Middle Road". In Davidson, B., Slovo, J. and Wilkinson, A. (eds.) *Southern Africa: The New Politics of Revolution.* London: Penguin.

_____ 1992. "Negotiations: What Room for Compromise", *African Communist,* 130:3rd quarter.

_____ 1995. *Slovo: The Unfinished Autobiography.* Randburg: Ravan.

Slovo, J. and Mbeki, G. 1963. "Operation Mayibuye". In Karis, T. and Carter, G. (eds.) *From Protest to Challenge: Documents of African Politics in South Africa, 1882–1964.* III:760–8.

Sparks, A. 1994. *Tomorrow is Another Country.* Sandton: Struik.

Suttner, R. 2001. *Inside Apartheid's Prison.* Durban: University of Natal Press.

Trevor, U. 1994. "Question of an Uprising of the Whole People", *African Communist,* 97:62–73.

Turok, B. 1974. *Strategic Problems.* Canada: Liberation Support Movement.

Umkhonto We Sizwe. 1961. "Founding Leaflet". In Karis and Carter (eds.):716– 7, 760–8.

_____ 1986. "Editorial: *Umkhonto We Sizwe* – People's Army", *Sechaba,* February.

_____ 1989a. "Declaration of the OAU Ad-Hoc Committee on Southern Africa on the Question of South Africa", *Sechaba,* October.

_____ 1989b. "ANC Statements", *Sechaba,* November.

Waldmeier, P. 1990. *Financial Times* (Johannesburg), February 12.

Unpublished Works

Barrell, H. 1993. "Conscripts to Their Age: ANC Operational Strategy, 1976–1986". D.Phil dissertation. University of Oxford.

Callinicos, L. "Reinventing the ANC: The Shift to Armed Struggle and Oliver Tambo's Role in Exile, 1961–64".

Gunnarsen, G. 2002. "Leaders or Organisers Against Apartheid: Cape Town 1976–84". Ph.D dissertation. University of Copenhagen.

Saeboe, M. "Paradox of Exile: The ANC and MK in Angola, 1976–89". MA dissertation. University of Natal.

Tambo, O., Mbeki, T., Slovo, J., Mabhida, M., Gqabi, J. and Modise, J. 1978. "Report of the Politico-Military Strategic Commission".

Culture(s) of the African National Congress of South Africa: Imprint of Exile Experiences

Raymond Suttner[1]

When the African National Congress (ANC) was unbanned in 1990 a number of ideological, inter-generational and organisational strands that had broadly, and in varying ways considered themselves part of the liberation movement, came together as members. By "broadly" reference is made particularly to affiliates of the United Democratic Front (UDF, formed in 1983). These in turn comprised a variety of tendencies and organisational formations (Seekings 2000; Lodge and Nasson 1991; Van Kessel 2000). In these organisations, it was common to hear coded references and indications of affiliation to the ANC. In addition, there were a variety of other people who wanted to join the ANC once it became legal. Just over a year after unbanning, half a million people were signed up (Rantete 1998:12–15).[2]

Unsurprisingly, there were complexities attached to post-1990 integration of these various elements, since the organisations that now were "one" had distinct styles of work and historical experiences informing their practice. Yet these differences were outweighed by the overall euphoria surrounding unbanning. Continuing state harassment of the organisation demanded unity. Consequently, the complexity of combining the component parts may not have been given adequate weight. In efforts to stress unity in the face of state attempts to undermine the ANC and the broader liberation movement, commonality was understandably emphasised, often at the expense of difference.

ANC: One Organisation Comprising Multiple Identities

It is only possible to understand some of the mass activities of the late 1970s and 1980s by virtue of the survival of traditions of support for the ANC or what it was believed the ANC represented. These traditions persisted in varying degrees and forms in different places and times. The bearers may have been old grannies in isolated townships or ANC activists banished to remote villages or located in well-known townships (Frederickse 1990:157; Mochele interview 1992). At other times it was newly released political prisoners (e.g. Mati in Coetzee *et al* 2002:53; Seekings 2000:30; Serache interview 2002). But the "traditions" that survived and survive are diverse in character. Members of any organisation not only have distinct political experiences that may have preceded their joining, but often religious beliefs of a variety of kinds, including "traditional" ones. They may, as part of these belief systems, observe various practices and rituals. These exist in a space both outside and at times overlapping with the organisation. There has been little discussion of how these belief systems interact, and what systems inform which decisions or actions for various people within the ANC (see Niehaus *et al* 2001).

It is important to appreciate the various components of the ANC in their own right since they represent distinct understandings of what it means to be in the organisation. Different experiences are likely to inform divergent conceptions of democracy within the ANC and in the society at large. Unless one appreciates these different cultural experiences, the distinct and multiple identities within a common identity, it will not be possible to understand the character of some of the differences and tensions that have emerged and may still emerge.

The various components also represent distinct practices and expectations of what it means to be an ANC member and what different people hope to derive from such membership. It may also define what describing the ANC as a "broad church" means, and what may be included or excluded from that concept at different times and under diverse conditions.

We can identify distinct overall characteristics attaching to various phases of the organisation's history, features whose relevance to this study lies in the extent to which they are an enduring part of organisational character or at least appear to be well established within the contemporary ANC. It is necessary for this emphasis because *the focus in this study is on the present*, though that can only be understood as part of a broader, complex history.

This raises controversial questions. One may ask whether the expectations and practices of an ANC member recruited in the dark days of the 1960s or 1970s were the same as those of a person joining in 1994 or afterwards. And can one always say that the expectations of persons recruited in difficult times, and that understandings of what it means to be part of the ANC, remain the same today?

What are expectations in this period when ANC membership may mean more in the way of benefits for some and next to nothing in terms of experiencing repression?

What is continuing in ANC traditions and what is new? What has disappeared and what continues to survive and why? On what basis, for example, are people designated or not designated as heroes, and what social purpose does this serve within ANC culture? (see Kriger 1995 on Zimbabwe). What aspects of a person's political life are singled out (and what downplayed) where there is such selection?

What elements of an organisation's traditions are celebrated and who is revered also have gender implications. If the organisation mainly celebrates activities in which males are predominant, such as military leaders, what implications does this have for gender equality?[3]

It may be that the character of the ANC is suffused with a masculine idiom (Erlank 2001 unpub.; Unterhalter 2000). The content and mode of construction of these masculinities over time needs to be unpacked. Related to this masculine and sometimes macho idiom may be the impact of conceptions of the "revolution" or being a "revolutionary" and their relation to "the personal". It needs to be asked to what extent people may have thought it necessary to suppress personal intimacy, or had this required of them, in the interests of a broader comradeship. If there is some validity in this question, how it impacts on concepts of parenthood, love and other questions of intimacy also needs interrogation (see Reddy and Katerud 1995 and Serache interview 2002, which represent conflicting experiences). If this tendency was present formerly, how does it play itself out today?

Relevance to the Unfolding Trajectory of South African Democracy

The various experiences, expectations and practices that make up the ANC may have significance for the type of democracy that unfolds in South Africa in the future.

This culture refers to a variety of phases and experiences, none of which has supplanted or totally displaced all others. Which cultural influence becomes dominant may well have consequences for conceptions and practice of democracy in South African society as a whole. This is because some types of experiences may tend towards greater popular involvement than others, greater internal democracy or more or less centralisation.

This chapter represents early work in progress. It outlines one aspect of these cultural experiences that is particularly influential in the development and present character of the ANC – that of exile and *Umkhonto we Sizwe* (the Spear of the Nation, popularly known as MK). This study also raises, in a limited way, the intersection between identity and belief systems that go with being in the ANC and systems that are part of wider identities of many of its members.

Exile and *Umkhonto we Sizwe*

With the banning of the ANC and initiation of armed struggle, in 1961, military and security considerations came to overlay organisational practice. Military and underground struggle cannot be based on the same organisational principles as open democratic activities. Security and secrecy are essential. Hierarchy is generally needed in an army and to a substantial extent underground. While these units could discuss and debate, opportunities for filtering through diverse opinions were obviously not as plentiful as were found in the open situations of the 1950s and 1980s onwards. Secrecy, as opposed to open discussion, became dominant. What was made public tended to conceal what diversity there may have been, behind official statements presenting a face of unity to the public.

It is not clear what the full impact was on the culture of democracy that had been developing in the period immediately before the banning of the ANC. The 1950s had seen its transformation into a mass organisation and campaigns that enhanced democracy, non-racialism and to a limited extent non-sexism (Lodge 1983; Suttner and Cronin 1986). Did conditions of exile, underground and armed struggle mean these emerging traditions were snuffed out? The answer may be quite varied and dependent on where people were placed and what type of work they did. Also, consideration must be given to new forms of cultural expression that conditions of exile gave rise to, the impact they have had and how enduring these proved to be.

Experience of exile in London was quite different from that in Angola, Zambia, Tanzania, Lesotho or Botswana, and the type of activities that people engaged in differed in the various centres, creating different norms and styles of work, and distinct relationships between members of the organisation (cf. Bernstein

1994; Israel 1999; Serache interview 2002). A person engaged in intelligence or security work would be more fully disposed to secrecy than someone promoting the ANC in public meetings or newspaper articles in London. But even in London, many people who "ran" underground operatives within the country, had to operate in "cloak and dagger" fashion (Suttner 2001:chs.2–3). These could not be open operations, since working conditions required conspiratorial methods and hierarchical structures whereby one section of the organisation (primarily based outside) communicated what had to be done inside the country. The outside/inside division was, of course, partially broken by incursions of Chris Hani after 1974 and Operation *Vula* in the late 1980s (Barrell:1990:29, 69) as well as by other lesser-known individuals (Serache interview 2002). In the case of Hani, it was an incursion by a leading official of the ANC and the South African Communist Party (SACP), just as Operation *Vula* also included leading officials of both organisations, Mac Maharaj and Ronnie Kasrils. All three had previously been "handlers" of other operatives within the country from outside.

The ANC of the 1960s was fighting for survival after reversals it had suffered. It confronted an enemy killing people in detention, and prepared to cross borders to chase after them. That enemy was able to infiltrate its agents into MK camps, where food was sometimes poisoned.

That this atmosphere was not always conducive to openness does not mean debate was excluded. It was constrained by these conditions, but it may be that the Morogoro consultative conference of 1969 and the Kabwe conference of 1985 resulted from debates, arguments and complaints amongst membership (Shubin 1999:84ff; Barrell 1990:26 regarding Morogoro; Williams 1994:29 regarding Kabwe).

It may well be that the level, character and intensity of debate depended on the type of work individuals were doing, whether they were in the military or not. But it would be a mistake to conclude that military discipline and structures necessarily precluded political discussion and debate. While these had to operate as disciplined forces, there appears to have been widespread political discussion in some situations in the camps, especially in political education courses (Sparg *et al* 2001; Moche interview 2002).

Exile was a vast and complex phenomenon extending over three decades and embracing a variety of experiences. Within the liberation movement it evokes contrasting emotions. Amongst those who were together outside, there are bonds forged over many decades and in difficult times, and sometimes a sense of veteranism compared with internal activists. Internal activists are sometimes seen as having only recently come to the movement and lacking the level of discipline provided in the militarily organised exiled movement (see quotation from Frene Ginwala in Hassim 2002:205–6 unpub.).

But, on the side of many internal activists, there is sometimes inadequate appreciation of exile experience, a sense that those from outside are out of touch with what is happening on the ground or without a feel for mass struggle. There is also often a sense that those who were inside faced the guns, while, implicitly, those in exile had an easy life.

What this research has revealed so far has been that the exile experience was extremely difficult, not only in the obvious hardships of MK camps. The very path to get there in the first place was often filled with pain and trauma of various kinds (Bernstein 1994; Moche interview 2002). This relates first to the consequence of the decision to leave that remained with people over the long period of separation from their country. Many had to leave behind lovers, husbands, wives or children, often without any explanation (Bernstein 1994; Duka 1974:chs.5–6). The conditions of exile often created fresh conditions of stress, that led to a variety of psychological and social difficulties relating to dislocation (Morrow 1998:509–10, 513; Said 2000:173 and ch.17 generally). It is all too easy to forget the physical hurdles generally encountered simply in getting to MK or into exiled structures, crossing hostile borders, sometimes facing arrest and interrogation in numerous countries along the way (Moche interview 2002). Similar logistical difficulties often confronted transport of MK for training in the early years (Shubin 1999:30). Some of this was related to the very qualified degree of support the ANC received from African states in its early years of exile, when many leaders preferred the Pan-Africanist Congress (PAC) (see Mandela 1994; Shubin 1999:131; Sellstrom 2002:408ff, 582).

Many of the people who arrived in exile were suffering the effects of multiple traumas, not least being the impact of assaults and tortures by apartheid authorities before they left. Obviously the conditions of exile made it very difficult, except for those based in major Western cities, to receive adequate treatment or counselling. The facilities available in many situations of exile made this hard to treat or even sometimes difficult to recognise the presence of such trauma (Pampallis interview 2002). It does seem, however, that some systems for treatment were in place in the camps, though the extent of their reach is not clear (Reddy and Katerud 1995). It appears, also, that the ANC Women's section made some effort to provide a measure of support (Hassim 2002:ch.3 unpub.).

In this chapter I refer to only three elements of the exile experience, that of the first MK recruits of the early 1960s, the generation of 1976, and some of the bureaucratic consequences of running a huge organisation in exile. Finally, I return to the question of survival of "traditional" belief systems that informed practices of some in MK in certain situations.

The First MK Recruits

These people (whom I understand were almost entirely men, though many women were recruited later, Hassim 2002:ch.3 unpub.; Cock 1991:162) were mainly products of ANC of the 1950s and early 1960s. In the strategic calculations of the time, it was expected that many would be out of the country for a few months and then return to train others. But the situation after the arrest of the top leadership at Rivonia in 1964 made this impossible and confronted the ANC with a long-term exile population.

Routes to MK were diverse and not all those who followed them were necessarily members of the ANC until then. Motivations were diverse, some seeking revenge, others being more seasoned in ANC politics and some escaping South Africa to avoid criminal prosecution. Still others were infiltrators sent by the apartheid regime. The ANC had to sort out the various categories and decide how best to train or restrain where necessary (see Reddy and Katerud 1995).

Many received training in the Soviet Union, others in China. Some lived for long periods in the Soviet Union and in various parts of Africa. The impact of all these external experiences on ways of thinking needs to be examined. To what extent and how did different political values and institutions of the countries where they were based impact on practices within ANC and organisational conceptions of the members concerned? What influence did these veterans come to have in the organisation as a whole? There was limited activity by some in the Wankie and Sipolilo campaigns in the late 1960s, when MK made attempts to reach South Africa via the then-Rhodesia together with ZAPU (the Zimbabwe African People's Union). What was their role in the organisation in subsequent years, particularly as they grew older? To what extent did they remain in the military and with what role and impact? Did their status as "veterans" confer any special authority on them?

Who were these early recruits to MK? It is well known that many were seasoned ANC cadres or members of the SACP and there was an overwhelmingly urban basis (Barrell 1990:12,13). While this may have been true, it seems that the rural component may not have been given adequate attention. Victor Moche (interview 2002) relates the conditions under which a Zeerust community committed each family to send one of their sons to MK. He first learnt this when he met the chief of the community who was visiting Dar-es-Salaam for an extensive period to check on the condition of his subjects.

> Apparently in their neighbourhood in Western Transvaal, the chiefs who were under pressure had decided they would support the movement, the struggle. So they had set up underground structures, which they linked to MK and its recruitment machineries. But being chiefs they had then called village councils, *lekgotla* as it is called. After persuading villagers that this was the right thing to do, they then levied a "head tax" on each household in terms of providing human power to join MK. So if you had a family of four young men, the eldest would be told, you will go to Gauteng to work for the family and you will send number 2 to school, number 3 is too young so he will stay at home and he will look after his parents and the cattle and number 4 will go to MK. So he [the chief] had been mandated to go out and see how they were doing. So he landed up with us [in Dar-es-Salaam] because he was not MK but a civilian.

The exact area from which these recruits came was Dinokana, around Zeerust. Many of the recruits were completely illiterate and "learnt their ABC in MK. Learnt everything they know in MK."

It appears that the process of joining MK was not an individual commitment at first. But it was not simply the chief ordering the villagers to provide men:

> There was a discussion among the elders to start with; within families there was discussion, so [those who joined MK] came out aware of what they had been assigned to do. But this was an assignment not so much by their selection, because they were

politically conscious and wanted to be in the ANC. It was an assignment because your family expected you to do this, your community expected you to do this. Now if that community just happened to be ANC, then you were ANC. So the politics of the community brought you into ANC politics.

Because of the illiteracy of these villagers, during infantry training in the Soviet Union, there had first to be translation from Russian into English and then also into Tswana. According to Moche (interview 2002) there was always re-translation during training, into at least two African languages. This lack of literacy in English did not signify anything about their level of political commitment. They "were involved in continuous discussion in the village and in MK they got other training in adult basic education, which combined with political education" (ibid).

This contingent of rural recruits was related not only to ongoing conflict between the government, seeking to implement Bantu Authorities and depose those chiefs that resisted (Moche interview 2002). It was also connected to the collision between the regime and Zeerust women resisting passes. The level of resistance supported by many of the chiefs of the area increased tension between them and the government (Lodge 1983:274; Hooper 1989; Walker 1991:205; Mbeki 1984:112).

The reference to the relationship between specific chiefdoms in Zeerust and MK is not meant to imply it represented a broad trend, though it may be wider than is generally acknowledged. I am also not implying that the overall social character of MK was fundamentally different from the conventional characterisation as primarily urban-based. The evidence presented here nevertheless points to some of the complexities in the social roles played by communities and specific actors, such as chiefs, in varying conditions.

The Generation of 1976

These youngsters left the country after the Soweto uprising. It is common to record that most "chose" to join the ANC. Exactly what considerations influenced this choice? In what sense was it a political decision, based on relatively sophisticated understanding? To what extent was it opting for the movement that seemed better organised, in particular more likely to ensure subsistence of such individuals outside the country?

One answer received, in a recent interview, appears to suggest that the average young person who left the country was unaware of the relatively better capacity of the ANC to support its cadres, compared with the PAC. The basis, on which youth were recruited to the ANC, if that was not already their choice, was through ideological discussion, often using black consciousness (BC) documents as a basis of debate (Serache interview 2002, who operated in Botswana in the 1970s). Obviously more interviews will need to be conducted, but there seems some logic in the assumption that most young people would not have known of the capacity of each organisation, being deprived of such information inside the country.

Many writers have suggested this group of youngsters were relatively unpoliticised, that many believed they were the first to take on the apartheid regime, and had little sense of South African political history (Bernstein 1994:xvii; Thandi Modise in Curnow 2000:36–7; Morrow 1998:499). Thus Hilda Bernstein writes:

> Each wave brought out its own type of people. Those who left in the late fifties and early sixties were mainly adult, often middle-aged, and highly political, with a history of engaging in public political struggle. Those of the seventies, and specifically of the huge exile wave after 1976, were overwhelmingly young, largely male; and though fired with political passion, they were often without real ideology or political programmes. They were of a generation who had been cut off from access to information about their own country, their own history, and from political theory and the history of struggle. The "elders" who might have passed on this knowledge were either themselves in exile, or on Robben Island or Pretoria Central prison. Or perhaps keeping discreetly quiet. ... The 1976 Soweto rebels came out with no history in their heads. They believed themselves to be the first revolutionaries, the first to confront the apartheid state; and their anger was often without political objective. They learned the history of their country only when they had left it – the long story of struggle, oppression and resistance. (1994:xvii-xviii)

This may well be exaggerated. The ANC did live on in the minds of very many people, even where it did not have an extensive organised presence. Also, some released political prisoners, such as the late Joe Gqabi played a formative influence in the political education of many young people (see Seekings 2000; Serache interview 2002). Nevertheless, much of the political development of these youngsters became the responsibility of the ANC, mainly in MK training and various political education classes (Davis 1987:59). An extensive component of the goals of the Solomon Mahlangu Freedom College was the provision of political education, in accordance with the perspectives of the ANC (Serote 1992; Pampallis interview 2002).

But the character of this induction into the ANC needs to be interrogated. To what extent were these youngsters imbued with a critical understanding of politics, as appears to have been the objective in the political education classes of Jack Simons (Sparg *et al* 2001:54)? To what extent was it primarily a politics of hierarchy where "the line" was conveyed from top to bottom and more or less compulsorily communicated? The answer is important in considering its implications for democratic development today and in the future. If it was primarily a "politics of hierarchy" it is more likely that what leadership says is what is believed, and dissent and even healthy discussion may be discouraged.

A further question that needs to be asked is in what way these youth impacted on and changed the ANC. What impact did BC have, through them, on the ANC thinking? Or must we treat this as an overwhelmingly one-way process of influence?

All of this needs to be located within a historical framework, the global climate of the time. Where young people were sent for training in former socialist countries, they usually went through courses in the brand of Marxism–Leninism then the official ideology of these countries. This has had considerable impact on the mode of analysis adopted by the students concerned and concepts of state and transition that have informed the organisation. And some of the discourse is still very much part of the ANC today (Moleketi and Jele 2002).

While someone like Jack Simons stressed a critical approach, the type of methodology deployed and the Marxism generally absorbed in the wider experience of members of the ANC may have been a barrier to critical thinking. Classical Marxism stresses the need to look at each problem afresh and that Marxism is not a dogma to be learnt by rote (as in Marx and Engels 1968:679). But being equipped directly or indirectly with Soviet-type Marxist training may often have been treated as a methodology ensuring "inevitable victory". These were referred to as the "tools of analysis". It needs to be asked whether this version of Marxist categories closed rather than opened or encouraged enquiry. (Obviously some would argue that Marxism is basically a "closed system" under any condition).

Furthermore, while someone like Simons used a Socratic method, encouraging classes to come to their own conclusions, that method requires some confidence and depth of knowledge on the part of the teacher. It means the instructor had to be ready for a variety of answers quite different from what he or she may have anticipated. The instructor had to be prepared to respond in a manner that encouraged diversity instead of stamping it into some mould of conformity with established policies and thinking. Someone with less depth and breadth of knowledge and confidence than Simons may easily have been tempted to shut discussion prematurely.

But the character of political education may have varied significantly. According to Victor Moche, political education conducted while he was in a camp in the Soviet Union was not only communicating Marxist views on the world. The main thrust of political discussion would be analyses of news bulletins. He did not see anything dogmatic in how people were taught and how they argued. They had to find ways of making sense of what they learnt was happening in various parts of the world (interview 2002). Thandi Modise's account of political education in camps in Angola at a later phase seems to confirm this: "Political education focused on events in Africa, and the history of the ANC. There wasn't too much about communism. I never met anyone who hated churches" (Cock 1991:152). Nat Serache, in contrast, reports that the political education he received in the ANC in Angola in the 1970s was "straight Marxism–Leninism", based on classical Marxist and contemporary Soviet texts (interview 2002). Also, as mentioned in regard to the earliest exiles, later ones were exposed to the modes of government and social orders of a variety of countries that acted as their hosts. What impact did this have on their ways of viewing and expectations from politics? It also needs to be asked how ANC concepts of collective leadership interfaced with different concepts of African culture and styles of leadership (Mandela 1994:20–1).

In addition, we need to examine to what extent concepts of organisation and relations between members of the organisation continue to be suffused with military concepts, long after the period of democracy has opened. Current ANC discourse is full of words carrying military connotations, including, "deploy", "marching orders", "line of march", willingness to "take orders from the organisation", the latter being a quality that evokes praise.

The ANC Bureaucracy

While not formally constituted as a government, the ANC in exile exercised many of the functions of a state in relation to its members. In many ways, the relationship between the national executive committee and membership had characteristics of dependency rather than active membership.

To carry out extensive welfare, military, educational, political and other tasks, an extensive bureaucracy was developed. Many members of the ANC in exile were primarily formed in this environment and had little experience of political activity within the country (Lodge 1983, 1988; Ottaway 1993). Ottaway writes (at 45–6:)

> The exiled ANC consisted of an informal government – the National Executive Committee – a military wing in the form of *Umkhonto we Sizwe*, and a bureaucracy manning the various departments. In Zambia and Tanzania, the ANC's bureaucracy ran farms, schools, and workshops; and in Angola, *Umkhonto* ran training camps. The Congress had diplomatic offices in London and representatives in many capitals around the world. What the external organisation did not have on a significant scale was a membership, that is, people belonging to the ANC and supporting its political goals but not directly working for it or being supported by it. Many ANC members in exile, particularly those in African countries, depended on the organisation for their survival. They were employees of a government bureaucracy, personnel of an army, or clients of a welfare state, not members of a political party.

In order to execute its tasks the ANC amassed substantial properties in a number of countries (Rantete 1998:4–6; Davis 1987:ch.2). In Africa, these sites were devoted to a variety of functions related to maintenance of official and military structures, provisioning of the membership and educational, welfare and health functions of various types. It has been noted that failure of other liberation movements to secure their means of subsistence for members resident in African states, especially Zambia, had been a source of tension (Davis 1987:38). The ANC sought to avoid this by provision of members' requirements through extensive agricultural developments as well as some small manufacturing and maintenance structures. This was achieved (with varying degrees of success), through considerable foreign funding and the development of skills of its members in the activities concerned (Sellstrom 2002; Morrow 1998).

Related to welfare functions is the question of what determined "career paths" in the organisation. Who obtained scholarships to which countries and how? On what basis was this decided? Who or what structures were able to access which resources and how were these dispensed? To what extent did ANC bureaucratic networks establish patron/client relationships, and if they did, have these relationships continued into the present, and with what consequences? According to John Pampallis, who taught at Solomon Mahlangu Freedom College in Tanzania for eight years, there was little evidence of people "jumping the queue" for scholarships. The key issue that determined whether or not someone secured an educational opportunity was whether they acquired the necessary qualifications (interview 2002). Whether or not this was a general experience or impression needs further research.

To what extent was SACP membership a path to these opportunities as well as a "route to greatness" within the ANC during the exile period (Suttner 2002)? A recent study on the SACP in exile, based on previously unavailable archival material, throws little light on these questions (Maloka 2002).

Part of the bureaucracy was ANC security. It is now acknowledged that there were substantial abuses by some ANC security personnel (see ANC 1996). Has this matter been fully aired (Ellis and Sechaba 1992; Ellis 1994)? Have all perpetrators been brought to book and to what extent have those wrongly abused or arrested received official and public acknowledgement? If there is a residue of bitterness due to some matters being concealed from the public and even family of the (wrongly) accused, it has implications not only for the ANC but for building a human rights culture today. It also means that some ANC security personnel may not have brought something qualitatively different into the relationship with their "partners" in the reconstructed security forces.

MK and the Combination of Belief Systems

In joining the ANC, receiving advanced military training and political education, many acquired skills never open to them inside the country. They

191

had access to ideas and scientific proficiency generally the preserve of whites. But very often these new skills and beliefs coexisted with a variety of cosmologies and belief systems preceding their involvement in the ANC.

How people related to various activities of the organisation may have been mediated by how they interpreted and related to their own cultural experiences prior to joining the ANC. These belief systems, of a variety of kinds, resurfaced at distinct times. In more than one interview, the question has arisen of access to healers to strengthen combatants or reduce prison sentences.

General Sandi Sijake relates how the MK group with whom he travelled in 1962 met with the late Elias Motsoaledi, who later became a Rivonia trialist. In preparing for the safety of their journey Motsoaledi would "take a broom and put some medication inside a bucket so that the combi would not be apprehended. Comrade Motsoaledi was one of the great communist leaders, but at the same time he still believed in his medicine".

> It was a bucket with some water. He would dip in a broom, a
> special medical broom, spray and put in, dip in and sprinkle
> around, dip in, sprinkle around saying whatever words people say
> to ensure that bad luck does not befall us. That was the basic thing
> he did with our combi before heading for Zeerust. (Sijake interview
> 2001; see also Mochele interview 1992)

These practices re-emerged in 1967, when there was talk of returning home as fighters. They were in a camp near Morogoro in Tanzania:

> People started to look around for traditional healers. There was a
> local chap, one of the Tanzanians, who was said to be able to treat a
> person and once treated a bullet would turn into water. A number
> of people, because they did not have money ... would trade some of
> their clothing [from the Soviet Union] for this medicine. (Sijake
> interview 2001)

This claim to turn bullets into water is, of course, a fairly common phenomenon, found amongst others, with Mlanjeni in the mid-nineteenth century in the Eastern Cape (Mostert 1992:1000), in the Maji Maji war against German occupation of Tanganyika (Iliffe 1995:196), amongst the Mbunda in pre-nationalist resistance in Angola (Davidson 1972:28–9) and in Che Guevara's experiences during his campaign in the Congo in the mid-1960s (Guevara 2001:14).

But the question arose again when the group met up with ZAPU comrades in Zambia:

> When we met with the Zimbabweans ... they insisted before going into Zimbabwe they needed to be strengthened with medication, ... while in Zambia. And also when they arrived home they would need to go to a traditional healer.... This would be someone who, when you arrive, you report to, "I have come back, I have returned home."

> Before we arrived [in Zambia] we didn't want this. Most of us dismissed this as rubbish. Then the leadership including OR [Tambo] and JB Marks said: "Look guys you are the ones who said you want to go home and you want to explore the route through Zimbabwe. To go through Zimbabwe we believe it is better for you to go through with people who are in the Zimbabwean liberation army ... you go through together with these people. This is their tradition. If you are to go with them you have to respect their tradition. Otherwise there is no way you can have a working relationship with them."

> As a result, we then had to go through this whole process ... You find one evening they make a fire, they prepare some food in front of one of the tents. There will be a string and a pot here with food without salt, corn in a small pot, the size of a meatball without corn bread, salt, piece of meat without salt and then some *mqombothi* [a traditional brew made for ceremonial purposes]. When you come there is this guy with a *big* tummy, *African personality*. Also this medicine in a bowl with water, he dips a broom and sprinkles you with this broom and then you jump, you walk over the string, and once you walk over, there is an incision here [points to chest] then he applies some medicine, then you get a piece of corn ball bread like and a piece of meat and go under a specific big tree, with a specific name which is said, usually, it is good for ancestors. In the old days they used to sit under that type of a tree. There is a lot of *mqombothi*, then you are ready to cross. (Sijake interview 2001)

Sijake argues that one should distinguish two types of access to "medicine". In the first case, individuals sought to strengthen themselves in order to prepare for battle. The second was an organisational agreement between ZAPU and

ANC. "It was formal, unlike if I just take my coat and approach a traditional healer and swop it for medicine". But performance of rituals associated with "traditional" beliefs and access to healers (*sangomas* or *inyangas*) may have been an accepted part of MK life and to some extent, exile life in general (Moche interview 2002; Morrow 1998:509).

These examples do not represent displacement of science by pre-scientific belief systems. It is, in reality, coexistence of more than one belief system. Resort to healers in order to strengthen combatants does not seem to have been regarded as a substitute for the deployment of firepower in the manner in which they had been trained.

Some time ago Jack Simons wrote that magic "begins where scientific knowledge ends" (1957:90). Many others indicate that notions of cause and effect that inform rituals in societies practising forms of magic are complex, and do not necessarily mean the denial of conventional scientific conceptions of cause and effect (Lienhardt 1961; Douglas 1966:59). In many cases, there is a coexistence of magical and scientific modes of belief and causation, one dealing with one sphere of existence and the other dealing with another realm.

Furthermore, too much can be made of the extent to which a scientific culture is in fact diffused within "science-based societies". Charlotte Seymour-Smith (1986:175) argues:

> In modern "scientific" cultures a large proportion of the population "believe" in scientific or technological phenomena without understanding them, a belief which is perhaps as magical or as religious as that held by a member of a simple society in the knowledge which the ritual specialists of the group possess. The scientific knowledge for which we all tend to take credit is in fact only understood and created by a very small proportion of the population.

With MK fighters (who used such resources), we are talking of something supplementary to scientific knowledge. This is not the same as individuals relying solely on the power of medicine. Medicine was seen as supplementing what they learnt in formal military training, with what some (though not all) regarded as an important additional source of strength. This is also quite different from a millenarian type movement, relying almost exclusively on the power of their beliefs as with the Israelites prior to the Bulhoek massacre (Edgar 1988).

Conclusion

This chapter represents an early attempt to extract qualities that may represent cultural traits of or throw light on the character of the ANC today. It has tried to show that beneath media reports alleging conflicts between different strands of the ANC lie complex cultural experiences which inform or condition the practices and expectations of members from a variety of backgrounds. But within each of these experiences there are many variations. The exile experience cannot be summarily categorised as militaristic, top-down and bureaucratic. It contains some diversity within a common experience. Likewise the internal experience, which is not covered in this chapter, cannot be simply typified as a golden era of popular democracy. Within each of these experiences or cultures there are many variants that qualify what may be seen as the general character of the period or the tradition it generated.

What will have to be further interrogated, as this research unfolds, is the extent to which cultures referred to, close off or open up certain options and what impact this has on the future development of South African democracy.

The chapter has also raised a wider issue relating to "non-political" or apparently non-political identities that nevertheless have a bearing on political practice. This is where access to multiple belief systems impact on political practice. This is not something whose significance has disappeared. It survives in numerous spheres of South African society, including trade unions and pre-match preparations of football teams, as well as popular discourse generally. While the question of access to healers has been referred to, the issues form part of much wider questions concerning the recognition of distinct identities and understanding how these relate to an over-arching loyalty to a national liberation movement.[4]

Notes

1   My thanks to the Swedish International Development Agency (SIDA) and the Nordic Africa Institute for funding the research of which this chapter forms a part. The Centre for Policy Studies in Johannesburg has provided me with a very hospitable and supportive research environment. Comments from Nomboniso Gasa, Shireen Hassim, Michael Neocosmos, David Masondo, Caroline Kihato, Sakkie Niehaus, Mugsy Spiegel, Martin Legassick, Peter Delius, Mandla Nkomfe, Phil Eidelberg, Monique Marks and

Krista Johnson have been very helpful. Not all will agree with the arguments now presented. Naturally I bear responsibility.

2   It is not clear how many were actually paid up. That was more strictly considered in later years.

3   This is not to say that all military figures are revered or treated with respect. Many former combatants are living in situations of great hardship and poverty (see Lamb and Mokalobe 2002 unpub. especially at 5; Xaba 2001:195).

4   Another form of the same phenomenon, dealt with in Suttner 2002, is that of initiation ceremonies performed on Robben Island.

References

African National Congress (ANC). 1996. *Appendices to the African National Congress Policy Statement to the Truth and Reconciliation Commission.* Johannesburg: African National Congress.

Barrell, H. 1990. *MK: The ANC's Armed Struggle.* London: Penguin Forum Books.

Bernstein, H. 1994. *The Rift: The Exile Experience of South Africans.* London: Jonathan Cape.

Cock, J. 1991. *Colonels and Cadres: War and Gender in South Africa.* Cape Town: Oxford University Press.

Coetzee, J., Gilfillan, L. and Hulec, O. 2002. *Fallen Walls: Voices from the Cells that Held Mandela and Havel.* Nakkadatelstvi Lidove Noviny; Robben Island Museum.

Curnow, R. 2000. "Interview: Thandi Modise. A Woman at War", *Agenda*, 43:36–40.

Davidson, B. 1972. *In the Eye of the Storm: Angola's People.* London: Longman.

Davis, S. 1987. *Apartheid's Rebels: Inside South Africa's Hidden War.* Johannesburg: Ad Donker.

Douglas, M. 1966. [1984]. *Purity and Danger: An Analysis of Concepts of Pollution and Taboo.* London and New York: Routledge and Kegan Paul.

Duka, N. 1974. *From Shantytown to Forest: Story of Norman Duka.* Recorded and edited by Dennis and Ginger Mercer. Richmond, BC: LSM Information Centre.

Edgar, R. 1988. *Because They Chose The Plan of God: The Story of the Bulhoek Massacre.* Johannesburg: Ravan Press.

Ellis, S. and Sechaba, T. [pseud]. 1992. *Comrades against Apartheid: The ANC and the South African Communist Party in Exile.* London: James Currey.

Ellis, S. 1994. "Mbokodo: Security in ANC Camps, 1961–1990", *African Affairs*, 93:279–98.

Frederickse, J. 1990. *The Unbreakable Thread: Non-Racialism in South Africa.* Johannesburg: Ravan Press.

Guevara, E. "Che". 2001. *The African Dream: The Diaries of the Revolutionary War in the Congo.* London: The Harvill Press.

Hooper, C. 1960. [1989]. *Brief Authority*. Cape Town and Johannesburg: David Philip.

Iliffe, J. 1995. *Africans: The History of a Continent*. Cambridge: Cambridge University Press.

Israel, M. 1999. *South African Political Exile in the United Kingdom*. Houndmills, Hampshire: Macmillan.

Kriger, N. 1995. "The Politics of Creating National Heroes: The Search for Political Legitimacy and National Identity". In Bhebe, N. and Ranger, T. (eds.) *Soldiers in Zimbabwe's Liberation War*. London: James Currey; Portsmouth: Heinemann.

Liebenberg, I., Nel, B., Lortan, F. and Van der Westhuizen, G. 1994. *The Long March: The Story of the Struggle for Liberation in South Africa*. Pretoria: HAUM.

Lienhardt, R. 1961. *Divinity and Experience*. Oxford: Oxford University Press.

Lodge, T. 1983. *Black Politics in South Africa Since 1945*. Johannesburg: Ravan Press.

_____ 1988. "State of Exile: The African National Congress of South Africa, 1976–86". In Frankel, P., Pines, N. and Swilling, M. (eds.) *State, Resistance and Change in South Africa*. Johannesburg: Southern Book Publishers.

_____ and Nasson, B. (eds). 1991. *All, Here, And Now: Black Politics in South Africa in the 1980s*. Cape Town: Ford Foundation and David Philip.

Maloka, E. 2002. *The South African Communist Party In Exile 1963–1990*. Pretoria: Africa Institute of South Africa.

Mandela, N. 1994. *Long Walk To Freedom: The Autobiography of Nelson Mandela*. Randburg: Macdonald Purnell.

Marx, K. and Engels, F. 1968. *Selected Works in One Volume*. Moscow: Progress Publishers; London: Lawrence and Wishart.

Mbeki, G. 1964 [1984]. *South Africa: The Peasants' Revolt*. London: International Defence and Aid Fund for Southern Africa.

Moleketi, J. and Jele, J. 2002. *Two Strategies of the National Liberation Movement in the Struggle for the Victory of the National Democratic Revolution*. [No publisher listed].

Morrell, R. (ed). 2001. *Changing Men in Southern Africa*. Pietermaritzburg: University of Natal Press; London and New York: Zed.

Morrow, S. 1998. "Dakawa Development Centre: An African National Congress Settlement in Tanzania 1982–1992". *African Affairs*, 97:497–521.

Mostert, N. 1992 [1993]. *Frontiers: The Epic of South Africa's Creation and the Tragedy of the Xhosa People*. London: Pimlico.

Niehaus, I., Mohlala, E. and Shokane, K. 2001. *Witchcraft, Power and Politics: Exploring the Occult in the South African Lowveld*. Cape Town: David Philip; London: Pluto Press.

Ottaway, M. 1993. *South Africa: The Struggle for a New Order*. Washington, DC: The Brookings Institution.

Rantete, J. 1998. *The African National Congress and the Negotiated Settlement in South Africa*. Pretoria: Van Schaik.

Reddy, F. and Karterud, S. 1995. "Must the Revolution Eat its Children? Working with the African National Congress (ANC) in Exile and Following its Return". In Ettin, M., Fidler, J. and Cohen, B. (eds.) *Group Process and Political Dynamics*. Madison: International Universities Press.

Said, E. 2000. *Reflections on Exile and Other Literary and Cultural Essays*. London: Granta Books.

Seekings, J. 2000. *The UDF: A History of the United Democratic Front in South Africa 1983–1991*. Cape Town: David Philip; Oxford: James Currey; Athens: Ohio University Press.

Sellstrom, T. 2002. *Sweden and National Liberation in Southern Africa. Vol 2. Solidarity and Assistance 1970–1994*. Uppsala: Nordic Africa Institute.

Serote, P. 1992. "Solomon Mahlangu Freedom College: A Unique South African Educational Experience in Tanzania", *Transformation*, 20:47–60.

Seymour-Smith, C. 1986. *Palgrave Dictionary of Anthropology*. Houndmills, Basingstoke: Palgrave.

Shubin, V. 1999. *ANC: A View from Moscow*. Mayibuye History and Literature Series No. 88. Mayibuye Books. Bellville: University of the Western Cape.

Simons, H. 1957. "Tribal Medicine: Diviners and Herbalists", *African Studies*, 16,2:85–92.

Sparg, M., Schreiner, J. and Ansell, G. (eds.) 2001. *Comrade Jack: The Political Lectures and Diary of Jack Simons, Novo Catengue*. Johannesburg: STE publishers and ANC.

Suttner, R. 2001. *Inside Apartheid's Prison*. Melbourne, New York: Ocean; Pietermaritzburg: University of Natal Press.

_____ 2002. "The Tripartite Alliance. Is it Falling Apart?" *Indicator SA*, 19,1:24–9.

_____ and Cronin, J. 1986. *30 Years of the Freedom Charter*. Johannesburg: Ravan Press.

Unterhalter, E. 2000. "The Work of the Nation: Heroic Masculinity in South African Autobiographical Writing of the Anti-Apartheid Struggle", *The European Journal of Development Research*, 12,2:157–78.

Van Kessel, I. 2000. *"Beyond Our Wildest Dreams": The United Democratic Front and the Transformation of South Africa*. Charlottesville and London: University of Virginia Press.

Walker, C. 1991. *Women and Resistance in South Africa*. 2nd ed. Cape Town and Johannesburg: David Philip.

Williams, R. 1994. "The Other Armies: Writing the History of MK". In Liebenberg *et al*: 22–34.

Xaba, T. 2001. "Masculinity and Its Malcontents: The Confrontation Between "Struggle Masculinity" and "Post-Struggle Masculinity" 1990–1997". In Morrell, R. (ed.): 105–24.

Unpublished works

Erlank, N. 2001. "Gender and Masculinity in African Nationalist Discourse 1912–1950".

Hassim, S. 2002. "Identities, Interests and Constituencies: The Politics of the Women's Movement in South Africa 1980–1999". PhD thesis.

Lamb, G. and Mokalobe, M. 2002. ""Soldiers of Misfortune': The Forgotten Warriors of South Africa's Liberation Struggle". Paper presented to conference on "Re-Conceptualising Democratisation and Liberation in Southern Africa". Windhoek, July 2002.

Interviews

Meshack Mochele, December 15, 1992, interview with Wolfie Kodesh Oral History of Exiles Project, Mayibuye Centre for History and Culture in South Africa.

Victor Moche, Johannesburg, July 23, 2002, interview with Raymond Suttner.

John Pampallis, August 5, 2002, interview with Raymond Suttner.

Nat Serache, August 31, 2002, interview with Raymond Suttner.

General Sandi Sijake, Stockholm, February 23, 2001, interview with Raymond Suttner.

Liberal or Liberation Framework?
The Contradictions of ANC Rule in South Africa

Krista Johnson

Social transformation in southern Africa has been shaped and constrained by, among other things, its history of settler colonialism and the anti-colonial nationalist movements that fought against it. Given the nature of the colonial/ apartheid regime and the impossibility of meaningful engagement and change through legal struggle, the national liberation movements of southern Africa were compelled to adopt an insurrectionary approach to change. Underpinned by Marxist and nationalist revolutionary theories and strategies, these liberation movements prepared themselves for a variety of struggles of a revolutionary kind, including the use of guerilla warfare, and envisaged insurrectionary change and a revolutionary seizure of power that would lead to a transition to people's power. Operating within the international context of the Cold War, with capitalism seemingly on the retreat and opportunities for independent states to advance development goals in a context apparently more favourable than today, the liberation movements prepared to seize state power and then use it to transform society.

Decolonisation, in the previous Portuguese colonies of Angola and Mozambique in the mid-1970s, Zimbabwe in 1980 and Namibia in 1990, and democratisation in South Africa in 1994, brought to power anti-colonial liberation movements that took control of the state machinery and reorganised themselves as political parties. But the inherited terrain on which the liberation movements found themselves was in many ways not the one they had prepared for. The independence process, particularly for Zimbabwe, Namibia and South Africa, was internationally monitored and legitimated, and led to the establishment of constitutional or parliamentary democracies in line with the Western liberal model. Thus the transfer of power came about through negotiation, not through insurrection, and in a changed, post-Cold-War international context in which the forces of globalisation and neoliberalism are hegemonic.

In the post-colonial era, the revolutionary liberation parties confront the challenge of bringing about transformation through parliamentarism and other "reformist struggles", armed with revolutionary strategies and theory that are not appropriate for this reality. The militaristic, top-down command that proved successful during anti-colonial struggle was hardly favourable for the durable strengthening of democratic values or norms, and has created new challenges on the difficult path to establishing robust, open and egalitarian structures and practices. In fact, confronted with the challenges of nation-building while at the same time consolidating their own power bases, national liberation parties have felt the need to centralise power and promote greater party and government autonomy, echoing pre-transition ideological commitments, in order to carry out complex and politically controversial economic reforms. Sadly, to varying degrees, these revolutionary liberation parties have transformed themselves into a new ruling conservative elite, often becoming the post-colonial enemies of democracy and freedom, a danger that Frantz Fanon (1963) warned against over 40 years ago. The political direction taken by liberation parties in several southern African countries also reveals the internal contradictions and limits to emancipation in anti-colonial resistance, and the parameters for social transformation in societies with a history of armed resistance to settler colonialism.

In 1994, South Africa's leading national liberation movement, the African National Congress (ANC), found itself on the unexpected terrain of reform, having come to power through a negotiated settlement that severely limited the possibility of bringing about radical social transformation. Since coming to power, the ANC government has adopted much of the neo-liberal logic of global capitalism, leading some critics to bemoan the ANC's "tragic leap to the right" (Saul 2000). Its emphasis on democratic forms of rule and good governance, the institutionalisation of individual rights and capitalist market economics through a constitutional dispensation, and the scaling back of the state's role in the economy have prompted other analysts on the left of the political spectrum to proclaim "it is the ANC that has now become the standard-bearer of liberal democracy in South Africa and the African continent" (MacKinley 2000).

Confirming Fanon's premonition of the revolutionary party and the national middle class in his chapter on "The Pitfalls of National Consciousness" in *The Wretched of the Earth*, Patrick Bond argues "Mbeki and his main allies have already succumbed to the class (not necessarily personalistic) limitations of post-independence African nationalism, namely acting in close collaboration with hostile transnational corporate and multilateral forces whose interests stand directly opposed to Mbeki's South African and African constituencies" (2002:1). But the quick dismissal of the ANC for becoming a liberal party by some leftist critics fails to explain the persistence of radical rhetoric and Marxist discourse, and how this may in fact contribute to rather than hinder the adoption of a liberal framework – particularly with regard to the reorganisation of state/society relations in post-apartheid society. Such perspectives also overlook areas where the ANC's philosophy diverges with liberalism, which has been particularly acute on the issue of socio-economic rights in South Africa.

In this chapter I argue that the ANC leadership, most of whom are former exiles and trained within the radical Leninist school of thought that gives primacy to the role of the vanguard party and the revolutionary intellectuals, are finding that the reorganisation of state/society relations along conventional liberal lines is quite compatible with their own understanding of the hierarchical relationship between rulers and ruled and the primacy of leadership over mass action in processes of revolutionary change. I will demonstrate that both agendas, anchored in the tradition of the nation-state, conceive of change in narrowly statist terms despite their anti-statist rhetoric. Furthermore, both visions of societal transformation and reorganisation are elitist in that they neglect the role of the popular masses in processes of change. Liberals advocate gradual, rational, managed change implemented by political leaders and an elite intelligensia. Leninist vanguardists push for faster, revolutionary change, but it is the role of an elite, revolutionary vanguard that is central to such change. Similarly, while both doctrines profess a stated belief in the rule of the people (that is, democracy), democracy is defined as a situation in which experts and elites represent the people, and are allowed to make the essential political decisions, promoting the rule of the few, at least supposedly, in the interest of the many. In reality, liberalism has always supported the rule of the best, defined not by birth status but by educational achievement, that is, a meritocracy. Vanguardism, too, constructs its own meritocracy, defined by a combination of educational achievement, proper political training and political lineage (in the case of African liberation movements).

This chapter will demonstrate that despite its radical ideology and rhetoric of popular democracy and people-driven transformation, the ANC shares with most elitist, liberal political parties a similar understanding of the role of leadership, representation and participation. It suggests that the challenge for those concerned with promoting popular democracy and participatory forms of development is not simply to oppose the liberal paradigm and advocate a more radical, leftist or even socialist alternative, but to transform the very basis of state/society relations by conceptualising new forms of political organisation that emphasise participation over representation, and horizontal, decentralised decision-making over hierarchical ones.

Revolution: Project of Social Transformation and Agenda for Political Change

> The transfer of state power from one class to another class is the first, the principal, the basic sign of a revolution, both in the strictly scientific and in the practical political meaning of the term. (V.I. Lenin)[1]

As a strategy for revolutionary change, Marxism-Leninism painted an insurrectional path to "national liberation" and political change, with the seizure of state power as the ultimate goal. It is this statist paradigm, of first seizing state power and then using it to transform society, which has dominated revolutionary thought for more than a century. Indeed, what the intense debates over "reform vs revolution" concealed was that both approaches focus on the state as the vantage point from which society can be changed.

As a model for national liberation movements engaged in anti-colonial struggle, Marxism-Leninism, but especially the writings of Lenin, were particularly appealing. Lenin followed Marx in insisting on the presence and active role of the working class in the struggle for democratic revolution. However, he argued that given its lack of cohesiveness and its limited focus, the working class requires the ideological and organisational guidance of a communist vanguard party in order to perform its historical role. Vanguardism, as a strategy for political action, gives primacy to leadership and hierarchical organisation over the decentralised and more spontaneous actions of the masses. It is a central component of Leninism's model of revolution as highly calculated and precisely executed by professional revolutionaries (1967:108). Democratic centralism is another defining principle of Leninism, premised on the belief that a unified, hierarchical organisational structure, whereby advice flowed from the bottom up and decisions from the top down, is the most efficacious.

> The determination of political decisions would therefore become the prerogative of the party while "democratic centralism" would serve as the guiding organisational principle to ensure discipline. Thus, where an individual might wish to dissent from a party decision in private, he or she would have to support that same decision in public. (Bronner 1988:178)

Lenin's preoccupation with tight organisation, controlled and planned revolutionary action, unity of purpose, and vigilance against counter-revolutionary forces led him to define the revolutionary vanguard in elitist and even undemocratic terms. Under conditions of revolutionary struggle, he believed the vanguard party would need to operate in great secrecy and may even be conspiratorial (1967:133). Lenin's own prescriptions were responding to the objective and subjective historical conditions that he and the revolutionary movement faced at the time. For example, his polemic against spontaneism in *What Is to Be Done?* was in direct response to what he viewed as the primitivism of various factions of the revolutionary movement, including the Russian labour movement, and their disorganised and spontaneous actions. It was written prior to the experience of the Soviets, which demonstrated the autonomous revolutionary ability of the Russian labour movement.[2] Similarly, these considerations on the function of the vanguard party and the role of democratic centralism have been frequently challenged within Marxism and outside it, particularly as these practices became distorted in the post-revolutionary Soviet Union, especially under Stalin.

But for our purposes, what is important to highlight is Leninism's appeal for African anti-colonial movements as a theory of proletarian insurrection against the bourgeoisie, and especially as the theory of anti-imperialism that it increasingly became; as well as where there may be points of agreement between Lenin's theory and liberal understandings of political change. Lenin proved particularly appealing to nationalist liberation movements throughout Africa which were struggling for political independence and self-determination of the oppressed black majority. In the context whereby colonialism was viewed primarily as a denial of sovereignty (rather than simply a denial of rights), Lenin's revolutionary strategy to seize power was particularly attractive. Freedom fighters and post-independence leaders such as Kwame Nkrumah were clearly not only inspired by Lenin but used him to interpret the national and global conditions they confronted. Ali Mazrui, who once dubbed Nkrumah "the Leninist Czar", argued that not only did Nkrumah emulate Lenin in his great belief in organisation, but his concept of African unity was "in a sense an extension of the Leninist principle of organisation" (1966:117). Mazrui's assessment of Nkrumah may be an extreme case, but many African freedom fighters were influenced by Lenin's teachings.

However, there was a rival path that the struggle for the self-determination of the peripheral areas of the world or decolonialisation could (and did) take, and this was the one mapped out by American liberal Woodrow Wilson. Wilsonianism was based on classical liberal presuppositions such as individual freedom and individual rights, an emphasis on procedural safeguards such as the rule of law, and an acceptance of the normalcy of political change and the inevitability of social progress. As Immanuel Wallerstein remarks: "the principle of self-determination, the centerpiece of Wilsonianism, was nothing but the principle of individual freedom transposed to the level of the inter-state system" (1995:109).

The liberal approach espoused by Wilson differed from that of Lenin's in that it favoured a "constitutional" path to decolonisation that would gradually and in an orderly way transfer power to Africans through negotiations between the imperial power and representatives of the people, instead of in a revolutionary/insurrectionary one. However, the intensity of the ideological conflict during the Cold War concealed some basic points of agreement. For example, both doctrines shared a similar understanding of who was to lead the struggle for self-determination. Wilsonian liberals saw the natural leadership of a national movement as lying in its intelligentsia and bourgeoisie. Leninists saw the leadership lying in a party or movement modelled on the Bolshevik party. The leaders could be (and often were) "petty bourgeois", provided they were "revolutionary" petty bourgeois. For liberalism and Leninist vanguardism alike, the task of political transformation could not be left to ordinary people, but required a select group of political elite to plan and execute the process. Liberals, Wallerstein explains,

> believed political change was inevitable, but they also believed that it would lead to the good society only insofar as the process was rational, that is, that social decisions were the product of careful intellectual analysis. It was therefore crucial that the actual policies

be conceived and implemented by those who had the greatest capacity for making such rational decisions, that is, by the technicians or specialists. It was they who could best elaborate the necessary reforms that could, and would, perfect the system in which they lived. (1995:149)

Indeed, liberalism has always been much more concerned with "rule of the best" than with "rule of the whole". Liberals defined the best not by birth status but rather by educational achievement. Similarly, Lenin's notion of an elite vanguard in the form of the party also ascribes to a select group of intellectuals the task of thinking and acting on behalf of the masses (Bronner 1988:178). While democracy was historically the objective of the radicals (socialists) – those who were truly antisystemic – the very notion of a revolutionary vanguard introduced an anti-democratic element into such radical struggles. Indeed, for Lenin, democracy was not something to strive for in the context of revolutionary struggle. Lenin argued that the "the broad democratic principle of party organisation" was "a useless and harmful toy" (1967 [1902]:136).

Following decolonisation, the two paths to independence produced opposing foreign policies, with liberal governments inclining towards the US camp and socialist governments leaning towards the USSR. However, the internal realities of the various states, particularly in the political arena, were quite similar. In terms of actual political structures, most of the states were either *de facto* or *de jure* one-party states or military dictatorships. Even when states had a multiparty system, post-independence politics tended to be dominated by one party, whose legitimacy to rule stemmed from their emergence from the decolonisation process as democratically elected representatives of the majority of the people. In southern Africa, a clear example of this is Zimbabwe, where the ZANU-PF's ability to maintain power since independence in 1980 paradoxically stems largely from the model of multiparty democracy which the ruling party has successfully manipulated. Richard Saunders has characterised Zimbabwe's political system as "a model which has mixed Western-style liberal democratic political constructs with ZANU-PF's increasing partisan domination of state and civil society, to produce a *pro forma* democracy that evokes little popular enthusiasm and diminishes active participation from ordinary Zimbabweans" (1995:6).

Once attaining state power and operating on the terrain of reform, vanguardism as an organising strategy in fact tends to organise society along similar lines to liberalism. Vanguardism encourages the liberal division between state and society, and the central role of the state and intellectuals in implementing reform. For example, as Hannah Arendt's analysis of revolutions describes, the ready-made programmes of the revolutionary vanguard party reasserted the hierarchical and oligarchic relationship between rulers and ruled by making a distinction "between the party experts who knew and the mass of the people who were supposed to apply this knowledge" (1963:264).

Furthermore, Lenin's vanguard party shares commonalities with all political parties, liberal and otherwise, by virtue of the nature of the party system as a form of political organisation whose primary function is representation, not participation. As Arendt argues:

> Parties, because of their monopoly of nomination, cannot be regarded as popular organs, but ... are, on the contrary, the very efficient instruments through which the power of the people is curtailed and controlled ... Hence, from the very beginning, the party as an institution presupposed either that the citizen's participation in public affairs was guaranteed by other public organs, or that such participation was not necessary and that the newly admitted strata of the population should be content with representation, or, finally, that all political questions in the welfare state are ultimately problems of administration, to be handled and decided by experts, in which case even the representatives of the people hardly possess an authentic area of action, but are administrative officers, whose business, though in the public interest, in not essentially different from the business of private management. (1963:269, 272)

This distinction between the party and popular-democratic organs, or the leaders and the masses, is one that Fanon (1963) warned anti-colonial movements against. Indeed the complex interplay that emerged during the liberation struggles between the imperatives of leadership, organisation and co-ordination on the one hand, and spontaneous, decentralised mass action on the other, continues to shape and limit the possibilities for transformation post-independence.

The Anti-Apartheid Struggle

The ANC conceptualised the revolutionary struggle in narrowly statist terms. Consistent with the dominant thinking about revolution for most of the twentieth century, the ANC perceived the winning of state power as the centerpiece of the revolutionary process, the hub from which revolutionary change would radiate. This was clearly conveyed by former ANC president Oliver Tambo, whose words and message became part of the movement's psyche when he stated:

> All revolutions are about state power. Ours is no exception. The slogan "power to the people" means one thing and one thing only. It means we seek to destroy the power of apartheid tyranny and replace it with popular power with a government whose authority derives from the will of all our people both black and white. (Tambo 1984:4)

The national character of the liberation struggle, and the focus on over-throwing the state, is understandable given the emphasis on self-determination and sovereignty in the struggle, which the black majority had been denied through apartheid. Indeed the ideologies of nationalism and pan-Africanism or black consciousness were quite strong within the ANC, and were used to stress unity and homogeneity against apartheid divisiveness. Nationalism identified the nation with the national liberation movement, as captured in the slogan "The ANC Is the Nation", further strengthening the conviction that the goal of the struggle was to achieve state power (Suttner 2002a:3).

The ANC has long been considered a "broad church" because it is said to comprise multiple, and often competing, political tendencies and beliefs. In addition, while the ANC was operating as a liberation movement in exile, a vibrant, mass, popular-democratic movement emerged inside the country with many of the organisations, most notably the trade union federation Congress of South African Trade Unions (COSATU), being aligned with the ANC. This mass democratic movement espoused other brands of Marxism such as workerism as well as the values of popular democracy and nonracialism, and generated organisational structures and forms very different to that of the ANC in exile. Once the ANC was unbanned in 1990 these competing political tendencies clashed with some of the practices and ideologies of the ANC in exile. Interestingly, despite the existence of a widespread popular-democratic movement that espoused alternative ideologies, many of the practices and ideologies of the ANC in exile became dominant within the organisation.[3] Although it is beyond the scope of this chapter, these competing political tendencies within the broad democratic movement continue to shape the possibilities for transformation in South Africa (see Johnson 2001).

The ANC's revolutionary strategy consisted of four pillars – international support, mass action, underground activity and the armed struggle. In practice the armed struggle was the central one of these four pillars. "It conformed to the Marxist-Leninist tradition, established in 1917, of seeking power by force rather than other means. Successful guerilla wars in Angola, Mozambique and Zimbabwe seemed to indicate that the same formula would succeed in South Africa" (Ellis and Sechaba 1992:200). With the turn to armed struggle, its reorganisation as an exiled liberation movement aimed at seizing state power, and its links with the SACP, the ANC was increasingly influenced by communist-style bureaucratic methods of work and a vanguard Leninist strategy with democratic centralism as its organising principle. Many ANC members received training in the Soviet Union as well as other socialist countries, and were taught Marxism-Leninism. Vivienne Taylor (1997:85) observed that many activists spoke about "studying the Marxist classics. Several mentioned gaining access to banned works such as Lenin's *What Is to Be Done?*"

Indeed, the pages of *Sechaba*, the ANC journal in exile, were full of references to Marx and Lenin. Lenin's *Two Tactics of Social Democracy*, and other works, were quoted at length as a "how to" guide for waging revolution. The ANC leadership also adopted Leninist language and phraseology. In an exchange with US-based Marxist scholar Robert Fatton over the direction of the ANC's struggle, Thabo Mbeki proudly proclaimed:

> The African National Congress is the vanguard organisation of the
> South African movement for national liberation. In its daily
> activities, it works to mobilise into action all national groups,
> classes, and strata that share an objective interest in the destruction
> of the apartheid system of white minority colonial and racist
> domination, the super-exploitation of the black working people,
> fascist tyranny, external aggression, and imperialist expansionism,
> and that are therefore willing to sacrifice for the victory of the
> national democratic revolution. (1984:611–12)

Indeed the ANC long considered itself to be at the top of the hierarchy of the broad anti-apartheid movement, believing, as Lenin did, in the primacy of political leadership and organisation over spontaneous, decentralised actions. "Invoking (Leninist) tradition", the ANC's Strategy and Tactics document adopted at Morogoro in 1969 clearly states:

> The primacy of the political leadership is unchallenged and
> supreme and all revolutionary formations and levels (whether
> armed or not) are subordinate to this leadership ... This approach
> is rooted in the very nature of this type of revolutionary struggle
> and is borne out by the experience of the overwhelming majority of
> revolutionary movements which have engaged in such struggles. ...
> The masses of the peasants, workers and youth, beleaguered for a
> long time by the enemy's military occupation, have to be activated
> in a multitude of ways not only to ensure a growing stream of
> recruits for the fighting units but to harass the enemy politically so
> that his forces are dispersed and therefore weakened. (1969)

The activation of the masses was the task of the ANC underground units that were developed along the Leninist model of an underground professional revolutionary vanguard. Elitist in character, these "advanced elements" acted on behalf of others that had to be awakened to their potential power. Perhaps it is symptomatic that an underground journal which was written and produced by three successive groups of underground activists in the 1970s was called *Vukani!* (Awake!) Without it being articulated at the time, clearly the groups had the idea or assumption that they possessed insights that were needed to waken the masses from their slumber. This vision and strategy promulgated by the underground units is reminiscent of one of the journals produced by Lenin called *Iskra,* meaning "spark", and Lenin's notion of small groups of professional revolutionaries serving as the vanguard for the masses.

Indeed, the top-down, bureaucratic organisational structure of the ANC in exile provided strong co-ordination, discipline and direction for the anti-apartheid struggle in the context of enormous military pressures and dangers of infiltration, but also introduced an elitist character to the struggle, and reasserted a hierarchical, oligarchic relationship between rulers and ruled. Reflecting on the impact of Marxism-Leninism on the ANC and the struggle, Ellis and Sechaba write:

The [Communist] Party's practice of democratic centralism, which it inculcated in the ANC, may also have contributed to the ineffectiveness of the armed struggle. In the end both the Party and the ANC in exile came to be run by a nomenklatura, an elite which, whatever its original merits may have been, grew distant from the mass of its supporters, lost their confidence, and did not listen to their voices. (1992:202)

The elitist nature of the ANC leadership surely contributed to its willingness to negotiate behind closed doors with the apartheid rulers in South Africa's transition to democratic government. The 1994 political settlement established South Africa as a liberal democracy, with a constitution that enshrines many liberal values – the rule of law, a bill of rights protecting fundamental freedoms, and an independent constitutional court. In the economic sphere, the ANC government has also moved to conform to dominant neoliberal prescriptions and the imperatives of the global capitalist economy with its macroeconomic framework "Growth, Employment and Redistribution" (GEAR). Since taking power, the ANC has shown such a willingness to transform South African society along liberal lines that South African liberals now claim some of the ANC leadership, most notably Nelson Mandela, as one of their own (Laurence 1998:49).

Indeed, liberals argue that the early members of the ANC were essentially constitutional liberals in outlook. Peter Walshe writes of them:

[They] were the products of missionary education – ministers, teachers, clerks, interpreters, a few successful farmers, builders, small-scale traders, compound managers, estate and labour agents. They were not trade unionists, nor were they socially radical ... they were setting out to attain what they considered their constitutional rights – equality of opportunity within the economic life and political institutions of the wider society. They believed Western and Christian norms to be closely interrelated, and accepted the Cape qualified franchise as their ideal. (Quoted in Welsh 1998)

For much of the history of the ANC and the anti-apartheid struggle, however, many black anti-apartheid activists were hostile towards liberalism. For example, Steve Biko, founder of the Black Consciousness Movement, wrote:

The biggest mistake the black world ever made was to assume that whoever opposed apartheid was an ally ... Although he [the typical

liberal] does not vote for the Nationalists (now that they are in the
majority anyway), he feels secure under the protection offered by
the Nationalists and subconsciously shuns the idea of change.
(Quoted in Laurence 1998:47)

Historically in South Africa, the term "liberal" was applied to whites who
opposed racial discrimination and favoured the extension of rights to the black
majority. Under apartheid, white liberals found their home in the old
Progressive Party (forerunner to the present-day Democratic Party). The
founding principles of the Progressive Party included many liberal tenets but
did not include a universal franchise, as at the time this was considered "too
radical" (Owen 2002). In the liberal tradition, apartheid was a denial of rights.
White liberals opposed racial discrimination and supported a nonracial
meritocracy, assuming this would produce equality of opportunity and
freedom from racial oppression. From the liberal perspective, reconciliation
between the races was viewed as a political necessity. Thus with the holding of
the first democratically elected government in 1994 and the subsequent
ratification of South Africa's new constitution in 1996, democratic change had
been achieved. For liberals, these events served as the end point in the struggle
for democratic transformation in South Africa.

The "ironic victory" that liberalism appeared to have won with the democratic
transition in 1994 did not signal the liberal triumph, however. In post-
apartheid South Africa, with the ANC increasingly becoming a centrist party to
make itself more acceptable in international circles, liberalism has become
decidedly illiberal, shifting its platform to the right. Liberalism is in a crisis, as
witnessed by the recent failings of the Democratic Alliance, the opposition
alliance that the liberal Democratic Party forged with the old apartheid voting
block represented by the New National Party (NNP); as well as South African
liberals' inability to engage with the stark realities of massive inequality and
demands for socio-economic rights.

Liberal Framework or Liberation Framework in Post-Apartheid South Africa?

The unbanning of the national liberation movements on February 2, 1990, came
as a surprise to the exiled leaders of the ANC. Quite dramatically the nature of
struggle had changed, and the national liberation movement found itself on the

unexpected terrain where political and diplomatic tactics were required rather than military ones. Having operated clandestinely for more than three decades, living with the fear of attack or assassination, the ANC had difficulty adapting itself to legality. As a liberation movement largely in exile and faced with enormous military pressures and dangers of infiltration by the apartheid regime, the ANC's commitment to a vanguard Leninist strategy that emphasised democratic centralism and top-down command proved successful in providing strong co-ordination, discipline and direction for the anti-apartheid struggle. The ANC's continued reliance on a Leninist mode of conceiving of the transition shaped its approach to political change in several ways. As Ellis and Sechaba explain:

> Its dogmatic pursuit of the Soviet line for so long had blinded it to certain realities and deprived it of some obvious assets. A good example of this is the strong dislike of the USA engendered by the Soviet connection, which caused the ANC to miss many opportunities to promote its cause in the world's most powerful country over three decades. (1992:198)

More importantly, by following the fundamentally insurrectionist Leninist paradigm of transition the ANC did not give enough weight to the range of transformations that are necessary to achieve fundamental change. As Raymond Suttner remarked:

> There is a tendency to devalue parliamentarism and other "reformist struggles" except insofar as these build up revolutionary momentum towards a decisive moment when there will be seizure of power. In other words, what you do at any particular moment prior to seizure is only important as a contribution to seizure not it itself. In that sense, we were poorly prepared by our theory for the type of conditions we in fact confront. (2002a:6)

While the Leninist paradigm of transition places little weight on reforms as structural possibilities of engagement and transformation, it also downplays the role of the masses, which meant the ANC was more inclined to accept an elite-pacted negotiated settlement. Indeed, the very notion of elite-pacting and negotiations is premised on the assumption that negotiations cannot be conducted by the masses themselves, at venues other than the bargaining table, but must be entered into on their behalf by a leadership that ostensibly speaks for them (Ginsburg 1996).

Shortly after its unbanning, the ANC came under tremendous international pressure to moderate its aspirations for socio-economic transformation and become more acceptable to powerful vested interests, as a precondition for achieving a smooth transition (Saul 1999:58). The "government-in-waiting" was compelled to become more liberal, to engage with capital, and to adapt to the seeming imperatives of the global capitalist economy. Membership in the SACP, which had previously been an advantage in the liberation movement – as they were seen as "the most advanced cadres" – now became a handicap. Nearly half of the national leadership of the SACP allowed their membership to lapse. Those who left made no critique of the party, nor of Marxism or communist practices (Suttner 2002b). Similarly, there has been no open debate or genuine introspection on the part of the ANC leadership on the implications of the demise of communism in Eastern Europe and the Soviet Union and the shifting terrain on national democratic revolution, despite the fact that the ANC has had three major conferences since its unbanning in 1990 (Zita 2002).

In contrast, the SACP and members of the South African left have engaged in considerable introspection and self-criticism. Joe Slovo's personal reflection on the history of Eastern European communism in his essay "Has Socialism Failed?" was later adopted as the party line. He acknowledged the lack of democracy in Eastern Europe, the failings of Stalinism, and the necessity of maintaining a multiparty system in a future South Africa (Ellis and Sechaba 1992:197). This process caused the SACP to modify its traditional line, dropping certain formulations such as "democratic centralism" that still remain part of ANC doctrine and discourse.

Ironically, one still finds the use of Marxist methodology or terminology in ANC circles or as the predominant mode of expression in ANC pronouncements. Indeed, the ANC leadership still uses the language of insurrectionism and militarism while pursuing an agenda of reform. It still has militaristic, top-down concepts of organisation, even though the terrain is no longer that of warfare. Its discourse is still Marxist while denying Marxism. Such observations have caused some SACP members to remark wryly, "the SACP abandoned Stalinism but retained Marxism while the ANC abandoned Marxism but retained Stalinism" (Suttner 2002b). The point is not to suggest that the ANC is Marxist-Leninist or even Stalinist. It is simply to show how ideological convictions that have their roots in the national liberation struggle can profoundly affect action by creating in political actors the psychological predisposition to interpret a situation in a given way.

For example, democratic centralism, tight internal discipline and strong central co-ordination continue to be the main organising principles of the ANC. An ANC discussion document on "Organisational Democracy and Discipline in the Movement" states that: "the ANC is not a federal organisation and ... central leadership structures occupy an important position in defining policy and implementing that policy which affects each level of organisation" (ANC 1997). Another discussion document states that: "the organisational forms and practices of the ANC have always been based on democratic centralism" (ANC 2000).

The continuation of such practices has prompted accusations that the boundaries for opposition and debate within government and within the ANC and the Tripartite Alliance have narrowed.[4] Some suggest there were early indications that the ANC leadership was developing an intolerance for divergent perspectives from within the ranks. Long-time ANC cultural activist Mike van Graan publicly stated what many others in the Alliance privately felt:

> Those of us who fought alongside you against apartheid thought that now we will have the space to create, to sing, to laugh, to criticise ... We were wrong. We now realise that space can never be assumed; it must be fought for. Of course, some of us will yield to the temptations you offer, many will conform to the new status quo (already self-censorship and fear of criticising the ANC is rife), some will go into exile and a few will say "nyet". (*Weekly Mail* May 7–13, 1993, quoted in MacKinley 2000)

Interestingly, the heated exchanges over lack of criticism and debate within the Alliance are very often framed within the Marxist-Leninist paradigm. Not only do the SACP and other leftist intellectuals couch their critique of the government's macro-economic policy GEAR and other neo-liberal policies of the ANC in Marxist rhetoric, but the ANC leadership including President Mbeki have been vocal in denouncing "the offensive of the ultra-left against our movement" as counter-revolutionary! (Mbeki in *Umrabulo* 17, 2002) One of the most recent examples of this was the paper "Two Strategies of the National Liberation Movement in the Struggle for the Victory of the National Democratic Revolution", written by two prominent ANC leaders, Jabu Moleketi and Josiah Jele. In the paper they lash out at what they perceive to be an "ultra-left plot" to unseat or at least undermine the ANC government, but base their critique overwhelmingly on Marxism-Leninism. In their critical analysis of Moleketi and Jele's paper, Mde, Craven and Bodibe (2002) argue:

> The irredeemably flawed methodology of analysis used by comrades Moleketi and Jele seems to have three basic strategies: McCarthyism, liberal usage of red herrings, and what can only be described as a Qur'anic approach to Marxism-Leninism. ... Throughout the document issues are confused rather than clarified by inserting long quotations from Marx, Engels and Lenin, which are so selective and ripped out of their historical context that they are totally irrelevant to the point the authors are trying to make. These comrades treat Marxism quite shabbily, not as a living body of historical and economic knowledge, but as a written bible of eternal truths to be pulled out of a hat and quoted extensively on any day, useful to silence the modern heretic.

Other key members of the ANC leadership, including Geraldine Fraser-Moleketi, Minister of Public Services, have "taken to lecturing the unions and advising them to read Lenin on the dangers of 'infantile leftism'" (Suttner 2002b:57). Similarly, in an exchange between ANC stalwart Peter Mokaba and SACP Deputy General Secretary Jeremy Cronin, the former, responding to the SACP's criticisms of the ANC's neoliberal agenda, challenged the SACP to "demonstrate their understanding of Marxism-Leninism, of socialism as a science and of socialist theory in the aftermath of the collapse of socialism". He continues:

> As I understand it, to be a communist does not merely consist in owning a membership card of the SACP and mistaking trade unionism for revolutionary class consciousness. The emergence of "communists" without Marxist-Leninism is a new and interesting experience. But it is dangerous. (Mokaba 2001:33)

Here again, Mokaba makes the Leninist distinction between trade unionism and revolutionary class consciousness, suggesting that the former (as practised by COSATU and also characterised as economism) can in fact work against the latter and against the ultimate goals of the national democratic revolution. It is an example of how Marxism-Leninism has been used to tame labour and shape the relationship between the government and the trade unions.

In addition, the ANC continues to use Marxism-Leninism and the notion of the ANC as a vanguard party acting on behalf of the "masses" to shape the new relationship between the state and society as well. This vision was most clearly articulated in the ANC discussion document "The State and Social Transformation", thought to have been written by President Thabo Mbeki, whose ideological and philosophical underpinnings are evident in much of the ANC's recent policies. The document represents a hybrid of dominant liberal precepts, such as an impartial state, and prominent features of liberation politics, such as an interventionist state, as well as the rhetoric of popular participation and people-driven development (Johnson 2002). The two frameworks can be reconciled given the consistent understanding of the role of leadership, and the relationship between rulers and ruled.

In line not only with liberal notions of a clear boundary between the state and civil society, but with vanguardist notions of a clear separation between the role of the leadership and that of the masses, the document reconstructs the terms of relations between civil society organisations and the state in a hierarchical and highly institutionalised fashion.

> The issue turns on the combination of the expertise and professionalism concentrated in the democratic state and the capacity for popular-mobilisation that resides within the trade unions and the genuinely representative non-governmental popular organisations. The democratic state therefore has a responsibility to ensure that this independent and representative non-governmental sector has the necessary strength to play its role in ensuring that the people themselves, and in their own interest, become conscious activists for development and social transformation. (ANC 1996)

In other words, the author ascribes to the state the role of knowledge producer, able to develop policy and set the agenda for social transformation. He restricts civil society organisations' role to that of mobilisation and implementing directives from above. He attempts to make a clear distinction between the government, or party experts, who "know" and the mass of the people who are supposed to apply this knowledge, leaving out of the equation the capacity of the average citizen to act and to form his own opinion.

This approach purports to be anti-liberal and to support a process whereby "the people become their own governors".

> The democratic movement must resist the liberal concept of "less government", which, while being presented as a philosophical approach toward the state in general, is in fact, aimed specifically at the weakening of the democratic state. The purpose of this offensive is precisely to deny the people the possibility to use the collective strength and means concentrated in the democratic state to bring about the transformation of society. (ANC 1996)

But it is also grounded in the liberal tradition of the state as a neutral arbiter whose responsibility it is to balance the competing interests within society.

> To the extent that the democratic state is objectively interested in a stable democracy, so it cannot avoid the responsibility to ensure the establishment of a social order concerned with the genuine interests of the people as a whole, regardless of the racial, national, gender and class differentiation. There can be no stable democracy unless the democratic state attends to the concerns of the people as a whole and take responsibility for the evolution of a new society. (ANC 1996)

Furthermore, by virtue of its impartiality, the democratic state is seen as the only legitimate expression of the interests of the whole nation, becoming coterminous with the "national interest" or the "public will". At the same time all other demands or proposals for social change emanating from outside the state are viewed as partial, subjective or sectarian, regardless of the legitimacy of the demands. At its core, this framework is inherently statist given its understanding of the primacy of leadership and the vanguard ruling party and that it leaves no room for popular political participation outside the state or the ruling party. Instead it advocates a corporatist arrangement whereby popular-democratic organisations are incorporated into the state, and all politics is reduced to state politics.

Concerning the most powerful, organised, and popular voice in civil society, the author warns:

> The instinct towards "economism" on the part of the ordinary workers has to be confronted through the positioning of the

legitimate material demands and expectations of these workers within the wider context of the defence of the democratic gains as represented by the establishment of the democratic state. ... If the democratic movement allowed that the subjective approach to socio-economic development represented by "economism" should overwhelm the scientific approach of the democratic movement towards such development, it could easily create the conditions for the possible counter-revolutionary defeat of the democratic revolution. (ANC 1996)

Interestingly, the ANC leadership continues to utilise the discourse of revolution and counter-revolution as well as Marxist liberation concepts of trade union "economism" to challenge the legitimacy of worker demands and define them as partial or sectarian. In conditions of struggle against the state it is clear the "economism" of trade unions can be limiting at best. However, in conditions after the attainment of state power, for the state to berate the trade unions for "economism" is to contribute to the suppression of their fight for democratic rights.[5] This is a clear example of how a revolutionary and indeed liberatory notion of the perils of sectarian struggles and the limitations of a working-class consciousness in the context of revolutionary struggle can be transformed into oppressive or reactionary ones in the context of reform.

Pressures to toe the party line and not be too critical of the leadership and its decisions have also come to bear on other organisations of civil society. Indeed, it was Nelson Mandela who first publicly led the attack on those organisations of civil society who seek to play the role of "critical watchdog" over the movement, and serve as channels for grassroots communities to voice their grievances and wishes (Mandela 1997). He referred to similar calls made in 1990, with the unbanning of the ANC, to retain the grassroots structures of the United Democratic Front (UDF) as an independent movement alongside the ANC. Mandela described such past and recent proposals coming from popular organisations within civil society as posing an "illegitimate challenge" to the leading political role of the ANC and the government (Greenstein 1998).

Indeed the ANC leadership and liberal politicians have found common agreement when it comes to promoting an apolitical role for civil society. This was clearly demonstrated during the 2001 Civil Society Initiative (CSI) conference convened by former National Party politician Roelf Meyer and attended by prominent national and international leaders, including former presidents Nelson Mandela and Bill Clinton. The theme of the conference as well as the overall initiative was one of encouraging the spirit of volunteering and self-help, promoting social partnerships between government and civil society organisations, and defining an apolitical role for civil society organisations as assistants to government in service delivery. In his address to the conference, Meyer explained:

> The CSI holds the view that in South Africa civil society forms part of a social partnership with the state and with business. It works alongside government and business to further the common national interest in a non-political arena.

Other speakers, many of whom are leading figures in the ANC, either inside government or outside of it, reiterated the basic message that civil society had to recast itself, move out of the political arena, and focus on voluntary service to communities.

Where the ANC leadership and liberalism have largely diverged has been around socio-economic rights and the issue of balancing political and socio-economic rights. This became clear during the South African Human Rights Commission's Inquiry into Racism in the Media in 2000.[6] On the need to balance the socio-economic rights of its citizens and poverty alleviation measures with pressures for economic discipline, liberals have remained rather silent, leaving this debate to occur mainly within the Tripartite Alliance. As Richard Calland (2002) has argued:

> Liberal thought can no longer cope with the imperative of contemporary politics and of the harsh global environment of massive inequality. Individual rights and freedoms, useful though they are in overturning dictatorships, are blunt instruments in the quest for meaningful socio-economic justice.

While the ANC leadership appears to have chosen a centrist path to transformation, justifying and legitimating its actions with revolutionary rhetoric and Marxist garb, the path is not yet fixed and there remains vibrant criticism, contestation and debate within the Alliance. On the other hand, liberalism has all but excused itself from the debate, largely consigning itself to the dustbin of history.

Conclusion

The purpose of this chapter has been to illuminate the complexity of the South African situation. I have sought to demonstrate the degree of subliminal ideological accord between liberalism and Leninist vanguardism as well as the extent to which the liberal framework is consistent with a Leninist liberation framework. I have argued that while we may characterise South Africa as a liberal democracy, the ANC is not particularly a liberal party, nor is its discourse or worldview grounded in liberalism. In contrast, I suggest that the ANC continues to use much of the liberation, insurrection discourse from the anti-apartheid struggle, which in the context of revolutionary struggle served a progressive role in broadening and strengthening the struggle, but in the context of reform is potentially reactionary. I suggest that the ANC leadership's training and adherence to Leninist principles of democratic centralism and the notion of the vanguard party have not hindered its willingness or ability to conform to the dominant liberal framework, but have in fact facilitated it. By understanding these peculiar dynamics of the South African context we can better appreciate the parameters and social constraints to transformation in southern African societies with a history of settler colonialism and armed resistance to it.

Notes

1   "Letters on Tactics". In Lenin, V. 1936–1938. *Selected Works: Vol. 6.* Lawrence and Wishart. Quoted in Turok 1980:3.

2   See Carlo 1973 for a discussion of the logical and historical inconsistencies of Lenin's work, especially *What Is to Be Done?*

3   For a discussion of these two strands and the factors that facilitated the ANC leadership in exile to become dominant, see Johnson 2001.

4   See MacKinley, D. 2000. "ANC Puts Party Before Democracy", *Mail&Guardian* February 6, 2001; "Authoritarian Leadership Alarms ANC Politicians", *Mail&Guardian* October 4, 1996.

5   I thank Mike Neocosmos for illuminating this point for me.

6   For a detailed analysis of these debates, see Johnson, K. and Jacobs, S. 2003.

References

African National Congress (ANC). 1969. "Strategy and Tactics of the ANC". Document adopted at the "Morogoro Conference", Tanzania 25 April – 1 May. www.anc.org.za/ancdocs/history/stratact.html.

———— 1996. "The State and Social Transformation". ANC Discussion Document (November). Johannesburg: ANC.

———— 1997. "Organisational Democracy and Discipline in the Movement". ANC Discussion Document (July). Johannesburg: ANC.

———— 2000. "Tasks of the NDR and the Mobilisation of the Motive Forces", *Umrabulo*, 8.

Arendt, H. 1963. *On Revolution*. London: Penguin Books.

Bond, P. 2002. "Thabo Mbeki's New Partnership for Africa's Development: Breaking or Shining the Chains of Global Apartheid?" Discussion paper (March). *Foreign Policy in Focus*. (www.fpif.org).

Bronner, S. 1988. "The Political Theory of Rosa Luxemburg", *New Politics*, 1,4:171–87.

Calland, R. 2002. "The Crisis of Liberalism", *Mail&Guardian*, Johannesburg, June 7–13.

Carlo, A. 1973. "Lenin on the Party", *TELOS*, 17.

Cronin, J. 2001. "A response to Peter Mokaba", *The African Communist*, Third/Fourth Quarter.

Ellis, S. and Sechaba, T. 1992. *Comrades Against Apartheid: The ANC and the South African Communist Party in Exile*. London: James Currey.

Fanon, F. 1963. *The Wretched of the Earth*. New York: Grove Press.

Ginsburg, D. 1996. "The Democratisation of South Africa: Transition Theory Tested", *Transformation*, 29.

Greenstein, R. 1998. "The State of Civil Society in South Africa". Johannesburg: Community Agency for Social Enquiry (CASE).

Johnson, K. 2001. "From Consensual Decision-Making to Conventional Politics: Popular Participation in Contemporary South Africa". Ph.D dissertation, Northwestern University.

———— 2002. "State and Civil Society in Contemporary South Africa: Redefining the Rules of the Game". In Jacobs, S. and Calland, R. (eds.) *Thabo Mbeki's World: Myth, Ideology and Politics in the South African Presidency*. Pietermaritzburg: University of Natal Press.

———— and Jacobs, S. 2003 (forthcomimg). "Democratisation and the Rhetoric of Rights: Contradictions and Debate in Post-Apartheid South Africa". In Nyamnjoh, F. and Englund, H. (eds.) *The New Politics of Rights in Africa*. London: Zed.

Laurence, P. 1998. "Liberalism and Politics". In Johnson, R. and Welsh, D. (eds.) *Ironic Victory: Liberalism in Post-Liberation South Africa*. Cape Town: Oxford University Press.

Lenin, V. 1967 [1902]. *What Is to Be Done?* Moscow: Progress Publishers.

MacKinley, D. 2000. "Democracy, Power and Patronage: Debate and Opposition Within the

ANC and the Tripartite Alliance since 1994". In Southall, R. (ed.) *Opposition and Democracy in South Africa*. London: Frank Cass.

Mandela, N. 1997. "Report by the President of the ANC, Nelson Mandela". Paper read at 50th National Conference of the African National Congress, December 16, 1997, Mafikeng.

Marx, K. and Engels, F. 1973 [1848]. *The Communist Manifesto*.

Mashinini, A. 1986. "Dual Power and the Creation of People's Committees", *Sechaba*, April.

Mazrui, A. 1966. "Nkrumah: The Leninist Czar", *Transition*, 26.

Mbeki, T. 1984. "The Fatton Thesis: A Rejoinder", *Canadian Journal of African Studies*, 18,3.

Mde, V., Craven, P. and Bodibe, O. 2002. "The Politics of Paranoia", *Mail&Guardian*, Johannesburg, November 1, 2002.

Meyer, R. 2001. Speech given at the National Civil Society Conference, April 24. Sandton, South Africa. www.idasa.org.za/csi/speeches.htm.

Mokaba, P. 2001. "Letter from Peter Mokaba", *The African Communist*, Third/Fourth Quarter.

Owen, K. 2002. "SA Liberalism Has Strayed into a Hall of Mirrors", *Cape Times*, Cape Town, July 4.

Saul, J. 1999. ""For Fear of Being Condemned as Old Fashioned': Liberal Democracy versus Popular Democracy in sub-Saharan Africa". In Daddieh, K. (ed.) *State Building and Democratisation in Africa*. Westport, Connecticut: Praeger Press.

Saunders, R. 1995. "Not by Votes Alone", *African Agenda*, 1,4.

Suttner, R. 2002a. "Unpacking the Meanings of "National, Democratic, Revolution" (NDR) Today". Unpublished paper presented to the Gauteng ANC provincial parliamentary caucus, June 26.

_____ 2002b. "What is the Character of the ANC?", *South African Labour Bulletin*, 26,2, April.

Tambo, O. 1984. "Presidential Statement", *Sechaba*, March.

Taylor, V. 1997. "Social Mobilisation: Lessons from the Mass Democratic Movement". Cape Town: University of the Western Cape Southern African Development and Policy Research Unit.

Turok, B. (ed.) 1980. *Revolutionary Thought in the 20th Century*. London: Zed.

Wallerstein, I. 1995. *After Liberalism*. New York: The New Press.

Welsh, D. 1998. "The Liberal Inheritance". In Johnson, R. and Welsh, D. (eds.) *Ironic Victory: Liberalism in Post-Liberation South Africa*. Cape Town: Oxford University Press.

Zita, L. 2002. "Is South Africa the Weakest Link in the "Imperialist" Chain?", *Umrabulo*, 14, April.

Contributors

Suzanne Dansereau is Assistant Professor in International Development Studies at Saint Mary's University in Halifax, Nova Scotia, Canada.

Kenneth Good is Professor in the Department of Political and Administrative Studies, University of Botswana in Gaborone.

Krista Johnson is Assistant Professor in the Department of International Studies at DePaul University in Chicago, Illinois, USA.

Amin Kamete is a Researcher at the Nordic Africa Institute in Uppsala, Sweden. Previously he was Senior Lecturer in the Department of Rural and Urban Planning, University of Zimbabwe, Harare.

Martin Legassick is Professor in the Department of History, University of the Western Cape, Cape Town, South Africa and Co-ordinator of the South African Democracy Education Trust (SADET) Project.

Henning Melber is a Research Director at the Nordic Africa Institute in Uppsala, Sweden.

Francis B. Nyamnjoh is Associate Professor of Sociology at the University of Botswana in Gaborone.

Roger Southall is Executive Director in the Democracy and Governance Research Programme of the HSRC in Pretoria, South Africa.

Raymond Suttner is the Manager of the "Hidden Histories" publishing series of the University of South Africa (UNISA) Press in Pretoria, South Africa.

Ian Taylor is a Lecturer in the Department of Political and Administrative Studies, University of Botswana and a Visiting Research Fellow in the Department of Political Science, University of Stellenbosch, South Africa.

Index

foreign involvement in 80–81
national development 72
opposition in 74–75
poverty in 81–83, 88
strikes in 86
structured autocracy in 73–77
workers' rights in 85
Botswana Democratic Party (BDP) xviii,
72–73, 88, 97, 98, 116
Botswana National Front (BNP) 97,124,
125, 126, 129, 130
and the Basotho Congress Party (BCP)
119–121
history of 127–128
Britain 3, 8
and Lesotho 118
Bush, George 2

Cachalia, Azhar 15
Central Kalahari Game Reserve (CKGR)
83, 84, 85
chieftaincy
and marriage 98–101
and minority tribes 106–110
and succession 104–106
female 101–104
in Africa 93–94
in Botswana 96–98
theories on 94–96
value of 96, 110–111
Chieftaincy Act 108
Chiluba, Frederick 4–5, 6
Chinamasa, Patrick 10
Chissano, Joaquin 7
Clinton, Bill 1, 17, 219
Civil Society Initiative (CSI) 219
Cold War 135, 200, 205
colonialism xiv, 200
colonial system xvi
Commonwealth Eminent Person's Group
170
Congress of Democrats (CoD) 140, 141

Congress of South African Trade Unions
(COSATU) 14, 15, 170, 216
and the ANC 208
Constitution
of Namibia 137–140
of South Africa 7
of Zambia 5
constitutionalism 7
Cronin, Jeremy 216
Cuba
model for armed struggle 157–158

decolonisation 143, 200
De Klerk, F. W. 170, 171
democracy
and chieftaincy (*See* chieftaincy)
assault on 59, 60, 66
British 3
conceptualising of xviii
definition of 202
electoral 3, 51
in Angola 6–7
in Athens 12–13
in Botswana 7, 17
in Malawi 6
in Mozambique 7
in Namibia 3–4
in post-colonial Southern Africa xix
in South Africa 7–8, 14 (*See also* UDF)
in Zambia 4–5
in Zimbabwe 47
liberal 3, 13
paradigm of xix, 116
participatory 13–14, 15, 172
representative 3
worker-led 172
Democratic Alliance 212
Democratic Party 212
Democratic Republic of the Congo 39, 142
Democratic Turnhalle Alliance (DTA) 138,
141
democratic values xiv